Trading Away

Our Future

Other Books by Raymond L. Richman

FISCAL SURVEY OF PANAMA
(with Milton C. Taylor)

FISCAL SURVEY OF COLOMBIA
(with Milton C. Taylor)

Other Books by Howard B. Richman

THE THREE R'S AT HOME
(with Susan Richman)

STORY OF A BILL:
LEGALIZING HOMESCHOOLING IN PENNSYLVANIA

RAYMOND L. RICHMAN
HOWARD B. RICHMAN
JESSE T. RICHMAN

Trading Away Our Future

How to Fix Our Government-Driven Trade Deficits and Faulty Tax System Before It's Too Late

Ideal Taxes Association
Pittsburgh PA

TRADING AWAY OUR FUTURE

A Publication of Ideal Taxes Association
www.idealtaxes.com
Pittsburgh PA

Printed in the United States of America
by United Graphics, Inc.
Mattoon, Illinois

ISBN: 0-929-44605-4

First edition

A B C D E

This book is dedicated to economists who
refused to conform to the
conventional wisdom:

Adam Smith,
Edward Chamberlin,
John R. Hicks,
John Maynard Keynes
Irving Fisher,
Milton Friedman,
and Herbert A. Simon.

TRADING AWAY OUR FUTURE

Contents

Preface

This book owes its existence to the authors' unhappiness with the ideological positions taken by an overwhelming number of economists on a variety of issues. Specifically, we take issue with their views on international trade and taxes.

We owe a great debt to earlier economists who took issue with accepted doctrines, persisted, and were vindicated in the ensuing debate over their revolutionary differences. We have in mind some of the great economists of the last century, men like John Maynard Keynes, Edward Chamberlin, Joseph Schumpeter, Irving Fisher, Milton Friedman and Herb Simon whose ideas broke substantially with then current doctrines and whose ideas in turn were debated and confronted by evidence, and through thesis, antithesis, and synthesis largely accounted for progress in economics as a science.

But many false ideas have endured without challenge, like the notion that free trade is always beneficial to both parties. We show that only balanced trade is always beneficial. When "free trade" is chronically in deficit, it can be disastrous. While economists blame wage stagnation on poor education, we show that it results from trade deficits. While economists minimize the role played by government policies in driving the trade deficits, we show that governments (both the US and foreign) have been driving the trade deficits and by doing so have been destroying American industry, savings, and future.

We also take issue with the accepted dogma about taxation, that capital gains are income. We show that they are income only when they are consumed and not reinvested. We take issue with the current theory on the burden of the real estate tax, showing that the tax is borne by the landowner and only impedes real estate investment when future assessment or rate increases are uncertain. We take issue with those who call the *Flat Tax* a consumption tax and show that it would not increase savings or investment nearly as much as would a true consumption tax. We point out that the latest variation of the *Flat Tax* put forth by a Presidential advisory commission as a way to increase growth and investment would do neither.

While most economists and policy makers know of no way to

bring down the US trade deficit without causing an economic slump, we put forward a comprehensive plan that would gradually reduce the trade deficits while causing a surge in American savings, investment and growth.

Some of the foregoing ideas are truly novel and without precedent, but we are indebted to a number of people who contributed to their development. Among them, Giuseppe Ammendola, adjunct professor of economics at New York University, who showed that the incentives given to private foreign investors when a tax loophole was passed in 1984 precipitated the growth of the trade deficits; and Bob McIntyre of Citizens for Tax Justice who testified in congressional hearings and predicted that the incentives to foreign investment incorporated into the 1984 legislation would increase the trade deficits, cost Americans jobs in export- and import-sensitive industries and convert the United States from a creditor nation to a debtor nation. How true and how sad that nobody listened.

We also owe an intellectual debt to American University economics professor Robert Blecker who called our attention to the negative effects of dollar appreciation on manufacturing investment, to University of Maryland professor of international business and former Director of Economics at the U.S. International Trade Commission Peter Morici who called our attention to the danger posed by Chinese currency manipulations, and to Argus Group principal Dan Mastomarco who called our attention to the sizable economic benefits available by switching to a border-adjustable consumption tax.

We would also like to especially thank Molly Inspektor, our editor at Ideal Taxes Association, whose invaluable help, copy editing, and great cover art greatly improved the appearance, organization, and content of this book. We also appreciate very much that Giuseppe Ammendola, Bob McIntyre, Dan Mastromarco, Uri Halfon, and Jim Bolton took the time to read early versions of this book and give us valuable feedback. All errors that remain are our own, and we take responsibility for them.

Last, but not least, we owe a debt of gratitude to our wives, Wilma, Susan, and Patricia, for their patience and forbearance that allowed us the time to research and write this book.

Introduction

TANSTAFL [There Ain't No Such Thing as a Free Lunch] is the name of the student-run snack bar in the Pierce residential student dorm of the University of Chicago. The name references the fact that the use of the term in economics was popularized by Milton Friedman, the Nobel Prize-winning former University of Chicago professor.
                                                                    -Wikipedia

A basic principle of economics is that there is no free lunch. Benefits are accompanied by costs. This book is about the costs and benefits of US trade and tax policies. We believe that the policies which have produced and sustained the enormous US trade deficits have many more costs than benefits. Those who think that the Chinese, Japanese, Saudis et al. are giving the United States a free lunch when they sell more than they buy are engaged in short term thinking that ignores huge long term costs.

With the dollar falling steadily, foreclosures rising, and credit tightening, by the fall of 2007 Americans were beginning to realize that the large American trade deficits were indeed a problem. When former Federal Reserve Chairman Alan Greenspan came out with his memoirs, he was peppered with questions about the trade deficit and the future of the dollar. In an interview with German *Stern* magazine, Greenspan said it was "absolutely conceivable that the euro will replace the dollar as reserve currency, or will be traded as an equally important reserve currency."[1] When questioned by Lesley Stahl on the CBS television program *Sixty Minutes* about where his own savings were located, he admitted that he had diversified them so that a large proportion were in currencies other than the dollar.[2]

The future of the dollar was looking grim. The strength of a currency is largely based upon the productivity of the economy that uses it. In the short-run, a country can borrow in order to prop up its currency, but in order for a currency to be strong in the long-run, that country must export about as much, or more, than it imports.

Unfortunately, during the decade from 1996 to 2005, the last ten years of Greenspan's reign at the Federal Reserve, the US trade deficits steadily increased as a percentage of GDP. The financial flows that sustained these deficits did not go to expand the US capital stock — they mostly financed consumption of foreign goods. Japan and China and other Pacific Rim nations stole industry after industry from the United States. America's manufacturing investment declined so much that by 2004 and 2005, net investment in American manufacturing actually went into negative territory, meaning that US manufacturers were not even investing enough to replace wearing out machinery and plants. The US manufacturing workforce declined steadily, so that by 2007 over a fifth of the US manufacturing jobs that would have existed given balanced trade had been lost. Those losing their manufacturing jobs often took less skilled jobs in the service sector, causing median wages to stagnate. In 2007, the United States was in a much weaker position to compete in world markets and the dollar had nowhere to go but down.

The decline of US manufacturing also had profound effects upon the US military, lengthening supply lines as more parts were sourced from abroad and reducing US capability to rapidly develop and deploy new weapons systems. The United States-China Economic and Security Review Commission 2007 report sums up the problem as follows:

> "U.S. defense contractors have merged and moved some manufacturing outside the United States. Sources of defense components are becoming scarcer in the United States, and the supply of American workers skilled in manufacturing these components is diminishing."[3]

While this was happening, most US elected leaders were ignoring the negative effects that our tax system was having upon the trade deficit and upon American savings. They were ignoring the fact that our tax system was subsidizing the foreign savings that were causing the trade deficits. They were ignoring the fact that our tax system was encouraging the consumption of capital. America needed to generate more of its own savings instead of borrowing them from abroad.

But the US government is not the only government that has contributed to the trade deficits. Recently some economists have begun to realize that the trade deficits are largely the result of a new form of mercantilism, dubbed "monetary mercantilism" by Joshua Aizenman & Jaewoo Lee in 2005, who defined it as "hoarding international reserves in order to improve competitiveness."[4] Under the old form of mercantilism, countries encouraged their exports and discouraged their imports in order to build up their gold hoards. Under the new form, which we call "dollar mercantilism," countries build up their dollar hoards as part of currency manipulations designed to encourage their exports and discourage their imports.

Here's how they do it. The dollar mercantilist governments borrow their own currency and then use it to buy dollars so that they can drive up the price of the dollar compared to their own currency in currency markets. As a result of the higher price of the dollar and the lower price of their own currency, their own products can then outcompete US products in world markets.

Because the dollars purchased by the mercantilist governments are not used to purchase US goods and services, demand for US produced tradables is kept artificially low. This new form of mercantilism intentionally produces trade deficits for the United States while allowing the practicing country to build up its manufacturing capacity at the expense of US industry.

Instead of keeping the purchased dollars in their bank vaults, the mercantilist governments loan them back to us so that they can earn interest on them. In effect, the mercantilist countries are lending us money to buy their goods, and just like a teenager with a new credit card, we are running up our balance with no thought to the future.

Japan gradually invented dollar mercantilism in the years following World War II. Beginning in the late 1990s, China copied the policy that had converted Japan from a weak and backward economy to a world powerhouse. In recent years, more and more countries have been joining the bandwagon, with the United States as their primary target. They have been accumulating dollar assets in order to manipulate currency values and preserve the conditions that produce trade surpluses for them and trade deficits for us.

Although the evidence of manipulation was mounting, as recently as 2007 most economists were still in denial. Free-trade ideology was still blinding them to the severity of the problem and the fact that the market forces that they expected to correct trade imbalances were being blocked by government policies. They were explaining away the causes of the trade deficits. They were minimizing the costs of the trade deficits. They were minimizing the role of the mercantilist policies, pursued by Japan for a half century and by China for over a decade, that had undermined the productive capacity of the United States and converted the United States from the world's leading creditor to the world's leading debtor. These economists were still equating globalization, the signing of the General Agreements on Tariffs and Trade and the creation of the World Trade Organization, with free trade. These and other agreements had reduced barriers to trade but had not prevented countries from pursuing mercantilist policies to our detriment.

Even though in private Greenspan was protecting himself against a fall in the dollar, his public analysis stumbled with most economists. In his 2007 memoirs, *The Age of Turbulence,* Alan Greenspan took the view that the increased trade deficits were no great problem but were the result of increased international specialization that has been going on since before the industrial revolution, what we now call *globalization.* He wrote, "It is the focus of a worldwide fear that America's external imbalance – the dramatic gap between what a nation imports and what it exports – will precipitate both a collapse of the US dollar's foreign-exchange value and a world financial crisis." He wrote that while the concern is not groundless, "it is easy to exaggerate the likelihood of a dollar collapse."[5]

Nowhere in his book was there any recognition that the trade deficits had depressed US manufacturing investment, making it more and more difficult for the United States to compete in the world market place. Nowhere was there any recognition of the strong role played by governments in creating and sustaining the trade deficits, distorting free market forces.

As advocates of free markets, we generally approve of relying on the free play of market forces to provide the highest level of welfare for Americans. But we discovered that *free trade*, normally beneficial, had become an ideology blinding the United States establishment from seeing key causes of the trade deficits and their disastrous consequences. The trade deficits are sustained by government policies, both US government tax policies and foreign government mercantilist policies, not by the free play of market forces. We have to face it. While trade often benefits all, when it comes to government-driven trade deficits, *there ain't no free trade!*

We must act now! If the correct actions are taken, we may still avoid the worst consequences of our failed economic policies. That task will involve direct action to balance trade, ending our tax subsidies for foreign savings, and changing our tax system to encourage American savings and investment. If we address the trade deficits now, then the United States, together with other advocates of democracy, will continue to dominate the world's economy. If not, then resolutely nondemocratic China will dominate. The world's future is in the balance.

Part I: The Trade Deficit

The lion was once the king of beasts. He stalked the jungle for his food. He was lean, fast, and strong. Then the edge of the jungle became populated by people. They were aware of the lion and to keep him at arms length, they started setting out food for him every day. For the lion, that was easier than hunting prey. He became lazy. He put on weight. His muscles atrophied. He became the pet cat. But the people eventually tired of feeding the cat. He had to return to the jungle and tried to hunt, but his prey easily outran him. He would starve to death unless he again became lean, fast, and strong. We don't know the end of the story.

Manufacturers' advocates William R. Hawkins and Alan Tonelson of the U.S. Business and Industry Council Education Foundation have had a much better grasp of what is happening than most economists. They must be tired of explaining the problems, again and again, for over a decade, being proved right, again and again, and then ignored. Mr. Hawkins holds graduate degrees in both economics and history. He started out working as a congressional staff person on defense issues, but is equally interested in US economic and political security. As we will relate in Chapter 3, Mr. Tonelson, a graduate of Princeton with a BA in history, makes predictions about mercantilist country behavior that have been ridiculed by prestigious economists but turn out to be correct.

Labor leaders have been advocating fair trade as an alternative to free trade for decades, but without really understanding what has been causing the trade deficits. Democratic presidential candidate Senator John Kerry blamed the deficits on the lack of a "level playing field" (i.e., low wages, child labor, subsidies, etc.), but lack of a level playing field may affect the level of trade and what products are traded but has little or nothing to do with the trade imbalance. Indeed, the current tilt of the playing field may be a consequence rather than a cause of the current trade deficits. Some suggest imposing tariffs, but tariffs, followed by counter-tariffs, affect only the level of trade not the balance of trade.

Trade imbalances are, as we shall show, a strictly monetary phenomenon. The trade deficits will continue as long as foreign savings keep flowing into the United States at a greater rate than US savings flow into foreign countries.

In this part, we explain why and how the inflow of foreign savings is causing our trade deficits and we suggest ways that those inflows could be reduced. We deal with the history, the consequences, and the causes of the trade deficits and some solutions that would eliminate them. We will dispense with the old paradigm. We will not be discussing free trade vs. fair trade, but balanced free trade vs. manipulated and imbalanced trade, and how to achieve balanced trade.

1. Why Trade Deficits Matter

*Once when Jacob was cooking a stew, Esau came in from the open,
famished. And Esau said to Jacob, "Give me some of that red stuff to
gulp down, for I am famished."... Jacob said, "First sell me your
birthright." And Esau said, "I am at the point of death, so what use
is my birthright to me?" But Jacob said, "Swear to me first." So he
swore to him, and sold his birthright to Jacob. Jacob then gave
Esau bread and lentil stew; he ate and drank, and he rose and went
away. Thus did Esau spurn his birthright.*

                                    -Genesis, Chapter 25, JPS translation

Our focus in this chapter is on the growing problem posed by the trade deficits. In the short term, the trade deficit is deindustrializing the United States while allowing some US residents to enjoy extraordinarily high living standards that are not justified by American productivity. In the long term, the trade deficit is not sustainable. It will likely lead to the collapse of the dollar, depression, and conversion of the United States to a second-rate power.

Not only will the United States feel the pain, but other countries will as well. Because other countries are dependant upon the US dollar as a reserve currency and because they are dependent on exports to the United States to sustain their own economies, the eventual collapse of the dollar could wreak havoc on the economies of the whole world.

Trade deficits cannot occur unless foreign governments or private investors are willing to finance them. There must always be a balance of payments. Deficits on trade and services have to be made up through a countervailing flow of funds. Indeed, the flow comes first because importers have to be sure of funds to purchase goods abroad. That flow of funds can sometimes include gifts, but it is usually made up of loans. When there is a trade deficit there is an equivalent flow of foreign savings in the opposite direction. In this book we will use "foreign savings" and "foreign financial capital" to refer to the flow of funds into the United States that finances the US trade deficits.

These inflows caused the dollar to rise to an artificially high level in

2002 as compared to a broad index of other currencies (an index calculated by the Federal Reserve). The high value of the dollar kept foreign goods cheap and stimulated US imports. It kept American goods expensive and discouraged US exports.

Normally, trade deficits are self-correcting. When a country begins to run a trade deficit, its currency declines in price in world currency markets. This makes its goods less expensive and foreign goods more expensive. But several of our trading partners, including Japan and China, manipulate currency values, keeping the American dollar overvalued relative to their own currencies in order to perpetuate and grow our trade deficits with them. They do this by sending the excess of dollars they earn back to us, by buying US government bonds and other US assets, in effect lending us the money to buy their goods. The Japanese and Chinese governments account for about two-thirds of the foreign-government-caused component of the trade deficits.

WHY BALANCED FREE TRADE SHOULD BE OUR GOAL

Are trade deficits a problem? Some economists are flippant. Why would a country want to exchange goods of greater value than it receives? And if a country willingly sends you goods of greater value than you send it, what is your complaint? Because most economists believe that trade deficits are a short-term phenomenon, their analysis of the costs and benefits of trade deficits has been restricted. In the short term, the country running a deficit benefits from higher consumption than would otherwise be possible, and the country exporting more than it imports consumes less than it otherwise would. But there are long term costs to accepting long-term trade deficits.

There are economic models which show that in the long run the situation reverses, with the country that "gave away" goods in exchange for IOUs better off, and the country which accepted the "free" goods worse off. A minimum standard for ensuring that trade does benefit all is that trade should be relatively in balance.

When trade is in balance, all countries benefit. Each country specializes in what it does best; exchanging those products for products it could not produce as cheaply as the selling country. As a result of such specialization, each country is enabled to use or consume a greater quantity of goods and services than it would have been able to do in the absence of trade. Classical economist David Ricardo in 1821 summarized the case for free trade as follows:

> Under a system of perfectly free commerce, each country naturally devotes its capital and labour to such employments as are most beneficial to each. This pursuit of individual advantage is admirably connected with the universal good of the whole. By stimulating industry, by rewarding ingenuity, and by using most efficaciously the peculiar powers bestowed by nature, it distributes labour most effectively and most economically: while, by increasing the general mass of productions, it diffuses general benefit, and binds together, by one common tie of interest and intercourse, the universal society of nations throughout the civilized world. It is this principle which determines that wine shall be made in France and Portugal, that corn shall be grown in America and Poland, and that hardware and other goods shall be manufactured in England.[1]

The advantages of international trade based on comparative advantage have long been clear. Each country specializes in what it can produce most efficiently and exchanges those goods for goods other countries produce more efficiently. When trade is in balance, both countries enjoy higher standards of living. Each country gives up a bundle of goods it can produce more efficiently for a bundle of goods the other country produces more efficiently. This raises the living standards of workers in both countries.

In this context, government interventions that distort market incentives are unambiguously bad. For instance, a tariff that limits trade would prevent otherwise beneficial exchanges from taking place and this would make both countries worse off than they otherwise would be. By the same token, an export subsidy that encourages trade would merely shift prices downwards on the subsidized good, giving a free benefit to those receiving the good.

Note that Ricardo assumes that trade is in balance. Therefore, the losses to those who lose their jobs as a result of being displaced by imports are more than offset by gains to those who produce for export. In addition, the standard of living in each country is raised.

Ricardo's comparative advantage argument leaves little room for chronically imbalanced trade, and no reason for it to persist. From this perspective, imbalanced trade is akin to a failure of supply to meet demand. It is analogous to a store stocking more goods than it can sell. Eventually prices will adjust, and balance will be restored.

For more than two centuries, the leading economists believed that an optimum trade balance would be produced by a policy of free trade. They even rationalized it by developing a theory that if all countries were on the gold standard (each currency convertible to gold at a specified weight), market forces would automatically cause prices to fall in the trade deficit country and rise in the trade surplus country and thus restore the balance of trade. They reasoned that the export of gold in settlement of the trade imbalance would force a reduction in the money supply in the deficit country causing wages and prices to fall and vice versa in the surplus country. In 1935, however, John Maynard Keynes argued that wages and prices were relatively inflexible and predicted, on that basis, that the adjustment in the deficit country would be accompanied by widespread unemployment and depression.

In 1972, the United States, faced with the loss of gold reserves, went off the gold standard and was followed by the rest of the world adopting the current system of flexible exchange rates. Economists believed that under a system of flexible exchange rates, the currency of any country experiencing substantial trade deficits would decline relative to the currencies of the trade surplus countries. This would make imports more expensive in the country experiencing the trade deficits, reducing its demand for imports, and make its exports less expensive to foreigners, increasing their demand for its exports. Over time, at least, balanced trade and purchasing power parity would be maintained. The only problem with this argument is that it has empirical holes. Why has the US trade deficit persisted for more than two decades? What delayed the natural adjustment? Enter strategic trade theory and the currency manipulations of the dollar mercantilist nations.

"Strategic Trade" versus Free Trade

In modern economic theory, the classical comparative advantage justification for free trade has been complicated by other factors. It is no longer considered to be a complete treatment of the topic. As Paul Krugman wrote in 1987:

> Free trade is not passé, but it is an idea that has irretrievably lost its innocence. Its status has shifted from optimum to reasonable rule of thumb. There is still a case for free trade as a good policy, and as a useful target in the practical world of politics, but it can never again be asserted as the policy that economic theory tells us is always right.[2]

There are a series of "what if" questions that the classic comparative advantage story does not address. As economists have addressed these questions, the case for free trade has become more complex, and imbalanced trade has become a more obvious problem.

The classic model assumes that comparative advantage is fixed. This makes sense when it comes to comparative advantage derived from natural resources but makes much less sense for complex manufactured goods. What if, by contrast, comparative advantage develops over time as firms learn how to produce goods more effectively? The classic model assumes that markets are perfectly competitive. What if they are not? What if the assumption that trade must balance is modified to allow the accumulation of debt and financial assets?

The consequence of asking these questions has been a set of "if" statements. As Harry Truman famously complained, most economists have two hands, and are likely to say "on the one hand... but on the other hand...." If certain conditions apply, then free trade remains optimal (or at least appealing). If other conditions apply, then governments have an incentive to engage in "strategic trade" policies that subsidize exporters, protect domestic markets, etc., in order to alter the terms of trade in favor of the domestic economy.[3] In other words, some of the time, non-free-trade or "strategic trade" policies allow governments to boost the national economy. Typically, though not always, this gain is at the expense of other national economies.[4]

What kinds of costs are imposed? One version of the strategic trade model focuses on competition between firms in two countries to make sales to a third country. Because the market is not perfectly competitive, there are oligopoly profits to be made by the firm that makes the sale. If one country can distort the terms of competition (e.g., through a subsidy to its exporters or by driving up the value of the currency of the other country), it can drive the other country out of the market, and realize the profits all by itself.[5]

Another way of characterizing the case for strategic trade builds on ideas of "external economies," because there are almost always "knowledge spillovers." For instance, getting better at making computers has allowed the Chinese government to get better at making weapons much more rapidly. Subsidizing one industry can have payoffs for other industries.[6]

The simplest case, however, is one that focuses on just two countries and monetary mercantilism. The mercantilist country runs a surplus for a while with the target country and invests the surplus received from trade in income-producing assets of the target country. Eventually the mercantilist country has substantially higher consumption because it is able to spend some of the profits from the foreign investment on consumables. The target country, eventually, has a lower level of consumption because it is paying for the mercantilists' consumption.[7]

Although strategic trade writers eschew the term, their analyses suggest that mercantilist policies can pay off. Contrary to the classic comparative advantage analysis, beggaring-thy-neighbor is often in the national interest. As Paul Krugman and other authors in the strategic trade literature note, these theories can be (mis)read as giving the green light to mercantilism.

Mercantilism and Imbalanced Trade

Mercantilism was an economic philosophy that dominated government policies from the sixteenth to the eighteenth centuries. It equated a country's welfare with an increase in its stock of gold and treasure. To a large extent, this was the result of the discovery of Aztec gold in the new world. Spain prospered by the shipment of treasure from the new world and became the dominant world power. The evidence thus appeared to justify the mercantilist view that equated gold and treasure with national power.

The mercantilist countries of the 16ᵗʰ through 19ᵗʰ centuries sought to export more than they imported in order to build up their gold hoards. During the sixteenth century, the Spanish gold taken from its American colonies was used to pay for goods made in England, France, and other countries. England and France grew economically while Spanish industry foundered, leaving Spain a second rate power.

The beginnings of economics as a science is often dated from the publication in 1776 of Adam Smith's *An Inquiry into the Nature and Causes of the Wealth of Nations* in which he criticized the underlying concept behind mercantilism. A nation's wealth, he argued, was not its gold, but its product. Smith was correct. The Spanish were clearly wrong to think that stolen gold would produce any long-term benefit. But the British and other mercantilist countries were not completely wrong. By building up their industries at Spanish expense, they turned themselves into economic superpowers and brought down the power of their military rival.

Mercantilism is a beggar-thy-neighbor trade policy. From the standpoint of the world economy as a whole, free trade is a far better policy. After Smith, removing any and all barriers to exports and imports became one of the first great "scientific" economic policies because it was shown that all parties benefited from trade.

Our problem is that the United States is currently the country being beggared. Strategic trade of various types can lead to real long-term changes in US competitiveness. Recent economic rethinking of the theory of international trade reveals that mercantilism can succeed in raising the long-term standard of living of those in countries practicing it.

The United States experienced chronic trade deficits for the past three decades, but the dollar did not fall relative to the currencies of the trade surplus countries. Economists, having raised free trade to a dogma, never counted on countries deliberately accumulating dollar reserves and dollar assets in order to manipulate currency values so as to maintain their favorable trade balances (dollar mercantilism). They also never counted on countries introducing policies, as the US government has done, that subsidize foreign savings over domestic savings. By investing their trade surpluses in US assets, Japan, China, South Korea, and several other countries are preventing any correction to the trade imbalance. The result: chronic trade deficits in the United States.

Are those who run chronic trade surpluses with the United States gaining anything thereby? In the old days of gold mercantilism, the gold gained from trade circulated as money. In the new days of dollar mercantilism, the dollars that are "sterilized" from trade are loaned back to the United States and earn interest. As a result, the dollar mercantilist nations earn income on their US investments so long as the dollars they acquire retain value.

The classic model assumed away trade deficits and surpluses. However in 1997, Peking University economics professor Heng-Fu Zou, a Senior Research Economist for the World Bank's Development Research Group, showed, in an intriguing paper, that mercantilism can succeed on its own terms for a small economy. Accumulating foreign assets (running a trade surplus) leads to long term positive outcomes. "A nation with strong mercantilist sentiment ends up with large foreign asset accumulation and high consumption in the long run."[8]

Zou's paper has been almost entirely ignored by the profession. It runs contrary to the received wisdom. But its intuition is very simple. A mercantilist preference for asset accumulation has the effect of increasing future consumption. By saving more now, countries put themselves in the position of collecting additional interest and other income later. This can make their consumers better off in the long term. In addition to the normal gains from specialization and comparative advantage, they will also be able to consume profits from their savings. Other studies of the history of recent Asian mercantilism reach similar conclusions: mercantilism can pay off.[9] The principal neighbor being beggared by this beggar-thy-neighbor approach to trade policy is the United States, soothed into passivity by the enjoyment of cheap imported goods bought with borrowed cash.

There are other important long-term advantages that accrue to countries with chronic trade surpluses. What they lose in short-term consumption, they may, under some circumstances, regain in long term technological advantage. By strengthening their industry and undermining US industry, they enhance their economic power in the world. These countries sacrifice some domestic consumption in the short-term, but gain tremendously in terms of long-term growth. In contrast, the United States gains domestic consumption in the short term, but suffers deindustrialization and, eventually, a severe cut in living standards.

Relatively balanced trade is a necessary precondition for the full benefits of free trade. When trade is in balance, the gains of those in the export industries plus the gains that consumers get from lower prices exceed the losses of those in the industries adversely affected by imports. Workers who lose jobs in low-wage industries that compete with imports find better-paying jobs in expanding export-oriented industries. But when a country experiences growing and chronic trade deficits as the United States has done for three decades, good jobs and rising wages are created in the exporting countries while in the United States manufacturing workers lose their jobs and are forced to seek jobs in the service sector, putting downward pressure on wages. The damage done by the deficits is not that they caused unemployment but that they caused wages to stagnate and made the distribution of income more unequal. Had exports increased in proportion to imports, the workers who lost jobs in low-wage industries like textiles and shoes would have found more productive and better-paying jobs in expanding export-oriented companies like Deere and Boeing.

There are substantial and real advantages to free trade, but mercantilist or strategic trade policies can benefit US trading partners while hurting the US economy. If strategic/mercantilist policies were succeeding, we would observe precisely what we are observing: large chronic trade deficits and the destruction of US competitive advantage in industry after industry.

When US policy makers belief in free trade induces many to maintain that all is well, we risk undermining the conditions under which free trade can succeed. In an analysis of the strategic trade model, David Collie demonstrated that free trade can be sustained under only some assumptions about relative competitiveness, and in these circumstances free trade is sustained with the threat of a trade war.[10]

Other studies affirm this point in models that overcome the original theoretical conflicts of the strategic trade literature concerning Cournot versus Bertrand competition. Efforts to distort the terms of trade strategically can succeed in boosting national income only when other nations do not respond. Beggaring thy neighbor can work, but only if the neighbor is passive.[11]

By ignoring strategic manipulation of the terms of trade by our more mercantilist trading partners, the United States may create conditions in which strategic trade and mercantilism rather than free trade are in equilibrium for those countries. *We are trading away our future for a mess of mercantilist produced pottage!*

Effect on Manufacturing

There are many products involved in international trade. These include manufactured goods, farm products, raw materials, financial services, computer software, and much more. In this book we mostly focus upon manufactured goods because they constitute the bulk of what is exchanged in international trade and can be most easily tracked using the available statistics. Also, the same trends that have been occurring with manufactured goods have been occurring with most other products as well.

Some economists suppose that the United States is in the process of transitioning from being a manufacturing-oriented economy to a services-oriented economy. They are not worried by the trade deficit in manufactured goods because they think that our trade surplus in services will eventually overcome it.[12] Indeed America has been exporting more services than it imports. But the surplus in services has not even come close to overcoming the trade deficit in goods. In fact, our trade surplus in services has been following a similar negative trajectory to the trade deficit in goods, peaking at 1.2% of GDP in 1996 and falling to 0.7% in 2006. Whenever we discuss the trade deficit in this book, we are talking about the combined deficit in goods and services. That deficit has been going up.

Figure 1 shows the trend in the overall strength of the US dollar and for US exports and imports from the beginning of 1996 through the third quarter of 2007. From 1996 to 2002, the dollar rose relative to most of the world's currencies. Possibly as a result, US exports of goods and services fell. Since then the dollar has been falling against most currencies and US exports have been rising. When the dollar climbs (i.e., strengthens) as compared with other currencies, exports tend to decrease and imports tend to increase because US goods tend to get more expensive than foreign goods. When the dollar declines (i.e., weakens), imports tend to decrease and exports tend to decrease because US goods tend to get less expensive than foreign goods.

If US exports were the entire story, then the trade deficit would be on its way to solving itself. Even though US exports were rising, US imports were rising even faster, partly because US exports were

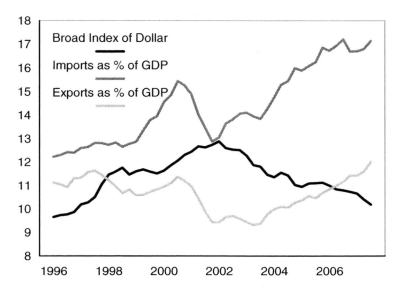

Figure 1. Dollar Strength and US Exports
The dollar peeked in the first quarter of 2002. Exports bottomed out in the first quarter of 2002. Imports rose throughout the period, except for a brief drop during 2000 and 2001. (Source BEA and Federal Reserve Broad Index of the Dollar with January 1997 = 10.0.

including an increasing percentage of imported components.

The trade deficit does not respond quickly to changes in the strength of the dollar. When the dollar was strong, foreign businesses increased their investment and American businesses reduced their investment. Then when the dollar fell, foreign businesses were still able to hold onto their market shares for quite some time, even at the new exchange rate. They did so by cutting their profit margins or by taking advantage of their increased productivity.[13]

As Figure 2 shows, the US trade deficit with China and Japan continued to grow, even though the depreciation of the dollar relative to the euro and many other currencies did cause the US trade deficit with the rest of the world to begin to fall in 2006. From the beginning of 2003 to the end of 2006, the dollar lost 21% of its value verses the euro (from .97 to .76 euros), but fell by only 1% versus the Japanese yen (120 to 119 yen) and by just 6% versus the Chinese renminbi (from 8.3 to 7.8 yuan). So long as some foreign governments, including the Chinese and Japanese governments, continue to manipulate their currency values in order to produce growing trade surpluses with the United States, the foreign-government-caused portion of the trade deficit will continue to climb steadily.

Trade deficits acquire a momentum of their own. When the exchange rate of the dollar goes up dramatically, it not only tends to

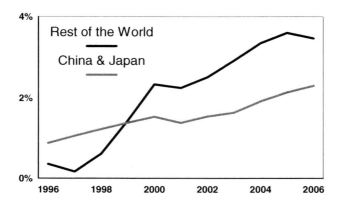

Figure 2. US Trade Deficit as Percent of GDP

The US trade deficit with China and Japan accounts for a steadily growing component of the overall trade deficit. (Source BEA)[14]

cause the trade deficit to go up, but it also tends to cause American manufacturing investment to go down. This lack of investment in manufacturing can, in turn, make future trade deficits worse.

When the broad index of the dollar rose dramatically during the period from 1996 through 2002, gross manufacturing investment declined steadily from 2.4% of GDP in 1996 to 1.3% of GDP in 2004 as shown in Figure 3, despite the fact that the cost of capital (as indicated by real long-term interest rates) was falling at the same time. In both 2003 and 2004 there was not even enough investment to replace wearing out plant and equipment as indicated by negative net investment those years. It wasn't until 2005 that manufacturing investment started a modest turn around, possibly in response to the weakening dollar that began in 2002.

Robert A. Blecker, a professor of economics at American University, performed the most extensive analysis of the effects of the exchange rate of the dollar (as measured by the broad index shown in Figure 1) upon American manufacturing investment. In a study published in the *International Review of Applied Economics*, he discovered that the exchange rate of the dollar was one of the four factors that caused manufacturing investment to change from year to year during the period from 1973 to 2004. Those factors were: (1) exchange rate of the dollar – higher exchange rate would cause less

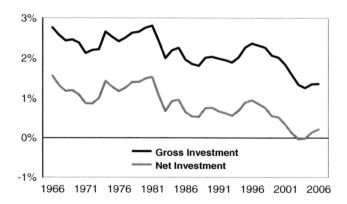

Figure 3. Manufacturing Investment as Percent of GDP
Fixed investment in America's manufacturing sector declined as a percentage of GDP from 2.4% in 1996 to just 1.3% in 2004. (Source: BEA Fixed Asset tables)

investment, (2) the cost of capital goods – higher interest rate would cause less investment, (3) the GDP growth rate – faster growth would cause more investment, and (4) cash flow from undistributed profits and depreciation allowances – more cash on hand would lead to more investment.[15] During the period from 1995 to 2004, the rising exchange rate of the dollar proved to be such a powerful factor that it drove manufacturing investment downward, despite the fact that falling long-term interest rates were making capital goods less expensive.

In a July 2006 speech based upon this study, Blecker pointed to the accumulating evidence of the decline in manufacturing investment. He said:

> According to my estimates, the rise in the value of the dollar since 1995 – which is a major cause of the trade deficit – has discouraged investment in US manufacturing to such an extent that the capital stock of the manufacturing sector was 17% lower in 2004 and new investment in US manufacturing was more than 60% lower in 2004 than they would have been if the dollar had not appreciated. Although the remaining manufacturing capacity is highly efficient, it accounts for a shrinking portion of US employment. Thus, the trade deficit does not simply cause a temporary reduction in output, but also a permanent loss of manufacturing capacity that can have long-lasting negative effects on the country's future productive capabilities.[16]

In 2006 Dan R. Mastromarco, a principal in the law and economics consulting firm Argus Group, pointed out that we are also losing our technological edge in manufacturing as evident from the decline in the number of engineering doctorates awarded to Americans by American graduate schools. He wrote:

> When manufacturing moves overseas to China, India, East Asia, or Europe, it takes engineering know-how because engineers will ply their trade where the action is – outside the United States. While venerable U.S. engineering institutions still maintain their foothold, more than half of their doctoral degrees are awarded to foreign students.[17]

Imbalanced trade shifts manufacturing from the importing countries to the exporting countries. Figure 4 shows that in 1965, the United States had a larger percentage of its civilian workforce employed in manufacturing than Japan (27.0% compared to 24.8%).[18] Since then manufacturing employment has been declining throughout the world as a percentage of the workforce, due to the increased productivity of modern technology, but it has been falling more rapidly in the United States than in Japan and Canada, two countries that have similar wage rates and technology levels as the United States.

By 1970, Japan had passed the United States with 27.4% of its civilian population engaged in manufacturing, compared to 26.4% in the United States and Canada a distant third at just 22.3%. By 2006, the United States had fallen far below Japan and even below Canada, with just 11.3% of its civilian workforce engaged in manufacturing. (Japan had 18.3% and Canada had 12.9%.)

The loss of manufacturing jobs does not translate into unemployment in the US economy; it translates into lower median wages. The displaced workers eventually find jobs but at an average lower wage. When former Ford workers now flip burgers for much lower wages, good jobs were lost even though unemployment did not rise.

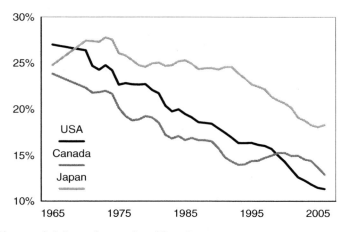

Figure 4. Manufacturing Employment

Manufacturing employment, as a percentage of the civilian labor force has been falling more rapidly in the United States than in Japan or Canada. (Source: Bureau of Labor Statistics)

In 2005, three economists (Erica L. Groshen, Bart Hobijn, and Margaret M. McConnell) performed a study for the Federal Reserve Bank of New York where they estimated the number of jobs it would take to produce the net imports coming into the United States. They estimated the loss of jobs to have been at most 3.3 million jobs in 2003, which was about 20% of the total US manufacturing workforce at the time. Rather than point out that 1/5 of US manufacturing jobs had been lost, they minimized the extent of the problem as being just 2.4 percent of total US employment:

> First, we determine that the offshoring of jobs has been a limited phenomenon: Our comprehensive estimate of the number of jobs embodied in US net imports is small relative to total employment in the United States – 2.4% of the total, at the most – both historically and in recent years. Moreover this estimate is sometimes positive and sometimes negative, suggesting that international trade does not necessarily mean a loss of jobs for the United States.[19]

It is true that manufacturing jobs can be gained from trade as well as lost. When trade is in surplus, jobs are gained, when trade is in deficit, jobs are lost. When the trade deficit diminishes, as it sometimes does, the number of jobs lost decreases. Unfortunately, in recent years, the job loss has been growing.

Given the increase in the trade deficit in goods and services from 4.6% of GDP in 2003 to 5.8% in 2006 and the increase in civilian employment from 138 million jobs in 2003 to 144 million in 2006, we extrapolate that if Goshen et al. conducted the same study today, they would find that by 2006, the trade deficit had caused a loss of up to 4.4 million jobs (27% of the 2006 manufacturing workforce).

Those who lost their factory jobs did not remain unemployed but competed for and found other work. Their competition had the effect of bringing downward pressure on wage rates in general. The resulting wage stagnation and worsening of the distribution of income has contributed to increased income inequality in the United States over the last three decades.

The decline in manufacturing and other exportable production associated with the trade deficit is compounded by its long-term effects on American competitiveness. The loss of entire industries (e.g., television, computers and shoes) to competitors in other countries makes it difficult for the United States to reenter those markets later. A variety of economic models incorporate the benefits of building upon what already exists (factors such as increasing returns to scale and the roles of intellectual property and learning-by-doing). By continuing and allowing policies that sustain the trade deficit, we prevent American firms from gaining the scale and competitive advantage that they might otherwise achieve, and we destroy firms that previously had a competitive position (and would not have lost it were trade in balance).[20]

Other Explanations for Loss of Manufacturing

The vast majority of economists believe in free trade so much that they have blinded themselves to the obvious cause of the loss of American manufacturing jobs: the government actions that drive the trade deficits. Instead, they have either minimized the problem or have offered alternative explanations.

Some have argued that the nearly full employment in the American economy is evidence that the effects have been minimal. But the damage done by the deficits is not that they caused unemployment but that they caused wages in the United States to stagnate and made the distribution of income more unequal. The workers displaced by imports found jobs at lower wages, which is what the "law" of supply and demand predicts.

Some have argued that American manufacturing jobs were displaced by technological changes. This argument is suspicious on its face. We have had technological changes throughout the past two centuries with no negative effects on the level of wages; indeed, wages rose continuously because of the increasing productivity that technological change produced. However, recent decades have been marked by widening disparities and a stagnation in median wages. The major problem is that most new products are not being produced in the United States. Instead, we import them and boost the trade deficit instead of manufacturing employment.

Some economists believe that America's current wage stagnation has been the result of the poor performance of our educational system. College graduates, especially those in scientific, technological, medical, and professional fields, have indeed realized substantially increased employment at high wages. It is argued that too few of our students go on to college, and therefore they qualify only for lower paid jobs. The argument is not convincing. You don't need a college degree to build airplanes with Boeing (highly labor-intensive); you don't need a college degree to build a Deere tractor or a Caterpillar bulldozer. Those are all big exporters and they all pay high wages. The trouble is that they and hundreds of other American firms are not exporting enough.

None of these explanations is as likely as the obvious conclusion that the trade deficits are responsible. By allowing the trade deficits, we have been deindustrializing our country.

Effect on Income Distribution

The US economy was enjoying full employment in 2006, but the millions of workers displaced by the trade deficits reentered the job market and the increased number of workers looking for jobs resulted in lower wages for all workers with the exception of those insulated from foreign competition such as Wall Street brokers, professionals, professors, and federal government employees *inter alia*! This is one of the principal reasons for the wage stagnation and the worsening distribution of income observed during the past two decades. The average wage adjusted for inflation in all private industry rose 2.2% per year from 1948 to 1978 but only 1.3% per year from 1978 to 2005. Although exports create jobs, the effect of trade deficits is to cause the loss of more jobs from imports compared with the gains from exports.

Had exports increased during the past two decades in proportion to imports, the workers who lost jobs in low-wage industries like textiles and shoes would have found more productive and better-paying jobs in expanding export-oriented companies like Caterpillar, Deere, Boeing, Harley Davidson, Intel, Texas Instruments, GM, and Ford. Balanced trade would have raised the incomes of US workers without harming our trading partners.

Federal Reserve Chairman Ben S. Bernanke disputes our interpretation. In a long 2007 speech devoted to the growing income inequality problem within the United States, he acknowledged that loss of jobs in import-competing industries was indeed occurring, but argued that such jobs would be replaced by jobs in exporting industries. Specifically:

> International trade, another aspect of globalization, may also have differential effects on the economic well-being of U.S. workers, even as it tends to raise real wages and incomes on average. For example, some empirical research suggests that, in the 1980s and 1990s, increased international trade reduced the profitability and hence the demand for labor in a number of industries that employed relatively low skilled workers (Borjas, Freeman, and Katz, 1997; Sachs and Shatz, 1994). Of course trade has increased the *potential* [italics added] markets for other domestic industries, leading to higher demand and thus higher real wages for workers in those industries.[21]

Although this argument sounds plausible, it had a 760 billion dollar hole in it in 2006. The word "potential" is key to understanding his fallacy. If trade were in balance, then what Bernanke said would be perfectly true. Unfortunately for American workers, the jobs in exporting industries are only "potential" jobs, not actual jobs, *because of the trade deficits!*

DANGER OF HARD LANDING

As a result of the trade deficits, the United States has been buying consumer goods on credit, going further and further into debt since the middle of 1985. This position of the United States is particularly dangerous because much of our debt is to a rising power and potential enemy in the international system – China. This is an almost unprecedented development, but the best parallels do not bode well for continued American power.[22]

There are two possible ways that the United States could come out of debt. In the "soft landing" scenario, we could work our way out of debt by producing goods and services for export. In this scenario,

American investment in trade-oriented goods and services increases in order to increase exports and to replace goods and services that Americans are buying from abroad. The trade deficit gradually improves.

Unfortunately, with more and more countries joining the Chinese and Japanese in buying dollars in order to build up their exports at our expense, and with China moving into more and more of our remaining industries, including automobiles, unless we take steps to fight dollar mercantilism, it is unlikely that a soft landing will take place while the United States still has industries left that can compete in world markets.

The alternative to the "soft landing" is the "hard landing." Once the run on the dollar begins, the dollar would fall to a fraction of its former value — the longer the hard landing is delayed, the less of our industry would be left at the time it takes place. The less industry left, the harder the landing, and the slower the recovery. After the hard landing, things would suddenly be different in the United States.

Other countries have gone through currency crashes, so what would happen is really not a mystery. Prices in the stores, especially prices of foreign-made goods, would go sky-high. In just one month, the cost of imported goods could double, triple, or quadruple. Interest rates would skyrocket. Some retail stores would fail because of the sudden decline in demand for their merchandise. The housing market would go bust, partly because of the skyrocketing mortgage rates and some home owners would sell their homes for a fraction of what they had once been worth. People who had taken out variable rate loans would face much higher interest costs and many would go broke, no longer able to pay the interest on their debts. The sudden growth in business and personal bankruptcies could cause many banks to fail. Energy prices, especially gasoline prices, would skyrocket.

The news would not be altogether bad. There would be a great boom in the secondhand industry. Secondhand stores would move into some of the buildings vacated by closing banks and retail stores. Our remaining manufacturing industry would be working around the clock, absorbing some of those who had just lost their jobs in the financial, real estate, and service sectors.

The United States would have a very tough year, but the following year would see the beginning of a recovery which would continue, unless we were to enact stupid economic policies that would prevent it. Those foolish policy options might be quite enticing. Whichever political party would be presiding at the time of the crash would likely be out of power for a couple of decades and the other party would fall back on its radical fringe.

If the Republicans were in power during the crash, then the left-wing big-government enthusiasts at the fringe of the Democratic party would likely turn America into a socialist state that would sap American incentive.

If the Democrats were in power, then the right-wing isolationists at the fringe of the Republican party would likely turn American into a country isolated as much as possible from the world economy. They would encourage import-competing industries (using tariffs) and discourage exporting industries (possibly with export restrictions).

The Argentine experience could be an example of what to expect. In 2002, the Argentine peso collapsed on world currency markets to about a quarter of its former value, giving Argentina a 10% inflation rate in a single month (March, 2002) and a decline of GDP of about 11% in a single year. Then, from 2003 through 2005, the Argentine economy recovered rapidly, growing by about 9% per year.

The Argentine government's mistakes during their recovery were rampant. In order to raise government revenue, the Argentine government imposed tariffs on imports, which encouraged the growth of inefficient import-competing industries. At the same time, they discouraged exports, especially beef exports. In March of 2006, President Kirchner actually banned beef exports (in order to reduce the prices paid by Argentine consumers). He later rescinded the outright ban, but still kept export controls that reduced beef exports to 70% of their 2005 level. As a result of similar mistakes under Peron after World War II, Argentina was one of the slowest-growing economies of the postwar twentieth century.

Some economists have argued that since the United States debt, unlike third-world debt, is denominated in our own currency, the dollar would not crash very far, nor would the effects be severe. They may be ignoring the fact that interest rates in the United States would likely skyrocket as a result of the sudden decrease in foreign savings coming into the country. They also may be ignoring the fact that a dollar crash would send stock markets plummeting throughout the world, thrusting the entire world into recession or depression.

It is true that we would not have the post-crash third-world problem of paying an increased amount of principal to repay our debt. We would have a different problem that could be equally severe, a skyrocketing interest rate on our debt. Since January 2006, the Federal Reserve has been holding US short-term rates above long-term interest rates causing foreign investors to gradually move their financial holdings into short-term holdings. The payments on short-term holdings go up as US interest rates rise, as would the debt payments by those Americans who have borrowed using credit cards or adjustable-rate loans. The rise in interest payments would drive many Americans into bankruptcy and they would take some financial institutions down with them. The Federal Reserve might try to alleviate these problems by intentionally inflating the dollar, but monetary inflation would cause its own set of problems.

The main problem is that our exports would not increase fast enough to slow the fall in the dollar. Although American automobile companies and some others would increase their production, we would still be importing oil and consumer goods at much higher prices. There would not be a sufficient increase in exports to stabilize the dollar until new investments in American production would come on line.

Paul Krugman argues that the extensive US investments abroad would result in an increased flow of income from abroad which would stabilize the dollar.[23] He might be right, but on the other hand, the crash of the dollar would cause a stock market crash around the world. While there would be an increased flow of income from abroad, it might not be enough to stabilize the dollar.

When the Argentine peso collapsed, few other countries were affected, but the effect of a dollar collapse would be worldwide.

Although we could export our way to continued prosperity in the "soft landing" scenario, a hard landing would mean a worldwide recession or depression. Increased demand for Asian exports in the United States helped the Asian Tigers recover from their currency crashes in the 1990s, but there would probably not be much increase in demand for American products from a depressed world economy.

Crashes tend to overcompensate. They often go beyond the minimum amount necessary in order to correct an imbalance. The wishful thinking by economists that the dollar crash would be mild may just be another example of the wishful thinking that got the United States into this mess in the first place.

In this chapter, we have shown that the trade deficit has been disastrous for the American manufacturing sector. We have assumed, given the growing trade deficits, that other American products involved in international trade have been similarly affected. Dollar mercantilism has taken a major toll on the US economy.

Investment in the manufacturing sector has been declining, which has destroyed good-paying jobs and led to an increasing inequality of income. Unless we deal with the trade deficit, we will face a steady decline in our tradable sectors. At the same time, we will face a growing likelihood of a sudden hard landing characterized by high interest rates, high inflation, and a high level of bankruptcies. The consequences of the hard landing could be the end of the United States as the world's predominant power. China, already the rising international power, is granted an additional weapon by our debt and deficits – the capacity to undermine the US financial system and produce a hard landing any time it decides to dump dollars on world currency markets.

2. Roots of the Trade Deficit

Warren Buffett once told a story about two islands, Squanderville and Thriftville. The citizens of Thriftville work hard to produce twice as much as they consume and export the rest to Squanderville in return for Squanderville's IOU's. Some pundits in Squanderville see future problems coming, but are ignored.[1]

A trade deficit occurs when a country buys more from abroad than it sells. How did the United States get the trillions of dollars worth of foreign exchange needed to pay for the excess of imports over exports: the trade deficits incurred during the past two decades? In 2006 alone, we imported $760 billion more in goods and services than we exported. The short answer is that foreigners lent us the money to buy their goods. The word "lent" should not be taken too literally but it is a fair description of the process. What foreigners did was to buy US stocks and bonds or put their savings into US bank accounts. This flow of savings from abroad provided the foreign exchange that our importers needed to pay for their imports.

Our imports equal the sum of our exports plus the flow of savings from abroad. What we pay for our imports equals what we earn from our exports plus what foreigners lend us. Payments to and from any country and the rest of the world must always be in balance. That is what is meant by the concept "balance of payments."

The US balance of payments for 2006 was calculated by the Bureau of Economic Analysis in two different ways, as shown in Table 1. That year, the United States imported about $811 billion more than it exported as measured by the *Current Account Balance*. That year, foreigners purchased about $805 billion more of American assets than Americans purchased of foreign assets as measured by the *Financial Account Balance*. The two are just about equal because they both measure the same thing. Trade deficits are financed by foreign capital flows; one mirrors the other.

Whenever the United States is running a trade deficit, foreigners are saving dollars and sending those savings to the United States to buy American assets (unless we ship gold).

Table 1. US International Transactions in 2006
[Billions of dollars] (Credits +; debits -)

Current Account

Balance on Goods	-838
Balance on Services	80
Balance on Income	37
Unilateral Current Transfers	-90
Balance on Current Account	-811

Financial Account

US-owned assets abroad, net	-1055
Foreign-owned assets in the United States, net	1860
Balance on Financial Account	805

(Source: Table 1, U.S. International Transactions Accounts Data, Bureau of Economic Analysis)

THE TRADE DEFICITS & FOREIGN INVESTMENT

Anything that reduces our trade deficit reduces foreign investment flowing into the United States and anything that reduces foreign investment flowing into the United States reduces the trade deficit. Most non-economists think that the trade deficits cause the flow of foreign savings into the United States, but most economists realize that the opposite is true.

Here's why. Whenever the United States is running a trade deficit, the value of its imports is greater than the value of its exports, so foreigners are getting a surplus of dollars for the surplus of goods that they sell us. Foreigners then have two choices: (1) they could exchange those dollars for their own currency or (2) they could save them, such as by using them to buy US Treasury Notes or by putting them in dollar-denominated bank accounts.

If they decide to exchange the dollars, they would take those dollars to a currency market where people trade currencies. With so many more people trying to sell dollars than buy dollars, the price of the dollar would go down (weaken). As the dollar would weaken, American goods would become less expensive to foreigners and foreign goods would become more expensive to Americans. The change in relative prices would cause foreigners to buy more American goods and Americans to buy fewer foreign goods. This would continue until the surplus of dollars disappears on the foreign exchange market. In other words, whenever foreigners don't save dollars, currency values adjust until a trade deficit is eliminated.

If they, instead, choose to save the dollars by putting them into financial investments or dollar-denominated bank accounts, then the trade deficit could continue and become chronic. Long-term trade deficits are always the result of foreign savings, and never the result of any other factor; not differences in wage rates, nor differences in working conditions; nor changes in educational levels, nor changes in tariffs. The international price of the dollar in currency markets would be affected by such factors, but not the trade deficit in the long-term.

There are two kinds of investment, fixed investment and financial investment. Fixed investment builds the economy where the investment is taking place, making it easier for that economy to pay off the foreign loan. It is illustrated by the building of the steel mills and railroads in the United States in the 19th century with the help of British investors, the European recovery after WWII financed by the US, the building of a new factory in South Carolina by BMW, and the fixed investment of American corporations in China. In all of these instances, fixed investment involved creating new productive capabilities.

Financial investment is illustrated by Daimler-Benz buying Chrysler, or by foreigners purchasing US stocks and bonds, or by foreigners putting money into dollar-denominated savings accounts in foreign banks that the foreign banks in turn place tax-free into US financial assets. Unlike fixed investment, foreign financial investment simply shifts control of productive assets from people in one country to those in another.

A HISTORY OF THE TRADE DEFICITS

The broadest measure of the trade balance is called the Current Account Balance. It is predominantly the trade balance in goods and

services, but is adjusted for usually small quantities measuring transfers between countries (such as gifts) and income flows between countries (such as profits repatriated by American corporations abroad).
Turn the chart upside down to see the amount of foreign savings flowing into the United States. Whenever the current account balance goes
down, the amount of foreign savings flowing into the United States
goes up, and vice-versa.

The graph shown in Figure 5 starts with 1960, the earliest year
readily available from the Bureau of Economic Analysis. The graph
doesn't show the late nineteenth century when foreign savings were
pouring into the United States to finance investments in our infrastructure and industries. Nor does it show how the World Wars of the
Twentieth Century and their aftermath caused American savings to
flow abroad.

Figure 5 does show that America was running a positive current
account balance until 1970. As a result of overly-rapid Federal Reserve money creation, inflation increased and caused the 1971 trade
deficit. Speculators began buying gold in anticipation that the dollar
value of gold would have to increase. As a result of being on the gold
standard, there was a serious loss of US gold reserves.

In December 1971 the dollar was devalued against European

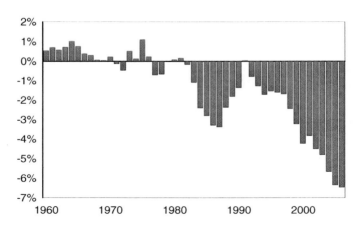

Figure 5. Current Account Balance as Percent of GDP
Since the early 1980s, the United States has spent more abroad than it has
sold, and borrowed more abroad than it has loaned. (Source: BEA)

currencies by eight percent and the price of officially traded gold went up to $38 per ounce. A little more than a year later, there was a run on the dollar and the dollar was devalued another ten percent. Although Germany and others tried to bolster the dollar, they were unsuccessful. A month later, exchange rates were allowed to float (i.e., to be determined by demand and supply) and the era of flexible exchange rates was born.

For the most part, what replaced the gold standard worldwide was the US dollar standard. In the first years of that standard, from 1971 through 1980, the current account balance hovered around zero. From 1981 through 1990 the United States ran a current account deficit indicating that foreign savings were pouring into the United States. That deficit peaked at 3.4% of our GDP in 1987, declined for several years, abruptly went away in 1991, and then came back. From 1995 to 2006 it grew steadily reaching 6.2% of GDP in 2006.

Since trade deficits are mirrored by inflows of foreign savings, it is necessary to understand what factors caused foreign savings rates to change during each of the four periods that we will examine. In other words, why did foreigners prefer to save the dollars they earned from their increased exports to the United States, instead of spending them by increasing their imports from the United States?

There are two kinds of foreign savings that flow into the United States, private foreign savings and foreign-government savings. Private savings flow into the United States in order to take advantage of what are perceived to be good opportunities for investment in US fixed assets such as stocks, bonds, and savings deposits. For the most part, private savings are motivated by the pursuit of high returns on investment. When US interest rates go up, private foreign savings tend to increase, when US interest rates go down, private foreign savings tend to decrease. Foreign government savings flow into and out of the United States for reasons unrelated to interest rates, as we shall discuss later.

In this chapter we focus on three factors that have contributed to the US trade deficit: monetary policy, tax treatment of private foreign savings, and dollar mercantilism. We will discuss the modern history of the trade deficit starting in 1982 and will break it up into 4 periods. We will show that the increased foreign savings from 1981 through 1984 was caused by the Federal Reserve raising US interest rates (i.e. tight monetary policy to fight inflation), which encouraged private foreign savings to flow into this country. We will next examine US policies regarding tax treatment of private foreign savings, policies that we believe have been important drivers of the trade deficit since 1984. Foreign savings briefly stopped coming into the United States in 1991 because of Gulf-War related gifts. From 1996 to 2005, inflows of foreign government savings financed the majority of the trade deficit, driving down US interest rates. We conclude by examining 2006-2007, years in which the trade deficit stabilized and then went down because of a partial switch by foreign governments and private investors from dollar savings to euro savings.

We will discuss the changes that occurred in terms of the simple supply and demand graph shown in Figure 6, which shows how long-term interest rates are determined. This graph describes the relationship between the supply of savings, and demand for those savings, as mediated by price (the interest rate). The graph shows that interest rates are determined by the intersection between the combined supply of domestic and foreign savings and the demand for those savings

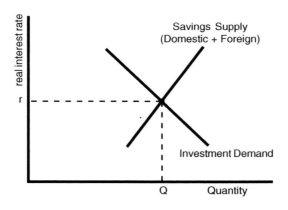

Figure 6. How Interest Rates are Determined
Long-term interest rates are determined by the intersection between the supply of savings (domestic & foreign combined) and the demand for fixed investment

by businesses and home buyers for gross fixed investment (their purchases of such things as structures, equipment, and software). Prices are normally set by the intersection between supply and demand, and interest rates are the price of borrowing money.

What Figure 6 says is that business and other long-term investors (such as home buyers) borrow money for fixed investment and get that money from a combination of domestic and foreign savings. When interest rates are low, investors can afford to borrow more money, and they do; conversely, when interest rates are high, there is less demand for fixed investment. On the supply side, when interest rates are high, there is more incentive to save since savings earn a higher rate of return; conversely when interest rates are low there is more incentive to consume on credit, which results in less savings available for long-term fixed investment.

1981-1984: PAUL VOLCKER CAUSES THE TRADE DEFICIT

From 1981 through 1984, the Federal Reserve under Chairman Paul Volcker tightened the money supply in order to reduce the inflation rate from 10.4% in the first quarter of 1981 down to 3.3% in the third quarter of 1984. In order to combat inflation, Volcker took money out of circulation by issuing lots of Treasury Notes (without having the Fed buy those notes on its own account). Contributing to this ex-

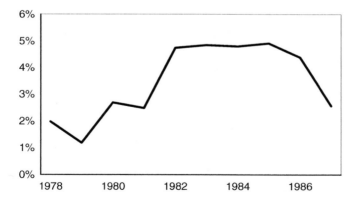

Figure 7. Federal Government Borrowing as Percent of GDP
From 1981 through 1984, Paul Volcker tightened the money supply by selling government bonds in order to control inflation. (Source: Federal Reserve)

panded government borrowing were the substantial Reagan budget deficits. As shown in Figure 7, the additional value of Treasury Notes put into circulation by the Federal Reserve was almost 5% of GDP each year from 1982 to 1984.[2] The number of bonds in circulation represents government borrowing (i.e. reduced domestic savings).

In line with this increased government borrowing, the interest rate multiplied from a real interest rate of 2.3% (on 10-year Treasury Notes) in 1980 to a real interest rate of 8.7% in 1984 as shown in Figure 8. The higher interest rate encouraged private savings. Personal savings rose from 7.2% of GDP in 1980 to 8.0% of GDP in 1984 and foreign savings increased from 0.1% of GDP in 1980 to 2.4% of GDP in 1984. The growth in foreign savings is mirrored by the increasing trade deficit.

Volcker's policies bear joint responsibility for these early trade deficits with Reagan's increasing US budget deficits. The federal government of the United States had been running a sizable budget deficit for several years before Volcker decided to tighten the money supply by selling US Treasury bonds. Up until Volcker's action, the federal budget deficit was causing inflation, but was not substantially increasing real long-term interest rates. Volcker eliminated the inflation, much to his credit, but his action had the effect of increasing interest rates, which, in turn, encouraged foreign savings to flow into the United

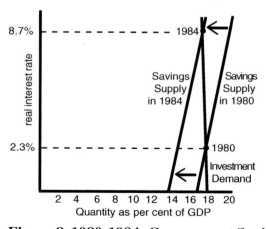

Figure 8. 1980-1984: Government Savings Falls
As the FED sold government bonds it decreased government savings and the interest rate increased.

States, contributing to the trade deficit.

1984-1986: CREATING TAX BREAKS FOR FOREIGNERS

In 1984 interest rates were very high: the US needed additional savings, whether from domestic or international sources. Instead of increasing US domestic savings (e.g. by cutting the federal budget deficit) the Reagan administration looked for ways to facilitate the flow of savings from abroad. Donald T. Regan, US Secretary of the Treasury, requested and received from Congress a seemingly minor policy change. Regan removed all remaining US taxes from the interest earned by foreign investors. From the perspective of the trade deficit, we believe this could make Regan the worst Treasury Secretary in United States history.

At Regan's request, the United States enacted one of the most foolish tax loopholes of all time, the private-foreign-savings tax loophole. Before 1984, most private foreign savers paid a withholding tax on any interest earned in the United States. Unless they were operating from a country that had a tax treaty with the United States that specified a lower taxation rate, they paid the United States a 30% rate of taxation on interest earned.

Regan asked congress to eliminate the 30% withholding tax in order to create a new tax loophole just for private foreign savers.

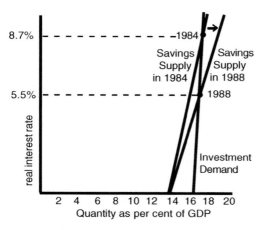

Figure 9. 1984 to 1986: Foreign Private Savings Increase

The creation of a tax loophole for foreign savers in 1984 caused increased foreign private savings to flow into the US. That flow still continues.

After the loophole, they paid nothing, zip, zero, nada, so long as their investments were purely financial, and not direct.[3] But perhaps Regan was not entirely to blame; earlier Secretaries of the Treasury had negotiated tax treaties that were just as foolish.

The Tax Treaties

The removal of the withholding tax concluded a process that had been going on for decades: the reduction of US government taxation upon foreign investment income earned in the United States. Tax treaties exist to resolve the potential for double taxation of income earned on foreign investments. Given their sovereign power over their citizens, some governments tax their citizens on their income wherever earned while others tax their citizens only on their income earned domestically, excluding income earned elsewhere. From the enactment of the US income tax, the United States has been in the first category but has allowed a credit on income taxes paid to foreign governments. In 1919 the International Chamber of Commerce of the United States endorsed the credit for foreign taxes as a measure that all governments should adopt. It called on the League of Nations to take measures to eliminate the "evils of double taxation."[4] That was a very sensible proposal but unnecessary in that US companies operating abroad were already sufficiently served by the US government's unilateral action of allowing a credit for foreign taxes paid.

In 1939, Sweden became the first country to unilaterally exempt interest earned by foreigners from taxation. After World War II, several other European countries followed suit in an attempt to attract foreign loans to help with postwar rebuilding. The treaty negotiated by the United States and the United Kingdom in 1945 provided for reciprocal exemption of interest on bonds and royalties at the source. As a result, when the Soviet Union later wanted to earn interest on its dollar reserves, it put those dollars in British banks. The British banks could then loan the same money to Americans without having to pay any tax to the United States on interest earned.

As the United States negotiated similar treaties with other European countries, similar accounts were established in banks throughout Europe. These accounts were increasingly funded by private individuals who wanted to lend dollars to Americans tax free. The resulting dollar-denominated bank deposits in European banks came to be called "eurodollars."

Our treaty with the Dutch in 1948 allowed the exemption of interest, royalties, and dividends at the source, but was later amended to permit a 15% tax on dividends. In 1955 our treaty with the Dutch was extended to include Dutch territories, including the Netherlands Antilles (NA), which ended up opening up a huge tax loophole in which US corporations would locate a subsidiary in the Netherlands Antilles for the purposes of borrowing money free of US tax (their tax liability to the Antilles would just be 1%). Many treaty shoppers and tax cheats also took advantage of the tax loophole opened by this treaty, as pointed out by Giuseppe Ammendola in his 1994 appropriately titled book about the 1984 tax loophole: *From Creditor to Debtor: The U.S. Pursuit of Foreign Capital – The Case of the Repeal of the Withholding Tax*:

> The US/NA Treaty was not just used by legitimate residents of the two countries or by third country investors who practiced treaty-shopping. It is widely assumed that many U.S. citizens used the benefits provided by the US/NA treaty to circumvent U.S. tax laws. The mechanism was similar to one used by third-country residents. The only difference was that the U.S. citizen would set up a shell company in a tax haven country protected by stringent bank and legal secrecy laws. From there the shell company would establish a Netherlands Antilles finance subsidiary and take full advantage of the benefits for residents provided by the US/NA treaty. The existence of another layer (the non treaty tax haven country) would render any IRS investigative effort more arduous.[5]

Even so, in 1984 exempting interest at the source was the exception not the rule. Almost all of our tax treaties permitted the taxation of interest levied by the source country, albeit at fixed rates of 15 percent or less. The exceptional treaties should have been renegotiated to close the loopholes that they had created for tax cheats and treaty shoppers, but instead, in 1984 at the behest of Secretary of the Treasury Donald T. Regan, Congress unilaterally expanded the tax loophole so that all nonresident foreigners, including foreign banks all over the world, could receive tax-free interest income from the United States.

We currently have tax treaties with 62 foreign governments. Although most US treaties are negotiated by the Secretary of State, tax treaties are negotiated by the Secretary of the Treasury. Almost all of our tax treaties include a provision that they can be terminated unilaterally by either country. As a result, they are very easy to renegotiate and are often renegotiated. Less than one-third of our current treaties (20 of 62) have remained unchanged since 1983.[6]

So, why did the United States enact this tax loophole? There were two reasons. One was to help American banks compete with European banks in the growing eurodollar market. The other was to attract foreign money to fund President Reagan's budget deficits. We shall discuss each in turn.

Eurodollar Market

Regan wanted to help those US bankers who sought a share of the transactions in the growing eurodollar market. He figured that if the United States offered tax-free interest, those putting their money into the eurodollar market to avoid taxes would switch to American banks.

His plan, however, did not end the eurodollar market, which has actually kept growing. The modern eurodollar market is fed with money from Americans who illegally earn tax free interest by depositing their money in foreign banks as well as by foreign governments wishing to avoid the possibility of having their reserves frozen should they come into conflict with the United States.

The failure of American banks to capture the eurodollar market in succeeding years led to similar attempts to lower the cost of foreign borrowing, such as by lowering the reserve requirement on large scale certificates of deposit and lowering FDIC insurance premiums on most large bank deposits.[7] Nevertheless the eurodollar market has continued to grow, and has spread from Europe to banks around the world.

There was, and still is, a simple way to end the eurodollar market. Simply terminate or renegotiate our tax treaties and reinstate the withholding tax on interest paid to foreigners. Bob McIntyre of Citizens for Tax Justice urged that the Netherlands Antilles tax treaty be terminated at the 1984 House of Representatives hearing on the proposed tax loophole to remove the withholding tax. In addition, without the benefit of hindsight, he made the same basic argument that we present in this book, specifically:

> Now, on the first issue, the question of whether we want more foreign capital into the United States. One thing that has to be understood is that in deciding what to do with the dollars we are sending overseas to buy imports, foreigners have two choices: They can either buy our goods or they can buy our assets. That is, they can either spend dollars on the products that Americans make or they can lend dollars back to us for capital investment purposes.... (B)y discouraging foreigners from buying our goods, as the current approach does by making investments in our assets more attractive, we have contributed substantially to our enormous trade deficit and cost thousands of Americans their jobs in export- and import-sensitive industries.... (W)e will soon move into a position of being a net international debtor - along the lines of Third World countries.[8]

McIntyre's prediction that the US would soon be a net international debtor came true in 1985. as shown in Figure 10. He was not the only one at the 1984 hearings who warned that Regan's proposal

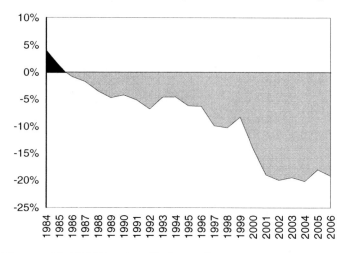

Figure 10. US Foreign Debt as Percent of GDP
The United States changed from being a net creditor to being a net debtor in the middle of 1985. (Source: BEA)

would strengthen the dollar which would cause increased trade deficits. Roberto C. Mendoza of Morgan Guaranty Trust stated:

> Among all the evidence that we have heard today, no one has disputed the fact that [this proposal] would strengthen the dollar. The only question is by how much.[9]

Pursuit of Foreign Capital

Regan ignored the warnings of McIntyre and Mendoza because he wanted to entice foreign savings so that the budget deficits produced by President Reagan's tax cuts would not cause higher interest rates which could crowd out private investment. He created a long-term economic problem for the United States (trade deficits) in order to achieve a short-term policy aim.

The loophole went into effect on July 19, 1984, and was still in effect when this book was written, although the authors of this book had already initiated a movement to eliminate it.[10] The advantage to foreigners is especially high when they live in a jurisdiction, such as Hong Kong, which completely exempts interest earned abroad from taxation. For example, at the beginning of 2007 when the US interest rate was about 5% and inflation was about 3%, the American saver would earn about 2% interest before taxes. For an American in the 35% tax bracket, 1.75% would go to pay US taxes leaving just 0.25% in real interest after taxes. The resident of Hong Kong would earn a real interest rate of 2%, eight times as much. He could even borrow yen from Japan at a half percent interest rate, convert the yen to dollars (bidding up the dollar to an artificially high exchange rate relative to the yen in the process), and then invest those dollars tax free in the United States at a slightly higher interest rate, and make a huge profit as part of what has come to be known as the "Japan Carry Trade."

As a result of this tax loophole, more foreign private savings came flowing into the United States. The savings and investment graph for 1984-1986 in Figure 9 illustrates how increased foreign savings may have caused the long-term US interest rate to fall. Despite the lower interest rate, foreigners increased their savings in the United States from 2.4% of our GDP in 1980 to 3.3% of GDP in 1986. We think this reflects the lower effective interest rates that foreigners paid. The lower interest rates, in turn, may have caused American personal savings to fall as a percentage of GDP from 8.0% of GDP in 1984 to 6.0% of GDP in 1986.

Figures 8 and 9 illustrate an important economics principle. When supply falls, as in Figure 8, price (in this case interest rate) tends to rise, whereas when supply increases, as in Figure 9, price tends to fall.

Ironically, we can find no mention of this tax loophole in Donald Regan's autobiography about this period.[11] Either he considered the action to be insignificant, or he hoped that history would not notice his mistake. Indeed, if it were not for Ammendola's 1994 book, it might have been forgotten.

Former Wall Street Journal editor Robert L. Bartley's book about the same time period extols supply-side economics, but doesn't mention the tax loophole. Bartley includes an entire chapter about the growing trade deficit. He attributes the inflow of foreign private savings into the United States entirely to supply-side economics making the American economy more attractive to foreigners, and not at all to the tax loophole.[12]

Supply-side advocates seem to be experiencing a case of collective amnesia about the 1984 tax loophole that subsidized the inflow of foreign private savings and thus contributed strongly to the decline in real long-term interest rates, the decline in American personal savings, and, through the consequent trade deficit, the decline in our capacity to compete in world markets.

The impact of abolition of the withholding tax extended far beyond its consequences for US Treasury revenue and the associated incentives to avoid paying taxes. Along with abolition of the withholding tax, went the elimination of all interest income reporting requirements. US banks were no longer required to report to the IRS the interest earned by nonresident aliens. This sounds minor, but it isn't. This means that foreign investors can hide income earned in the United States from taxation in their home countries, making that income essentially tax free. The elimination of the withholding tax made US banks an appealing tax dodge destination.

Some claim that eliminating the withholding tax had little impact because the United States already had treaties with some countries that provided for low or no taxes on interest earned. But the reporting requirements issue gives the lie to this argument. Even where tax treaties already provided for low taxes on interest in the United States, elimination of the withholding tax allowed foreign investors to avoid tax payments to their home governments.

In 2001 and 2002, the IRS almost fixed this reporting loophole. However, banks and their allies vigorously and successfully resisted proposed IRS regulations that attempted to require *reporting* of interest to the IRS for forwarding to foreign governments. The regulation would have allowed those governments to begin collecting tax revenue on this interest. Daniel J. Mitchell of the American Heritage Foundation claimed that this policy "threatens [the] economy and financial markets,"[13] when instead it would have merely facilitated payment of *existing tax obligations* that foreigners already owed. Opponents of this policy erroneously claimed that it would lead to "double-taxing cross-border savings"[14] when it could not possibly do so. Because of the elimination of the withholding tax, the US *does not tax these savings at all*.

Even if the US does not reinstate the withholding tax, a simple legislative or regulatory provision that required reporting of *all* interest income could have a substantial effect on the trade deficit. Stephen J. Entin of the Institute for Research on the Economics of Taxation suggested that a change to reporting income could lead to a shift of "$400 billion in foreign saving out of the United States."[15] To Entin, this was cause for alarm. From our perspective, turning away illegal tax dodges, perhaps in conjunction with a renewed withholding tax appears to be a promising approach to cutting the trade deficit.

The Free Movement of Financial Capital Ideology

The US Treasury Secretaries that followed Regan ratified his tax loophole by writing new tax treaties with foreign governments such that the United States would not tax their citizens' interest earnings in the United States while they would not tax American earnings in their countries. They adopted, as a philosophy, a radical version of the free trade ideology, that the flow of financial capital between countries (which causes trade deficits) *should* go untaxed just as the flow of goods between countries should be free from tariffs.

In 1997, the Pacific Rim countries known as the "Asian Tigers" discovered just how destructive the free flow of financial capital between countries can be. First speculative capital flowed into their countries. This capital bid up their stock markets and other assets, raising the exchange rate of their currencies. Their bankers found it advantageous to borrow US dollars from foreign banks at rates much lower than domestic interest rates and then lend those dollars for the purchase of real estate and securities. Banks in Japan, Europe and North America became major creditors of institutions in Thailand, South Korea and Indonesia and the obligations were for the most part payable in dollars.

As their currency values went up, the Asian Tigers lost market share to Chinese exports in world markets. Despite growing trade deficits, their economies boomed. What became known as the Asian miracle attracted foreign private speculators to invest in Asian stocks and bonds. The inflow of foreign capital led to stock market and real estate bubbles. Later, when the capital flowed out, their economies were thrust into deep depressions that were aggravated by the fact that their debts were denominated in suddenly much more expensive dollars.

The crisis started on July 2, 1997, when Thailand was forced to allow its currency, the baht, which had been pegged at a rate of 25 to the US dollar, to engage in a free fall against the dollar. Others, too, had pegged their currency to the dollar. The flight of foreign capital caused a collapse in real estate and security prices. The Thai stock market registered a collapse of fifteen percent in just one day. Besides Thailand, the economies of Indonesia, South Korea, and other Asian countries fell into depression. The fall in the exchange rate made the dollar obligations too onerous and the tigers had to default on their obligations. The International Monetary Fund came to their rescue, but that did not prevent repercussions as far away as Russia and Brazil.

The crisis has not been forgotten, even though the economies of Indonesia and South Korea rebounded in short order. In 2006, Thailand followed the example of Malaysia and imposed controls on the withdrawal of foreign investment. Most of the Asian Tiger governments have also been accumulating dollars both in order to protect their currencies from future currency collapses and also in order to insure that their countries would experience trade surpluses, not deficits. The finance ministers of Indonesia, Malaysia, the Philippines, Singapore, Thailand and newcomers Vietnam, Laos, Myanmar, Brunei and Cambodia met in Thailand as recently as April 2007 to consider the problem of the money pouring into their countries from abroad and to devise a common policy to deal with the threat of another crisis.

Economists, have continued to hold to the free movement of capital ideology, despite the growing empirical evidence against it. In 1990, Lawrence Goulder clearly stated the theory held by most economists to this day. According to his theoretical framework, capital most efficiently moves to where it is most beneficial, absent any taxes or other governmental interference that might inhibit capital movement. In line with this theory, he conducted a simulation of the effects of a possible reinstatement of the US withholding tax, the tax that had been eliminated by Regan's tax loophole in 1984. If foreign governments were to respond with their own taxes upon interest paid to Americans, he found, the result would be losses in US residents' aggregate welfare as well as losses in global economic efficiency.[16]

His simulations, however, were seriously flawed. They left out important effects that he discussed toward the end of his paper – the role of the withholding tax in curtailing tax fraud and the fact that many foreign governments still tax foreign savings. The actual effect of the 1984 removal of the withholding tax was to produce an artificial incentive drawing capital to the United States where it would be completely tax free not only from US taxes, but also, through tax cheating, from the countries where the capital originated.

Recently, economists have begun to discuss the growing empirical evidence that the flow of financial capital can be very detrimental to the country receiving that capital. In November 2007, Eswar S. Prasad, Raghuram G. Rajan, and Arvind Subramanian found that the more a nonindustrial country was importing financial capital, the slower its growth. In their abstract they wrote, "Surprisingly, we find that there is a positive correlation between current account balances and growth among nonindustrial countries, implying that a reduced reliance on foreign capital is associated with higher growth." This was indeed a surprise to the many economists who believe that financial capital benefits the recipient country. They concluded that the deleterious effect of the foreign capital is due to the resulting higher exchange rate that makes the recipient country's exports less competitive in world markets. They wrote:

> To summarize, we have presented evidence that capital inflows can result in overvaluation in nonindustrial countries and that overvaluation can hamper overall growth. To bolster this claim, we have shown that overvaluation particularly impinges on the growth of exportable industries.[17]

Despite this strong empirical evidence that foreign financial capital hurts nonindustrial countries, they suggested that the inflow of financial capital may benefit industrialized countries, like the United States. But the private-foreign-savings tax loophole was detrimental to the United States for exactly the same reason that financial capital hurts nonindustrialized countries. It strengthened the dollar and made US products less competitive in world markets.

Although we are for untaxed trade between countries (i.e., no tariffs), we are not for untaxed flows of capital between countries. And we are certainly not willing to subsidize the destructive inflow of financial capital into the United States, which is what Congress did in 1984 when it enacted the private-foreign-savings tax loophole at the urging of Treasury Secretary Donald T. Regan.

The idea that financial capital movement between countries *should* always go untaxed is foolish. There are times when countries should encourage that inflow through tax breaks and times when countries should discourage that inflow through high taxation.

When a net inflow produces fixed investment, as did the inflow of

capital to the United States during the 19th century or the inflow of
capital that helped rebuild Europe after World War II, it can lead to
economic growth that more than makes up for the resulting trade deficits. Governments would be wise to subsidize such an inflow by unilaterally eliminating their taxes on that capital. But when the net inflow
of financial capital leads to financial bubbles and a deteriorating manufacturing sector, as occurred with the Asian Tigers during the 1990s
and after Regan's foolish 1984 tax loophole, governments would be
wise to discourage that inflow through taxation.

1991: GEORGE H.W. BUSH REDUCES FOREIGN SAVINGS

In 1991, George H.W. Bush temporarily stopped the flow of foreign savings to the United States. He did so partly through a recession
and partly because he received huge gifts from the Persian Gulf nations in return for using American troops to liberate Kuwait from Iraq.
Normally, the flow of funds that finance a trade deficit consists of
loans (i.e. foreign savings), but the flow of funds that financed the
trade deficit in 1991 consisted of gifts, not loans.

Investment tends to be cyclical. Every 5 to 10 years, the level of
investment slows. George H.W. Bush was the victim of one of those
slides. In 1991 and 1992, fixed investment declined to 13.4% of GDP.
Such rates are strong compared to the 5.5% rate of fixed investment
in 1933, at the depths of the Great Depression, but weak compared

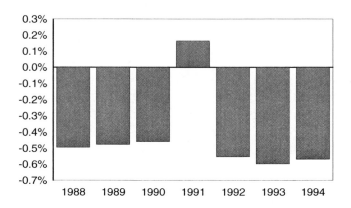

Figure 11. Transfers as Percent of GDP
Gifts from Persian Gulf nations to pay for the liberation of Kuwait reduced
foreign savings that were being loaned to US in 1991. (Source: BEA)

to the 15.4% to 17.4% range of the 1980s. Still, the recession was enough to get Bush defeated with "It's the economy, stupid" becoming Clinton's campaign focus. We do not recommend sending the United States into an investment slump in order to solve a trade deficit, especially since fixed investment is the engine of long run growth.

Also, in 1991 and continuing into the first part of 1992, Persian Gulf countries gave the United States gifts in order to pay the cost of US troops liberating Kuwait during the Persian Gulf War. Foreign savings is measured by the *current account deficit* and has three components, the largest and most variable of which is the trade deficit in goods and services. The other two components are income from other countries and unilateral current transfers between countries. The gifts to the United States from the Persian Gulf countries directly reduced the transfer component of the current account deficit by .73% of our GDP from 1990 to 1991, as shown in Figure 11.

As shown in Figure 12, the savings and investment graph for 1990-1991, the simultaneous fall in foreign savings and gross fixed investment resulted in very little change in the interest rate. Personal savings did not change much either, only rising by a minuscule 0.2% of GDP (from 5.2% to 5.4%).

Some might suggest that the United States perhaps rent its pow-

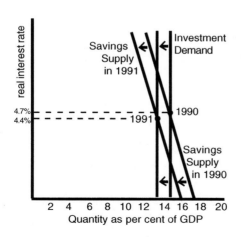

Figure 12. 1990-1991: Investment & Foreign Savings Fall
In 1991, investment demand decreased, while at the same time transfers to the U.S. by the Persian Gulf nations caused foreign savings to fall.

erful military as a mercenary force to rich countries in order to reduce the level of foreign savings. This isn't a prospect that anyone ought to hope for, however.

1996-2005: DOLLAR MERCANTILISM

In a March 2006 lecture entitled *The Global Saving Glut and the US Current Account Deficit*, Ben S. Bernanke, Chairman of the President's Council of Economic Advisors and future Chairman of the Federal Reserve Board, explained that a "global savings glut" was largely responsible for the US trade deficit and that one of the important causes of that glut was the buildup of dollar reserves by governments pursuing export-led growth strategies. Specifically Bernanke said:

> In practice, these countries increased reserves through the expedient of issuing debt to their citizens, thereby mobilizing domestic saving, and then using the proceeds to buy US Treasury securities and other assets. Effectively, governments have acted as financial intermediaries, channeling domestic saving away from local uses and into international capital markets.[18]

The idea that there is a "global savings glut" is a bit deceptive. The countries sending their savings to the United States deliberately prevent those savings from being available to borrowers in their own countries. The Chinese government simply orders its banks not to make many loans to Chinese citizens.[19]

The situation in Japan is a bit more complicated. The Japanese central bank has been increasing its money supply at such a slow rate that it has been producing deflation, the opposite of inflation. Deflation discourages borrowing (such as borrowing for consumption) because loans must be paid off with more valuable future yen. As a result of deflation, Japan even went through a decade-long depression from 1992 to the end of 2002, which reached its depths in 1997 and 1998 when the Japanese economy experienced negative growth. During that depression, unemployment rose steadily from 2.1% in 1991 to 5.4% in 2002, as shown in Figure 13.

According to Milton Friedman, writing in 1997, the Japanese Central Bank could have cured the depression if it were willing to expand the money supply, making more credit available for their own citizens to borrow.[20] *Finally* in 2002, they boosted the Japanese money supply by 36% in a single year.[21] The result was that Japan's unemployment rate began a turn around in 2003, as shown in Figure 13.

The one time increase in money supply in 2002 coincided with Japan's lowest savings rate of recent decades, 25.9% in 2002. Perhaps the Japanese central bank was discouraged by the falling Japanese savings rate. They returned to their deflationary monetary policy and Japanese savings rates climbed steadily back up, reaching 28.0% in 2006.[22]

Some economists disagree with Milton Friedman's analysis that deflation and inflation are essentially monetary phenomena. For example, in a 2005 book Hans Genburg, Robert McCauley, Yung Chul Park, and Avinash Persaud argued that the mercantilist governments are virtually forced to engage in dollar reserve accumulation in order to prevent deflation. They argued that if these countries were not buying dollars to weaken their currencies, then their strengthening currencies would produce lower import prices and higher asset values which would contribute to deflation.[23]

We don't buy this argument. Many countries, including the United States, have experienced strengthening currencies without experienc-

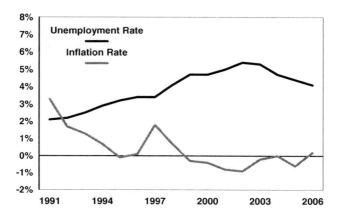

Figure 13. Japan's Unemployment and Inflation Rates
The above graph shows Japan's unemployment rate as a percentage of the total labor force and its inflation rate. (Source: IMF World Economic Outlook Database)

ing deflation. Milton Friedman's analysis has been proven correct again and again in the effective monetary policy actions of the US Federal Reserve to bring down inflation and prevent deflation.

The real issue, in our view, is that without dollar mercantilism the mercantilist nations would have to change their economic policies. Instead of discouraging consumption and imports, they would have to encourage their own people to consume more goods and services, including imports from abroad. These countries choose mercantilism, and the United States lets them do so.

When a country wants to increase its exports to the United States, without increasing its imports from the United States, it puts the dollars earned by the trade surplus into dollar reserves. The Japanese government sends its country's savings to America by borrowing yen and then using those yen to buy dollars in the foreign exchange markets. The Chinese government pegs the renminbi (sometimes abbreviated RMB) to the dollar and uses its country's savings to buy up all excess dollars. These actions:

1. Bid up the price of the dollar so American goods will be more expensive for their consumers.
2. Keep down the price of their currency so that their goods will be less expensive for American consumers.
3. Bid down American interest rates, so that Americans buy more goods on credit, including more imports.

Both the Chinese and Japanese governments have been buying dollars and investing them in the United States in order to bid up the world price of the dollar and thus the price of American goods in world markets and at the same time to bid down their currencies and thus the price of their goods in world markets.

What Japan's and China's development strategy involves is not trade: just selling, not buying. Balanced trade can grow indefinitely, forever! But sooner or later, mercantilism means that one's trading partners become impoverished, which spoils the market for exports. As we noted above, the growth rates of the Japanese economy have slowed. We would argue that was because incomes in its trading partners did not grow commensurately.

In recent years, several other Pacific Rim countries as well as India and Brazil have also begun sending their savings to the United States. According to Peter Morici, some of these countries are motivated by a need to lower the exchange rate of their currencies so that their exports to the United States can compete with Chinese exports.[24]

Nobody knows exactly how many dollars each foreign government has invested in the United States because many foreign governments, including China, take advantage of the private-foreign-savings tax loophole to invest most of their dollars in foreign banks who in-turn reinvest the same dollars under the bank's name in tax-free interest-paying assets in the United States. As a result of governments doing this, as pointed out by Robert McCauley writing in a 2006 issue of the *BIS Quarterly Review*, the Bureau of Economics Analysis (BEA) statistics dramatically underestimate the amount of foreign government savings in the United States.[25]

As recently as September 2007, the Federal Reserve may still have been unaware of the extent of the foreign government savings inflow. In a speech in Germany, Federal Reserve Chairman Ben S. Bernanke stated that only 47% of the US current account deficit from 2002 through 2006 could be attributed to what he called "official capital inflows." Specifically, he stated:

> From 1998 through 2001, even as the U.S. current account deficit widened substantially, official capital flows into the United States were quite small. During the years 2002 through 2006, net official capital inflows picked up substantially but still corresponded to less than half (47 percent) of the U.S. current account deficit over the period....[26]

His footnote for this data states:

> During 2002-06, gross foreign official inflows totaled $1,491 billion; net official inflows were only slightly less, as U.S. official outflows were negligible. Private foreign inflows net of private U.S. outflows totaled $1,659 billion during the same period...[27]

Our estimate is that over the period 2002 through 2006, foreign official inflows totaled $1,775 billion, which is 56%, not 47%, of the current account deficit over that period.[28] Our estimate comes from the reserves that foreign governments reported to the International Monetary Fund COFER database. Those statistics, which don't start until 1995, are illustrated in Figure 14.

Our estimate for calculating the foreign government contribution to the trade deficit actually underestimates that contribution. Only some countries report the allocation of their reserves to currencies to the IMF, so we assumed that the same proportion of dollars would be in the unallocated reserves as in the allocated reserves. In 2006, 65% of the allocated reserves were in dollars, so we estimated that the same proportion of the $1,705 billion in unallocated reserves would be dollars. But China, one of the countries that doesn't report the allocation of its reserves to the IMF, reportedly had much more than just 65% of its $1,066 billion of currency reserves in dollars at the end of 2006.[29] Even though our estimate is still too low, it is still much higher than Bernanke's estimate!

During the period from 1996 through 2006, when the current account deficit ballooned from $125 billion to $811 billion, we estimate that the amount of dollars that foreign governments added annu-

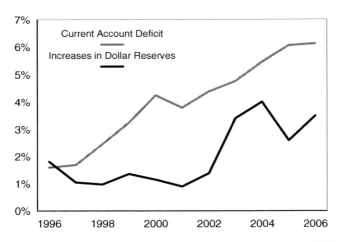

Figure 14. Trade Deficit and Dollar Reserves as Percent of GDP
Dollar mercantilism accounted for about half of the current account deficit during the decade from 1996 through 2005. The graph also includes 2006. (Source IMF COFER database & BEA)

ally to their reserves increased from about $142 billion in 1996 to about $464 billion in 2006, accounting for 51% of the current account deficit over the entire period.

As shown in Figure 15, in recent years the Chinese central bank has been accelerating the growth of its currency reserves (predominantly dollars). The effect has been to drive up China's trade surplus with the United States by a similar amount. For example, in 2006 China increased its currency reserves by $247 billion (from $822 billion to $1068 billion) and their trade surplus with the United States grew to $233 billion.

The foreign government reserve increases also tend to encourage increases in private foreign savings. For example, the Japanese Central Bank's purchases of yen help protect the speculators in the "Japan Carry Trade" who borrow yen from Japanese banks and then use those yen to buy dollars which they invest in dollar-denominated accounts. In a March 2007 report, the Peterson Institute for International Economics urged the Japanese government *not* to support these speculators in the future, writing, "Now that the yen has begun to strengthen, it is important that Japan not intervene to bail out speculators that engaged in the Japan carry trade when the yen was very

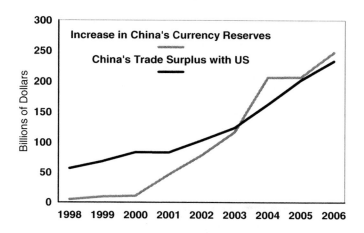

Figure 15. China's Currency Reserves and Trade Surplus with US
The Chinese government has been increasing the growth rate of its dollar reserves and its trade surplus with the US each year since 2000. (Source: reserves from Asian Development Outlook, 2003 & 2007; trade from BEA)

weak."[30] (The Japanese government is not the only government whose policies assist the Japan Carry Trade; the United States private-foreign-savings tax loophole that Secretary of the Treasury Donald Regan helped create in 1984 directly subsidizes it!)

Figure 16, the savings and investment graph for 1996-2005, illustrates the effect of increased foreign savings coming into the United States, partly due to dollar mercantilism. The additional savings helped to push down real long-term interest rates on 10-year treasury notes from 4.5% in 1996 to 1.3% in 2005. The falling interest rates, in turn, caused personal savings rates in the United States to fall.

Federal Reserve Chairman Ben S. Bernanke shares our assessment that the fall in US personal savings was at least partly due to the inflow of foreign savings. Like us, he points to the falling interest rate as evidence in support of that assessment.[31] However, some economists claim that the causal arrows we have drawn are drawn backward.

We have argued that the increasing supply of foreign government savings causes the trade deficits, but others attribute the deficit to increasing American demand for foreign savings. For example, Ronald McKinnon, a Stanford University economist, theorized that the trade deficit is caused by America's need for foreign savings because of the

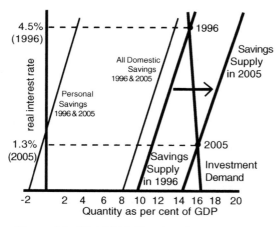

Figure 16. 1996-2005: Foreign Government Savings Increases
As a result of dollar mercantilism, foreign savings increased from 1996 to 2005, which caused interest rates and personal savings to fall.

falling rate of American private personal savings and because of our federal government's budget deficits. According to him, the "relatively high-saving East Asian countries are virtually forced to run export surpluses in order to lend their 'surplus' saving to the United States."[32]

Since both supply and demand can lead to changes in price and quantity, this is an empirical question. The implicit mechanism behind McKinnon's theory is that the falling rate of American personal savings drives up real interest rates, thus inviting foreign savings, just as the fall in government savings under Paul Volcker's Federal Reserve drove up interest rates and invited foreign savings from 1982-1984. However, his theory doesn't fit with the direction that long-term interest rates and personal savings have been moving since 1984. As Figure 17 shows, since 1984, the real long-term interest rate (rate of return on 10 year Treasury Notes after subtracting the GDP deflator) has been going down, not up, as the personal savings rate as a percentage of disposable income (disposable income is personal income after taxes) has been going down. Furthermore, during the 1990s when the Clinton administration and the Republican congress moved the federal government budget from deficit to surplus, the trade deficit

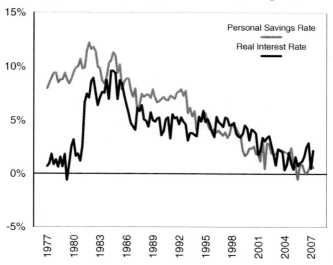

Figure 17. Personal Savings Rates and Real Long-Term Interest Rates
Both personal savings as a percentage of disposable income and real long-term interest rates (on 10-year T-Bills) fell from 1984 to the second quarter of 2007. (Source: Federal Reserve & BEA NIPA Tables)

continued to increase despite growing government savings. Professor McKinnon's explanation just doesn't fit the facts.

McKinnon was not the only influential economist who ignored the direction that interest rates had been moving. A similar hypothesis was presented by David Backus, Espen Henriksen, Frederic Lambert, and Chris Telmer in a conference paper that was so popular among economists that it was chosen for presentation at three different economic conferences during the 2005-2006 period.[33]

Like McKinnon they held that the fall in personal savings in the United States caused the trade deficit by inviting foreign savings. They explained that personal savings shifted as a result of a growing ratio between net worth and GDP. In other words, personal savings is a function of asset values. According to their hypothesis, when asset values grow in comparison to GDP, personal savings fall. They provide a scattergram which shows that where net worth is high relative to GDP, the personal consumption rate is high and thus the personal savings rate is low. According to them the high ratio between net worth and GDP "might reflect the performance of the economy as a whole." They ignore the fact that asset values (and thus the ratio between net worth and GDP) are, to a large extent, an inverse function of real long-term interest rates, partly because revenue producing assets compete in the marketplace with interest-producing long-term bonds and partly because houses are usually purchased with interest-bearing mortgages.

They explained trade surpluses among European countries by holding that those countries experiencing slow growth have falling investment rates combined with stable savings rates while those countries experiencing more rapid than average savings growth experience trade deficits. According to this explanation, countries needing money for investment have been drawing savings from those countries having a surplus of savings. They ignore the fact that the transfer of savings from one European country to another could be mediated by higher interest rates in the countries with higher investment rates.

The theory proposed by Backus et al. is wonderfully comforting to those who advocate a *do-nothing* approach. It implies that we are experiencing trade deficits just because we are prosperous. After all, if trade deficits are the product of rapid investment growth and trade surpluses are the product of slow investment growth, then trade deficits are simply an indicator of prosperity! Unfortunately, their theory doesn't fit well with reality once you leave Europe. It ignores the fact that China has been growing at a rapid 10% clip while at the same time experiencing large trade surpluses. It also does not explain why the United States trade deficit continued to expand throughout the economic investment slowdown from the third quarter of 2000 to the third quarter of 2003.

Their most striking omission is the absence of any mention of interest rates in explaining the phenomena that they discuss. Instead of reasoning from the obvious economics supply-and-demand equality that investment equals total savings (domestic plus foreign) with interest rate functioning as the mediating price, they use a different way of expressing the same equality which obscures the role of interest rates. There is a reason why they ignore interest rates. Almost all of the phenomena that they mention could be explained more simply by interest rates, except for the inrush of foreign savings into the United States which runs completely counter to the direction of change of interest rates.

We hold that foreign government dollar mercantilism has been pushing foreign savings into the United States, driving down real American interest rates which, in turn, drive down the rate of personal savings. We disagree with the theory of McKinnon and of Backus et al. that declines in US savings stimulate the influx of savings from abroad. Granger Causality Tests are a way to try to tease apart which variable is causing what over time. When we ran the Granger test for the 1996 through 2005 period, the results were unambiguously in favor of our explanation. Foreign savings are driving down US savings. When monetary mercantilist nations buy dollars, they often put those dollars into treasury notes, including long-term US bonds, causing long-term interest rates to go down. This, in turn, causes American personal savings to go down, not only because savings are less attractive at lower interest rates, but also because people tend to buy more consumer goods on credit when interest rates go down.

The value of assets, such as stocks and homes, goes up when interest rates go down. This occurs partly because people buy homes on credit and partly because the dividends paid by stocks look better when the returns from other financial instruments, such as bonds, are lower. Compounding these, when the value of their assets goes up, people think that they are wealthier and tend to borrow more money.

The inrush of foreign savings also makes credit much more readily available and less expensive to Americans. It was impossible to listen to the radio or watch television during this period without hearing advertisement after advertisement inviting people to borrow money. For all of these reasons, it is clear that the increased foreign savings lowered the rate of personal savings.

Like foreign private savings, foreign government savings go tax free. The US government has been encouraging foreign governments to send their savings to the United States with a special tax loophole that partly results from treaties that we have with various foreign governments. Foreign governments get to invest in the United States without paying any income tax on earnings, and our government gets to invest in their countries tax free. The only problem is that at the end of 2006, foreign governments had about $3,200 billion invested in dollar reserves, while the US Treasury and Federal Reserve, combined, only had $41 billion invested in foreign currencies.[34]

2006-2007: The United States gets a Breather

When Congress killed the Dubai Ports deal in March 2006, they were worried that US security would be endangered if the United States let an Arab company run six of our sea terminals. In a last-ditch attempt to salvage the deal, the Bush administration switched to economic arguments. They argued that scuttling the Dubai Ports deal would send a negative message to foreign investors who would withdraw their investments and hurt the US economy.[35] The Bush administration was correct that the Dubai Ports deal rejection would discourage some foreign financial investment. According to the Bank for International Settlements, OPEC nations reduced their dollar-denominated bank deposits and increased their euro- and yen- bank deposits starting soon after the Ports rejection.[36]

From the second quarter of 2006 and continuing in 2007, the dollar fell against the euro and most other non-mercantilist nation currencies. As a result, the US trade deficit began decreasing as a percentage of GDP. US manufacturers were starting to gain back lost market share, especially those companies that were selling products not yet being produced by mercantilist nations. For example, the *Wall Street Journal* reported that an American company producing lobster trap wire was gaining market share because its primary competition was an Italian company.[37]

The Japanese government only increased its foreign exchange holdings by 12% in 2007 and its trade surplus with the United States actually fell slightly from $53 billion over the first three quarters of 2006 to $50 billion over the first three quarters of 2007. But the Chinese government stepped up its foreign exchange holdings by 43% from $1,066 billion at the end of 2006 to $1,532 billion at the end of 2007. As a result, its trade surplus with the United States grew 13% from $164 billion over the first three quarters of 2006 to $185 billion over the first three quarters of 2007.[38]

If current trends were to continue, the mercantilist countries would, for a while, be de-industrializing Canada and Europe, instead of the United States. Some European politicians and business leaders were not pleased with the prospect. They were already starting to pressure the European Central Bank to do something about the rise of the euro versus the dollar.[39] The European Central Bank had three choices: (1) permit the deindustrialization of the European economies, (2) build up dollar reserves rapidly enough to move the problem back to the United States, or (3) join the United States in concerted action to end dollar mercantilism.

Meanwhile, according to British financial columnist Ambrose Evans-Pritchard, the Chinese government was threatening to sell massive amounts of their dollar reserves should the US impose tariffs upon Chinese goods. Pritchard referred to this as the "nuclear" option since the action would likely cause a sudden collapse in the US dollar that would hurt both countries.[40]

With the dollar falling in world currency markets and US inflation heating up in 2007, foreign governments were looking for ways to get as much of their dollar reserves as possible out of interest bearing accounts and into US equities. They hoped to get larger returns for their dollar reserves and also to preserve as much as possible of their assets should the United States currency crash or the United States decide to inflate away its debt. The US tax exemption for foreign government earnings, whether interest or dividend earnings, would subsidize their dividend earnings from these purchases.

In May 2007, Morgan Stanley estimated that Sovereign Wealth Funds, the funds set up by foreign governments to invest in foreign equities, had about $2,500 billion in assets, and would have about $12,000 billion by 2015.[41] These were dollar reserves that foreign governments had collected, much of it as a byproduct of dollar mercantilism. In May 2007 the Chinese government spent $3 billion to acquire a 10% interest in the Blackstone Group, a specialist in private equity takeovers. In December 2007 they paid Morgan Stanley, one of the most influential US banks, $5 billion for an eventual 9.9% of its common stock.

This new trend caused Patrick A Mulloy, a member of the United States-China Economic Security Review Commission, to argue in November 2007 testimony before the Senate Banking Committee that the United States should address the "mercantilist trade practices" of China and other Asian countries before we become a "Sharecropper's Society" (a term coined by Warren Buffett when describing the eventual result of our current trade policies).[42]

At the end of 2007, when this was written, the future was up in the air. The fall in the dollar's exchange rate was causing a slight turnaround in the US trade deficit and a slight improvement in American manufacturing investment, giving US manufacturing a breather. But there was also the possibility that the fall in the dollar could turn into a rout.

Much more likely was the possibility that the dollar purchases of the dollar mercantilist nations would eventually cause the US trade deficits to resume their upward course. Foreign governments were set to increase their purchases of US equities while gradually turning US businesses into socialist enterprises whose managers might eventually become foreign government agents.

FUTURE OF THE DOLLAR STANDARD

This chapter has involved a pretty intense economics lesson, but it really isn't very complicated. The United States trade deficits are caused by inflows of foreign savings in the form of financial investments. Our government has been encouraging those foreign savings through foolish tax loopholes, and foreign governments have been deliberately sending us their countries' savings as part of a dollar mercantilist strategy that is intended to manipulate their currencies and build up our imports and their exports.

The dollar standard, which began in 1971, could have worked without causing the deindustrialization of the United States were the accumulation of dollar reserves by any country limited to a small (reasonable) percentage of their imports and/or if the United States were to accumulate reciprocal reserves of foreign currencies. Absent those conditions, the dollar standard permitted dollar mercantilism, a deliberate policy to create, maintain, and perpetuate trade surpluses with the United States. As recent events show, countries that have accumulated large dollar reserves can use those reserves to pressure the US government and to purchase US equities.

In Chapter 3, we shall examine the analyses and solutions of trade deficit ostriches who fail to understand the causes of the trade deficit and of trade deficit eagles who do understand the problem.

In Chapter 4, we will present our favored solutions to the problem, solutions that will be designed to end the foreign financial capital inflows into the United States that cause trade deficits.

3. Ostriches and Eagles

*According to Wikipedia, the myth of lemmings following their lead-
ers over a cliff can be traced to a Walt Disney documentary entitled
"White Wilderness" which included footage of lemmings running
headlong over a cliff. It turns out that the Disney filmmakers who
produced the movie contrived this scene.*

The notion of people following their leaders into the abyss is not myth.
Millions of Germans, Englishmen, French, and Russians died in World
War I following an idiotic response by world leaders to the murder of
Austro-Hungarian Archduke Ferdinand in Sarajevo in 1914. Millions
of Germans followed Hitler who started World War II under the slo-
gan "lebensraum" and the myth of Aryan superiority. Millions of Russians followed Lenin and Stalin, disciples of Karl Marx, in creating a
Communist state that was supposed to wither away but instead assumed totalitarian powers and slaughtered and impoverished millions
of its own citizens.

Although the mythmakers who led their people off the metaphori-
cal cliffs described above were all politicians, their decisions were
grounded in political and economic theories that turned out to be in-
accurate, dangerous and wrong. Leaders and thinkers who misunderstand how the economy operates are likely to enact policies that
produce economic disaster. John Maynard Keynes famously suggested, "The ideas of the economists and political philosophers, both
when they are right and when they are wrong, are more powerful than
is commonly understood. Indeed, the world is ruled by little else."

Leaders and thinkers who misunderstand how the economy operates are likely to enact policies that produce economic disaster.
Most economists continue to argue that free trade is desirable. We
agree. But the policy prescriptions they advocate often amount to
nothing more than unilateral disarmament in the face of mercantilist
efforts to beggar-thy-neighbor (e.g., the United States) through strategic trade policy. Because economic theory and recent experience
shows that mercantilism can be successful, these are the policy prescriptions of ostriches. The promotion of free trade requires more

than smoothing the mercantilists' way.

We are persuaded that the trade deficit is a serious problem which deserves a serious policy response. We argued in Chapters 1 and 2 that it is destroying much of the American manufacturing base and being sustained by misguided and/or malicious government policies. Those selling us more than they buy are able to expand capability and accumulate capital that alters the terms of trade in their favor: they win in the long run with imbalanced trade. To the extent that these successes come as the result of the destruction of otherwise competitive American industry, the United States loses. US policymakers should be farsighted not sand-sighted. In confronting the challenge posed by the trade deficit, we need to be eagles.

THE OSTRICH ATTITUDE

The vast majority of economists believe strongly in free trade and have not yet realized the importance of ensuring balanced trade. They have been very slow to understand the causes of the trade-deficit and have sometimes been arrogant and condescending in their dismissals of those who do. For example, in a 1997 *Slate Magazine* column, free-trade advocate Paul Krugman arrogantly criticized a book review by fair-trade advocate Alan Tonelson, a fellow of the U.S. Business and Industry Council Education Foundation, as follows:

> Professional trade alarmist Alan Tonelson gave a particularly clear statement of the new fears in his *New York Times* review of *The Big Ten: The Big Emerging Markets and How They Will Change Our Lives*, a book by former Commerce Undersecretary Jeffrey Garten....Tonelson's claim is that as emerging economies grow — that is, produce and sell greatly increased quantities of goods and services — their spending will not grow by a comparable amount; equivalently, he is claiming that they will run massive trade surpluses. But when a country grows, its total income must, by definition, rise one-for-one with the value of its production. Maybe you don't think that income will get paid out in higher wages, but it has to show up *somewhere*. And why should we imagine that people in emerging countries, unlike people in advanced nations, cannot find things to spend their money on?[1]

The succeeding decade, and the rise of Chinese trade surpluses and dollar mercantilism, have shown Tonelson to be correct and

Krugman to be wrong. But to our knowledge, Krugman has never recanted or offered an excuse. Krugman's arrogance was further on display when he introduced his book entitled *Pop Internationalism* with the story of a conference he attended in which John Sculley, then CEO of Apple Computer, "described a world in which nations, like corporations, are engaged in fierce competition for global markets." He wrote, "I thought I knew something about international trade, and it seemed to me that Sculley had no idea what he was talking about."[2] This comment by Krugman seems particularly puzzling when put in the context of Krugman's own work, much of which involves the analysis of strategic trade and conditions in which countries do engage in fierce competition for global markets. Here Krugman's "realist" position on trade policy leads him to a position that denies what he otherwise acknowledges: that many politicians (and hence countries) tend to think in neo-mercantilist terms.

John Sculley's Apple Computer has to compete with computer manufacturers from around the world so he may indeed have had some idea of what he was talking about. We would at least give him the benefit of doubt. According to Krugman, "concerns about competitiveness are, as an empirical matter, almost completely unfounded" and "thinking in terms of competitiveness leads, directly and indirectly, to bad economic policies on a wide range of issues, domestic and foreign, whether it be in health care or trade."[3]

As prescriptions for US policies this may be wise. As an empirical description of the policies followed by other countries, it is blind. For instance, the United States-China Economic and Security Review Commission 2007 report noted:

> The push for reform in China's economy in the 1980's and 1990's appears in some cases to have reversed with a renewed use of industrial policies combined with a new class of super state-owned enterprises."[4]

Are Chinese policies to maintain "absolute control through state-owned enterprises"[5] good for China? We do not think so. Are Chinese policies that leverage state power to harm US companies and workers good for the US? Absolutely not.

Krugman also noted, "International trade is not a zero-sum game."[6] We agree. Comparative advantage fundamentally expands the overall trading pie. Our issue is not with this fact. Our concern is that a single-minded focus on the *potential* for gains from trade is blinding many US economists to the very real *manipulation* of trade engaged in by our competitors. Mercantilism and other distortions of international flows tend to shrink the pie that trade provides. In ignoring these threats, Krugman seems to be in denial that trade deficits can continue to exist for long periods and selectively ignores the mercantilist practices of such countries and Japan, China, and others, mentioning them only when their policies have failed.[7] For instance, Krugman describes the failed Japanese effort to corner the computer memory market through trade policies.

The only reference to mercantilism in his textbook on international economics is found in a box on page 542 entitled "Hume versus the Mercantilists." The mercantilists of the 16th through 18th centuries, as we pointed out, believed that a country's wealth depended on its ac-cumulation of gold which required a surplus of exports over imports. According to Krugman, "Hume's reasoning shows that a perpetual surplus is impossible." An inflow of gold drives up prices in the surplus country and drives prices down in the deficit country which tends to correct the trade imbalance.[8] Hume was wrong. If the goal of the gold mercantilists were to build their industry (not their gold hoard), they could have practiced the same system that the dollar mercantil-ists practice today by using the gold obtained from trade to buy assets in the trade deficit country.

According to Krugman, the possibility of mercantilism under a system of flexible exchange rates is similarly impossible. The flow of foreign currency into the surplus country would tend to depreciate the currency of the deficit country, lowering prices in the deficit country relative to the surplus country and raising prices in the surplus country. Krugman was ignoring the strategy that the dollar mercantilists have in fact been pursuing. Surplus countries simply stock up on the currency of the deficit country and use it to buy assets in the deficit country. These are acts which are appropriately called mercantilism because they are intended to perpetuate the surplus of exports over imports.

They short-circuit the normal market correction.

Free-trade advocates, like Krugman, have been slow to come to understand the causes of the problem of dollar mercantilism and the US tax subsidies of foreign savings that have sustained the trade deficits. As a result, the remedies that they have so far proposed (increasing domestic savings, jawboning, or doing nothing) have been entirely inadequate. We will discuss each of these methods in turn.

Increasing Domestic Savings

Some have supposed that the trade deficit could be reduced if the United States could increase domestic savings, either by lowering the government budget deficit or by increasing private savings. For example, in his 1990 book *The Age of Diminished Expectations: US Economic Policy in the 1990s,* Krugman argued that the trade imbalance would decrease if the American budget deficits were reduced.[9] Unfortunately, when Krugman's prescription of moving the American government's budget deficit to surplus was put into practice during the Clinton administration with a consequent reduction in US long-term interest rates, the increased inflow of foreign savings from the dollar mercantilist countries offset the effects of the balanced budgets, lowering interest rates so much that domestic savings decreased, not foreign savings.

Measures designed to increase private savings would similarly fail to reduce the trade deficit very much. Proposed measures have included putting a part of Social Security into private accounts, replacing income taxes with consumption taxes, and expanding tax-free retirement and medical savings accounts. Another way to increase savings would be to end the use of wealth-based means-testing in government programs such as Pell grants that penalize those college students and their parents who have saved to pay for their child's college education.

All of these alternatives would increase domestic savings and reduce interest rates, thus decreasing the flow of private foreign savings. However, increasing domestic savings will do nothing to stop foreign governments from deliberately putting their countries' savings into dollar reserves in order to maintain their trade-surpluses with the United

States.

To be clear, we support measures to increase domestic savings. The entire second part of this book focuses on changes in tax policy to encourage domestic savings. Our concern is that these measures will be ineffective in the face of dollar mercantilism unless accompanied by strategies to discourage financial inflows or otherwise address the trade deficit. We advocate measures to increase domestic savings in Part 2, but only when combined with measures designed to discourage dollar mercantilism.

A 2005 study by Erceg, Guerieri and Gust estimated that a one dollar reduction in the Federal budget deficit would reduce the trade deficit by 20 cents *or less*. In their review of literature, they noted that previous estimates of the relationship between the budget deficit and the trade deficit were much higher, sometimes as high as a one dollar budget deficit reduction reducing the trade deficit by 50 cents.[10] The difference may be due to the tremendous growth of foreign government transfers of savings over the last decade. Foreign governments do not much care about the interest earned on their savings. They are transferring savings in order to promote their exports and discourage their imports.

Jawboning

Some of the ostriches advocate that the Chinese and Japanese governments depreciate their currencies. This relies upon the cooperation of the very governments that are benefiting from dollar mercantilism. For example, Lester Thurow of MIT wrote in his 2003 book, *Fortune Favors the Bold*:

> The American trade deficit should and will eventually disappear, of course. On that issue there is no debate. But a hard landing ... would be a worldwide disaster. There is one, and only one, route to a soft landing however. Surplus countries have to use monetary and fiscal policies to stimulate their economies to grow faster.[11]

How much faster should China grow than it is already growing? Could Japan have really grown faster than it did from the fifties to the nineties? Growth isn't the answer. Instead, these countries need to increase their buying of imports, faster! Thurow is wrong that there are no alternatives. In Chapter 4 we will examine them.

Ben S. Bernanke, Chairman of the President's Council of Economic Advisors and future Chairman of the Federal Reserve Board, echoed Thurow's "one" solution in a March 2006 speech stating that the solution was to educate and convince foreign governments that it would be better to employ their savings to promote their own country's internal development than ours (as though the current system was to our benefit and not to theirs)![12] The real solution is to convince the Chinese and others that they would be better off using their "savings" at home than sending them to the United States. Yes, but how to convince them? Modern economic analyses of strategic trade (see Chapter 1) suggest that their policies may be providing benefits for the mercantilist economy. More than simple persuasion is required.

Bernanke noted in the same March 2006 speech that reliance on market forces, such as by reducing the budget deficit, had not and would not solve the trade deficit problem. But he failed to note the reason that those foreign savings were flowing to the United States. Private foreign savings were flowing to the United States because we were subsidizing them. Foreign government savings were flowing to the United States because those countries were pursuing the old mercantilist policy of deliberately promoting their exports and discouraging their imports.

It is almost as if our leading economists were wearing blinders – all flows are justified as free trade, even those that are deliberately designed to beggar their trading partners, provided they are not called tariffs or quotas. The Japanese and Chinese dramatic economic successes over the last several decades were the result of, or at least accompanied by, mercantilist practices. In the short run at least, mercantilism works. Cajoling won't work, unless accompanied by credible measures to end the mercantilist policies.

When China joined the World Trade Organization, it had to agree to let foreign banks come into China and issue credit cards. That would have opened up their domestic markets to imports by stimulating domestic economic demand. The Chinese government had said that foreign banks would be allowed to operate in China starting on

December 11, 2006. But just before the deadline, they made up new rules that prevented foreign banks from operating independently of Chinese government control and greatly restricted the business they could do.[13]

The United States-China Economic and Security Review Commission 2007 report argued that this is no isolated trend: "China's economic policies violate the spirit and the letter of World Trade Organization membership requirements."[14] In many areas China has worked to thwart World Trade Organization rules and maintain state control over the economy.

In December 2006, several Republicans had just been defeated in the midterm election by Democrats opposed to completely free trade, especially completely free trade with China. The Bush administration finally woke up to the fact that their failure to deal with Chinese dollar mercantilism could cost their party the 2008 election. For years, free-trade supporters had dreamed that the Chinese would eventually open up their markets to American products, such as American cars, but high tariffs on our cars and auto parts while the Chinese built their own automobile industry finally made it apparent that Beijing had no intention of ever doing so. So that month President Bush sent all of our government's top financial leaders to China (Treasury Secretary Henry Paulson, Federal Reserve Chairman Ben S. Bernanke, Secretary of Commerce Carlos Gutierrez, Labor Secretary Elaine Chao and Health and Human Services Secretary Mike Leavitt) to emphasize that we were serious this time. But, according to the close reading of the communique afterward by *China Stock Digest* editor Jim Trippon, the mission was an abject failure.[15]

If it could not get Chinese cooperation, the Bush administration hinted that it would file a complaint with the World Trade Organization. Indeed, shortly afterward, US Trade Representative Sue Schwabb announced that the United States indeed would be filing a complaint. The United States had earlier filed a complaint when the Chinese imposed a tariff on our auto parts. The complaint just caused them to lower the tariffs slightly. Jawboning hasn't worked, doesn't work, and never will work, even when we send all our government's top financial officials to do it simultaneously!

Do Nothing!

Many economists argue that the US economy benefits from the foreign government accumulation of dollar reserves. The US trade deficit reflects the willingness of foreigners to provide real goods and services to the United States in exchange for dollars. Dollars are cheap to print, and the ability to spend dollars instead of exchanging goods puts the United States in an advantageous position.

From our perspective, there are two problems with this analysis: (1) the dollar was already the world's main reserve currency in the 1970s when US trade was approximately in balance; and (2) we have difficulty imagining a scenario in which holding about a trillion dollars in reserve would be necessary for Japan or China.

In the short run we agree with the ostriches that the sand is a good place to hide; it is comfortable and cool. Why not stick our heads in the sand while the US economy appears prosperous? Why not? Because this is not a sustainable long-term approach. It ignores the coming tidal wave.[16] If we stick our heads too deep in the sand, we risk drowning. Doing nothing could make things much worse. Economists Nouriel Roubini and Brad Setser write:

> No doubt the dollar's position as the world's reserve currency and the depth of US financial markets creates an intrinsic source of demand for both dollars and dollar denominated assets. However, this could prove to be a mixed blessing. The dollar's privileged position could increase the risk that the world will finance large US trade deficits for too long, delaying the needed adjustment and making the eventual adjustment all the more difficult and unstable.[17]

Doing nothing leads to three basic problems: (1) it contributes to the decline of American productive capacity, particularly the ability of the US economy to produce tradable goods and services; (2) the current imbalances are not sustainable; (3) doing nothing will eventually lead to resolutely nondemocratic China replacing the United States as the world's dominant economic and political power.

One of the foremost political advocates of doing nothing has been former Republican vice presidential candidate Jack Kemp. Noting that he sits on the Board of Directors of many US corporations that do business overseas, he argued in 2006 that increasing world economic integration brings "democratic capitalism" to the world.[18] However, one of the main effects of our failure to deal with Chinese dollar mercantilism is that China has been growing by about 10% per year, while the US economy has only been growing by about 3%.

Does Kemp realize that China has a Communist government? In order to do business in China, American companies accept the Chinese government as a partner. The Chinese government has been, and continues to be a totalitarian regime. Sooner or later Jack Kemp and the corporations on whose board he sits will need to recognize that they may be strengthening totalitarianism, not democratic capitalism, when they build factories in China. Again, let us look at the reality.

After Mao's death in 1976, Deng Xiaoping approved a series of economic reforms that included private family farms and limited private enterprises but gradually encompassed large corporate enterprises. Foreign investment in jointly-owned enterprises became institutionalized. As a result of these changes, the role of the Communist party changed, and the provinces gained a great deal of power (independence too strong a word). The devolution of authority and decentralized decision-making brought great advances to many areas of the nation.

But such power coupled with the new institutions presents a great challenge to the continued monolithic control of the Chinese Communist Party (CCP). As Ross Terrill wrote in *The New Chinese Empire,* "At some point the CCP may become alarmed at the threat to Beijing's authority and seek to reverse the devolutions, at whatever economic cost, in order to save its own political skin."[19]

When Lenin in 1921 approved the New Economic Policy (NEP) that gave profit incentives to farmers and small private enterprises, he explained to his supporters that this capitalist-like policy was a necessary precondition to building communism. As a result of introducing some free-market incentives, agricultural and industrial production had been restored to its prewar levels by 1928. Stalin's abrupt abandonment of Lenin's New Economic Policy led tragically and inevitably to the relative stagnation and ultimate failure of the Soviet Union.

What gives us pause is that the Communist Party's leaders may consider free markets as a tactic. Marxists believe that all economies have to go through a capitalist stage. Once the development of that stage reaches the "right" level, the dictatorship of the proletariat can be imposed.

In December 2006, William F. Jasper discussed the striking parallels between Lenin's NEP and what the Chinese leadership calls "market socialism." He pointed out that journalists and professors were quick to call the Soviet Union of Lenin's time a "former" communist country. He pointed out that capitalists (Armand Hammer, Averell Harriman, and Henry Ford) rushed in to invest in the new Soviet Union. He also pointed out that communists today, including members of the CCP leadership, specifically compare "market socialism" to Lenin's NEP. According to Jasper, here is how Lenin summed up the strategy behind the NEP when explaining it to his fellow communists:

> The Capitalists of the world and their governments, in pursuit of conquest of the Soviet market, will close their eyes to the indicated higher reality and thus will turn into deaf mute blind men. They will extend credits, which will strengthen for us the Communist Party in their countries, and giving us the materials and technology we lack, they will restore our military industry, indispensable for our future victorious attacks on our suppliers. In other words, they will labor for the preparation for their own suicide.[20]

If one of the purposes of "market socialism" is indeed to build up the Chinese military, then it is clearly working. The Chinese military has benefited substantially from technology transfer. According to the 2007 United States-China Economic and Security Review Commission 2007 report:

> China's defense industry is producing new generations of weapon platforms with impressive speed and quality, and these advancements are due in part to the highly effective manner in which Chinese defense companies are integrating commercial technologies into military systems.[21]

The economic resources gained through mercantilist-encouraged export production help support Chinese military modernization. The Communist leaders who adopted "market socialism" cannot be unaware of Japan's enormous success with its export-based development strategy, keeping the yen undervalued and the dollar overvalued. That policy kept Japanese goods cheap and US goods expensive, resulting in a surplus of exports over imports. The Japanese strategy also included restricting the access of foreigners to the Japanese market. Japan relied on its own savings to supply the capital for its new manufacturing industries. China's strategy may be more Machiavellian, getting foreign capitalists to invest their own capital. Its success certainly must have succeeded beyond their most optimistic expectations.

Let there be no doubt. The factories the foreign capitalists build in China are not foreign factories. They are Chinese. They are located in China, and in nearly all cases the government is the dominant partner. Foreign capitalists built all the oil wells in the Middle East and about everywhere else, and when these were nationalized, they were paid off from the oil earnings which were theirs to begin with. The Arabs learned that foreign capitalists did not really own the wells they built in Saudi Arabia. The real owners were the Saudis. By decree, a piece of paper, they transformed foreign-owned oil wells into Arabian oil wells. We learned that lesson, too, when overnight German chemical plants in the United States became Anti-Hitler plants in World War II. Japanese owned factories in the United States, like Toyota, Honda, Mitsubishi, aren't Japanese; they're American. Should the Chinese Communist Party ever decide to nationalize its factories, they have ample precedent, domestic police power and even international law on their side.

China imports no capital except for socialist enterprises. The foreign firms provide the capital which shows up as Chinese imports. Not only do we pay for imports from our firms in China, but we pay for the exports of capital goods those factories need. Our trade deficit with China is even bigger than it appears. Much of our exports never earned any foreign exchange. The Chinese government provides domestic inputs like land and even buildings and is a partner in every foreign enterprise. Every one of those businesses is incorporated in

China. They are Chinese businesses run by foreigners to exploit foreigners.

REMEDIES PROPOSED BY EAGLES

The trade deficit eagles recognize the problem and diagnose it more accurately. They are leaders, lobbyists, and economists who have been examining the problem realistically and searching for effective solutions. Eagles include economists like Giuseppe Ammendola, Robert Blecker, Richard Duncan, Dan Mastromarco and Peter Morici, lobbyists like William R. Hawkins, Bob McIntyre and Alan Tonelson, and leaders include Warren Buffett, Pat Buchanan, US senators Max Baucus, Byron Dorgan, Chuck Grassley, Lindsey Graham, Charles Schumer, and Debbie Stabenow.

Even though they are more aware of the causes and the consequences of the trade deficits, some of the solutions that the eagles propose would not be effective. In the section below we discuss remedies the eagles have proposed. Some of these remedies are ones we do not think would be effective (fair trade and tariffs). We think that more effective options are available, including import quotas, and we discuss these approaches in detail in Chapter 4.

Fair Trade

Many eagles recommend leveling the playing field and putting more money in the hands of trade surplus country workers as a way to reduce the trade deficit.

Richard Duncan in his 2003 book (which he revised in 2005), *The Dollar Crisis: Causes Consequences and Cures* came closest to our view of the seriousness and causes of the trade deficits. He recognized that the problem is related to the "dollar standard" and "that it has allowed the United States to finance extraordinarily large current account deficits by selling debt instruments to its trading partners." He warned that the global imbalances will likely cause a great depression and will likely be the biggest economic story of the 21st century. He argued that global aggregate supply is beginning to outrun global aggregate demand as the countries pursuing export-oriented growth are producing more and more goods without a corresponding increase in income among worldwide consumers. Eventually, he predicted, US consumers will not be able to borrow more for consumption. Like other debtors they will be forced to pullback. His solution was to raise aggregate demand in the export-oriented countries through unionization of their workers and a global minimum wage.[22]

He expected the trade surplus countries to willingly agree to his plan, ignoring the fact that the export-oriented countries are pursuing a deliberate mercantilist policy of suppressing consumption in their own countries while building up consumption of their exports. As long as this policy is permitted by the United States and continues to be effective in growing their economies rapidly, why should they end these mercantilist practices?

During the 2004 election, Senator Kerry promised that he would call for an immediate investigation into China's worker rights abuses, suppression of unions, child labor, and the inflexibility of the exchange rate between the renminbi and the dollar. In May 2007, the Kerry program was put into a deal negotiated between the White House and Congressional Democrats. According to a report of the deal by Irwin M. Stelzer, the United States would require its trading partners to adopt various labor market and environmental reforms. The United States would then sue those trading partners who did not comply.[23] Enforcement of such an agreement would likely raise some of the costs of doing business in China, and the labor market reforms could increase the wages of Chinese workers and thus their demand for consumer goods, including their demand for American goods.

Fair trade by itself is not going to lead to balanced trade. When Kerry ran in 2004 he ignored the fact that the $161 billion trade deficit with China in 2003 accounted for only 24% of the total trade deficit that year. What accounted for the $106 billion deficit with Europe, 21%; $57 billion with Japan, 11%; and $47 billion with Canada, 9%? No child labor in these countries, no suppression of unions, no currency inflexibility, and they pay wages comparable to ours! As we have emphasized, trade deficits are monetary phenomena. While fair trade requirements might help address some monetary imbalances, they are insufficient by themselves. If the savings of newly-prosperous workers in foreign countries are sent to the United States, fair trade could ironically make the US trade deficit worse!

Tariffs versus Import Controls

Acting on the belief that the trade deficit is harming US interests, some eagles look for direct policy interventions to change the terms of trade. Although tariffs and import quotas both discourage imports, tariffs are much more likely to backfire.

American University professor of economics Robert A. Blecker was one of the first to advocate measures against those countries that were deliberately manipulating their currencies in order to keep them undervalued in relation to the dollar. In his 1992 book published by the Economic Policy Institute, he recommended using a tariff (which he called a "unit labor cost equalization surcharge" targeted against just those countries.[24] In a 2006 speech, he argued for either tariffs or auctioned quotas again targeted against those countries. He advocated that the tariffs or quotas be lifted once those countries abandon their currency manipulations.[25]

Blecker's solution was similar to what we will advocate in Chapter 4 except that we would use just auctioned import quotas tied to their imports of American goods. Such quotas would require that the other country import more US exports if they want to export to the United States; tariffs can lead to counter-tariffs which can reduce the other country's importation of US exports.

Peter Morici, a Professor of International Business at the University of Maryland, may have been the first to identify foreign buildup of dollar reserves as the main cause of contemporary trade deficits. He presented the problem clearly with excellent detail. For example, here is a cogent paragraph from his own summary of his 2004 paper, *Currency Manipulation and Free Trade:*

> China's currency manipulation creates a subsidy on its exports equal to nearly 9% of its GDP and 21% of its exports. This practice, along with the constraints the renminbi peg places on the currency policies of other Asian governments, is a major cause of the large and growing US trade deficit. Now exceeding $600 billion annually, the trade deficit is appreciably slowing US growth and jobs creation, and causing real wages to stagnate, even as productivity advances at a brisk pace.[26]

His solution, in a February 2007 op ed piece published in *Enter Stage Right,* was "countervailing duties" imposed on China under an existing law, suspended by the Reagan Administration in 1984, which allows the United States to enact tariffs against any closed-market economy.[27]

Pat Buchanan was one of the first political figures to recognize dollar mercantilism, although he did not give it a name. In his 2004 book *Where the Right Went Wrong*, he recognized the reason why Asian nations were buying up American assets, whether or not they were a good investment:

> Asian nations continue to accept and hold depreciating dollars in return for their goods for two reasons: To maintain and increase their share of the U.S. market and to continue to suck production out of the United States. This cannot go on indefinitely. We are approaching a precipice and the only question is when we reach it.[28]

Buchanan's solution was import quotas. He cited approvingly President Reagan's imposition of import quotas upon Japanese automobiles in order to save the big three automobile companies in 1985. Specifically, he wrote:

> Reagan intervened to save the industry by imposing import quotas on Japanese cars. Free traders denounced Reagan as a heretic. The death of Ford and Chrysler were of far less concern to them than fidelity to the free trade gospel of David Ricardo and Adam Smith.
> But Reagan's intervention succeeded. The U.S. auto industry was saved....[29]

Although Reagan's quotas were poorly designed because they limited the number of Japanese vehicles that could be imported into the United States rather than their value, their effect was almost entirely beneficial for the United States. The Japanese automobile manufacturers reacted in two ways: they concentrated their exports on high priced luxury vehicles like the Lexus and decided to produce their low-priced small cars in the United States. If they could not export more autos to the United States, why not produce them in the United States?

Even after the import quotas were withdrawn, the Japanese factories remained. Little by little, they came to use more and more American-made parts. By 2006, almost half of the parts used in Japanese automobile company factories in the United States came from American or Canadian suppliers, a significant amount though still much less than the 77% used by US and Canadian automobile factories.[30] Reagan's import quotas caused foreign fixed investment in the United States to the benefit of the American worker and the American economy.

Tariffs on steel imposed by President George W. Bush in March 2002 in order to save the American steel industry were not as effective. When Bush imposed tariffs ranging from 8% to 30% on different types of steel, China threatened retaliation, Japan was reported ready to retaliate with a tariff of about 30%, and the European Union threatened a wide variety of retaliatory measures and filed a World Trade Organization complaint. It is ironic that these were the very countries with which we have huge trade deficits! In November 2003, the World Trade Organization ruled against the United States on these tariffs, and in December 2003, President Bush withdrew them. More than import quotas, tariffs beget a backlash.

Business and labor organizations have long been advocates of import controls. William R. Hawkins, a fellow of the US Business and Industry Council Education Foundation proposed in 2001 that the United States "restrict imports so as to redirect American spending to the support of domestic production." He cited approvingly:

> Wynne Godley, Distinguished Scholar at the Jerome Levy Institute, Professor Emeritus of applied economics at Cambridge University, and a Fellow of King's College, has suggested the use of nondiscriminatory import controls which are allowed under Article 12 of the Uruguay Round GATT agreement. These might consist of "price based" measures such as "import surcharges, import deposit requirements or other equivalent trade measures with an impact on the price of imported goods." As Godley puts it, "the great advantage of import controls, as Keynes once said, is that they do stop imports from coming into the country."[31]

Indeed import quotas are one of the most effective ways to balance trade. In the next chapter we will recommend tying import quotas to the amount that the trade surplus countries import from us as a way to definitely balance trade over a period of years.

Congress Begins to Address Dollar Mercantilism

Public opinion in the US was tilting away from the international consensus in favor of free trade by 2007. Among the 47 "publics" surveyed by the Pew Global Attitudes Project in 2007, the United States public has the least favorable view of trade, with marked declines in support over the last five years. In 2002, 78 percent of Americans agreed with the statement that "trade is good for your country" but today only 59 percent of the American public has a favorable attitude toward trade.[32] This transformation of US public opinion is beginning to influence policy deliberations. Several US Senators, as discussed below, have begun to target dollar mercantilism.

The dollar mercantilist nations keep the international trade playing field from being level by manipulating the price of their currencies so that their countries' goods will be less expensive than US goods in world markets. Although some of them let their currencies float and some of them peg their currencies at a certain price versus the dollar, the mechanism is always the same. Their central banks borrow their own currencies, which they use to buy sufficient dollars to keep their exchange rates low versus the dollar. They then send the purchased dollars as savings to the United States

Several US senators are fed up with the US failure to address dollar mercantilism. In early 2007, Senator Debbie Stabenow, Democrat from Michigan, introduced legislation in the Senate entitled *The Japanese Currency Manipulation Act* which called for an end to Japan's "damaging currency policy." It directed the administration to come up with a plan to draw down Japan's excessive levels of currency reserves which maintain a ratio of the yen to the dollar that, according to the Automotive Trade Policy Council, provided the average imported Japanese car a $4,000 advantage and up to $10,000 for higher-end vehicles like the Lexus.[33]

On June 13, 2007, Democratic senators Max Baucus and Charles Schumer and Republican senators Chuck Grassley and Lindsey Graham introduced the Currency Exchange Rate Oversight Reform Act of 2007, a bill that was designed to deal with Japanese and Chinese currency manipulations.[34] According to Senator Schumer, the bill was designed to be "World Trade Organization (WTO) compliant and strong and effective."[35]

Although this bipartisan bill is designed to get the dollar mercantilist countries to stop their currency manipulations, it has all sorts of waffling provisions. It lets the Secretary of the Treasury determine whether a country is manipulating its currency and lets the Secretary of the Treasury designate a country as having changed its policy, whether or not any results have actually been achieved. There is nothing quantitative in any of these determinations. In view of the traditional support by the Treasury Department of the banking industry, this role for the Treasury Secretary would likely make the bill ineffective since reducing the trade deficit would likely cause interest rates to rise and bankers lose money when interest rates rise (both because many of their loans are fixed-rate and also because the values of the assets used to secure their loans tend to fall).

However, on the good side, it does include a strong definition of dollar mercantilism. Section 113 (a) part (3) reads:

> The Secretary shall designate a currency identified under paragraph (2) for priority action if the country that issues such currency is—
>
> (A) engaging in protracted large-scale intervention in one direction in the currency exchange market;
>
> (B) engaging in excessive reserve accumulation;
>
> (C) introducing or substantially modifying for balance of payments purposes a restriction on, or incentive for, the inflow or outflow of capital, that is inconsistent with the goal of achieving full currency convertibility; or
>
> (D) pursuing any other policy or action that, in the view of the Secretary, warrants designation for priority action.

After over a year of fact finding, it threatens some pretty tough actions should a currency ever get designated for "priority action," with a tariff imposed upon all goods coming to the United States from that country. That tariff would be administered under existing anti-dumping laws and would add to the cost of the imports from that country the amount that that country's currency is undervalued. But that tariff would be withdrawn whenever the Secretary of the Treasury finds that the country has made progress in its policies.

There are other interesting aspects of this bill. For one thing, it does not rely upon the World Trade Organization (WTO) rules for its authority, but instead upon our International Monetary Fund agreement with 183 other countries, which prevents a country from manipulating its currency in order to enhance trade. Specifically, Article IV of the IMF Articles of Agreement requires that countries "avoid manipulating exchange rates or the international monetary system in order to prevent effective balance of payments adjustment or to gain an unfair competitive advantage over other members."[36]

The bill also proposes that the Federal Reserve take action. Section 116 (a) (2) reads:

> (A) IN GENERAL- The Secretary shall consult with the Board of Governors of the Federal Reserve System to consider undertaking remedial intervention in international currency markets in response to the fundamental misalignment of the currency designated for priority action, and coordinating such intervention with other monetary authorities and the International Monetary Fund.

The Federal Reserve System is already supposed to be intervening in currency markets under its own account under existing laws in order to preserve the long-term health of the American economy. Unfortunately, recent Federal Reserve Board chairmen, ostriches all, have not done so. This bill might give the Federal Reserve the encouragement it needs to finally do its job.

With a Treasury Secretary committed to long-term economic health, the provisions of this bill could possibly work. However, if the Treasury Secretary puts the short-term good of the banking industry above our nation's long-term good, the provisions of this bill could easily be bypassed.

What is needed is a bill that enforces numerical targets and puts the long-term good of the American economy first. In the next chapter, we will discuss solutions that would get to the root of the causes of the trade deficit and would work. The eagles are right; it is time to act.

4. How to Balance Trade

A frog sits in a pot. Gradually the water gets warmer. Unknown to the frog, somebody has been turning on the heat. At first the frog swims around; the warmer water is pleasant. But then the water gets hot. The frog needs to do something soon or it will be too late. Although the frog's limbs have registered the fact that there is a problem, the frog's brain does not yet know that he is in trouble. Will he hop out of the pot while he is still able to do so?

Those involved in American manufacturing industries are feeling the heat, but Washington has not come up with an effective response. In this chapter we will discuss just what we would do to end the trade deficit.

We did not get into the present stew overnight, and getting out without getting burned will be difficult. Our moves need to be planned out as if we were in the middle of a tricky chess game. The key to success is that the trade deficit must be brought down gradually. The trick is to avoid extremes. Should the trade deficit persist for too long, we could lose most of our remaining manufacturing. If it ends too abruptly, the United States economy could be thrust into a high-inflation and high-interest-rate hard landing.

If we are not careful, the Chinese government could manipulate the level of savings that it is sending to the United States in order to force the United States into passivity. First they could suddenly jerk out dollar reserves. Then they could "rescue" the US economy by resuming their dollar purchases. In other words, they might "jerk-on-our-chain" by not letting us do things gradually.

The Chinese government has already been indirectly threatening to dump dollars should we enact tariffs.[1] Given the likelihood that most of China's more than $1 trillion of dollar reserves are being held in foreign banks outside of the United States, it would be very difficult for us to respond by freezing Chinese funds should they engage in such economic warfare.

We need to take the necessary steps in the proper order. The first step should be to eliminate the private-foreign-savings tax loophole and the provisions in our tax treaties that prevent or limit taxation of interest at the source. This would not only reduce the flow of private foreign savings and help the comeback of domestic savings and American exports, but it would also encourage the Chinese government to put its dollar reserves in American accounts where the United States could freeze their assets should they try to jerk them out.

The second step should be to enact Import Certificates or some other form of import limitation tied to exports that would bring trade into equality over a period of years. Import Certificates would solve the trade deficit steadily while producing a boom in American manufacturing investment.

The third step should be to take measures to prevent future dollar mercantilism. We could do so by taxing dollar reserves and by buying foreign currency reserves.

STEP 1: RESTORE THE WITHHOLDING TAX

As we discussed in Chapter 2, in 1984 the United States enacted one of the most foolish tax loopholes of all time, the private-foreign-savings tax loophole. Other tax loopholes have simply led to tax avoidance strategies, but this tax loophole invited the private foreign financial investment that is wrecking the manufacturing sector of our economy. Before 1984, private foreign savers from many countries paid a 30% withholding tax on any interest earned in the United States. Since enactment of the loophole, they have paid nothing.

As a first step, the United States should begin requiring that banks report all interest payments to the IRS, including payments to those that are at present tax free. The IRS almost changed the rules to do this in 2001 and 2002. Congress should pass a law requiring the changed policy. Simply recording interest income (and passing that information along to tax authorities abroad) would end massive tax fraud by foreigners who earn interest in the US, but fail to report that income on their taxes.

The next step would be to restore the withholding tax. If we delete §871(h,i,k) and §881(c,d,e) from the Internal Revenue Service code and either terminate or renegotiate our tax treaties with foreign governments, private foreigners would soon pay a 30% withholding tax on any interest earned in the United States on their financial investments. Almost all of these treaties include a provision that they can be terminated unilaterally by either country. As a result, they are very easy to renegotiate. When we renegotiate these treaties, they should be restructured to eliminate all limitations on our taxation of interest paid by Americans to nonresident foreigners.

We should also consider simply terminating all of these treaties and *not* renegotiating them. There is only one equitable and efficient way to achieve neutrality in where investment takes place. American residents, including corporations, should be taxed on their income wherever earned and given a tax credit for income taxes paid to the country from which the income originated. Foreign residents, businesses and governments, should be subject to the same rules and rates on income earned in the United States. This would end the discriminatory treatment enjoyed by special interest groups, especially the avoidance of taxes made possible by tax treaties.

If countries want to unilaterally give their citizens tax credit for foreign taxes on interest earned abroad, they can; traditionally, the United States and the United Kingdom unilaterally gave their citizens a tax credit on such taxes.[2] If countries want to seek foreign capital by unilaterally eliminating interest taxation at the source, let them. Several European countries did so in order to attract foreign private loans to help with rebuilding following World War II.

At present the inflow of foreign financial capital is damaging to the US economy. We should not give any incentives for foreigners to send their financial capital here! It may at first seem counterintuitive, but the financial inflows sustain the trade deficit and thereby discourage investment in productive enterprises producing tradable goods and services. Instead, of financing investment they merely finance consumption, while diminishing the long term prospects for the US economy.

Given the $4 trillion of private foreign capital earning interest in the United States in 2006 and estimating a 5% interest rate, elimination of this tax loophole and the relevant tax treaty provisions could increase United States annual income tax collections by as much as

$60 billion,[3] though the total would likely be offset by increased tax credits to Americans earning interest abroad since foreign governments would likely respond by raising their taxes on interest paid to Americans.

But more importantly, eliminating this loophole would discourage the inflow of foreign savings and raise American interest rates which would encourage American domestic savings. Eliminating this loophole would also lower the exchange rate of the dollar, making American exports more competitive in world markets and when competing with foreign imports in American markets.

Eliminating this tax loophole would also improve American national security. Before 1984, most foreign governments would put their dollar reserves directly into US assets where they would be tax free under the long-standing foreign government tax loophole. In those days, they would take a huge interest cut were they to put them into the dollar-denominated accounts of foreign banks.

However, since the passage of the private-foreign-savings tax loophole, many foreign governments have changed the location of their dollar reserves. Although the Japanese government continues to put most of their reserves directly into America,[4] those who are less friendly to the United States, including the Chinese government, avoid the possible freezing of their funds (as President Jimmy Carter did to Iranian funds in 1979) by putting their money into the dollar denominated accounts of foreign banks which in turn can put the money tax free into US assets under the foreign bank's name.

Figure 18 shows the current situation, assuming a 5% US interest rate. At this interest rate, foreign governments can earn just under 5% interest by putting their reserves into a foreign bank that in turn puts them into US assets, or they can earn 5% interest by putting their reserves directly into US assets. If they keep their dollars in foreign banks, they would be less likely to have their funds frozen should they come into conflict (economically or militarily) with the United States.

If we were to close the foreign-private-savings tax loophole and end the interest provisions of our tax treaties, the Chinese government would likely put a much higher proportion of their dollar reserves directly into US assets in order to earn about 5%, not 3.4% interest. Once invested in American assets, their funds could be frozen were they to suddenly start jerking our chain by pulling out their dollar reserves or were they to attack Taiwan.

STEP 2: IMPOSE IMPORT CERTIFICATES ON MERCANTILISTS

By the end of 2006, foreign governments had already accumulated about $3,200 billion in dollar reserves (about 24% of our GDP) with the dollar-mercantilist Chinese and Japanese governments having accumulated the majority. Unless we do something, these countries will keep accumulating and lending us more and more dollars while taking away what remains of our manufacturing industries.

In the fall of 2003, Warren Buffett in *Fortune*[5] and one of us in the Pittsburgh *Tribune-Review*[6] both looked at the problem and discovered that the United States, on its own without even needing to consult with any other countries, could eliminate the trade deficits. All we would have to do is tie other countries' exports to the United States to the exports that they accept from us.

Buffett's plan was endorsed by Senator Byron Dorgan in his 2006 book, *Take This Job and Ship It.* Dorgan wrote, "The plan that I believe we should employ to tackle these dangerous trade deficits and stop the wholesale export of American jobs is one offered by Warren Buffett."[7]

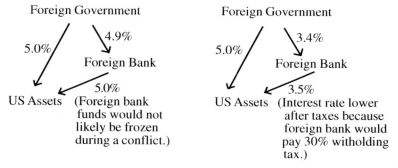

With Current Tax Loophole   If Tax Loophole Removed

Figure 18. Where Foreign Governments Put Dollar Reserves
Closing the loophole would encourage foreign governments to put dollar reserves directly into assets that US government could easily freeze.

Buffett's plan and our plan differ regarding how the Import Certificates would be issued. Buffett's plan would issue the marketable Import Certificates (ICs) directly to US exporters in proportion to their exports and then allow the exporters to sell the ICs to importers. Our plan would just have the US Treasury Department auction the marketable ICs directly to importers.

The Buffett Plan

In September 2006, Senators Byron Dorgan and Russ Feingold fleshed out the Buffett plan in bill form (Senate Bill 3899), which they named the *Balanced Trade Restoration Act of 2006*.[8] Their bill would have the Department of Commerce issue Import Certificates (which they called "Balanced Trade Certificates") directly to exporters.

Each $1 of exports (based upon the appraised value declared on the shipper's export declaration) would earn the exporter a $1 Balanced Trade Certificate which the exporter could then freely market to importers of goods to the United States. The value of imports allowed by a Balanced Trade Certificate would change over time. During the first year of the program, a $1 certificate would allow up to $1.40 of imports, during the second year, $1.30 of imports, the third year $1.20, and so on until by the fifth year $1 of exports would allow $1 of imports. The exporters would freely market the Balanced Trade Certificates to those who wished to import goods into the United States and the Department of Commerce would require that the certificates be submitted with imports.

Dorgan and Feingold's bill exempted oil and gas imports from the Balanced Trade Certificate requirement during the first five years and then phased them in thereafter. There is no economic reason, however, to exclude energy imports during the first five years of the Balanced Trade Certificate plan. America's exports should pay for all of our imports, including energy imports. The Balanced Trade Certificates would give Americans more incentive to conserve energy and increase their own energy production.

In the findings portion of their bill proposal, Dorgan and Feingold claimed that the plan would not violate WTO Rules:

(4) Article XII of the General Agreement on Tariff and Trade (GATT 1994), annexed to the Agreement Establishing the World Trade Organization entered into on April 15, 1994, permits any member country to restrict the quantity or value of imports in order to safeguard the external financial position and the balance of payments of the member country.

(5) In accordance with Article XII of the GATT 1994, the United States should take steps to restore balance to its merchandise trade, and safeguard its external financial position and its balance of payments.

The Richman Plan

Our plan differs from Buffett's plan in that we would have the Department of Treasury auction the Import Certificates, rather than have the Import Certificates issued directly to exporters. Also, the certificates would just be targeted to individual dollar mercantilist countries, as evidenced by their excessive amounts of dollar reserves. Here's how one of us described our plan in the original article:

> Is there any way to balance our trade? Let's take a clue from the fact that barter is always beneficial to both parties. Instead of "Free Trade" as the slogan, how about the slogan, "Free and Balanced Trade"? We could announce to countries with whom we have large chronic deficits that their exports to us in the future will be limited to, say, 110% of what we bought from them last year. If you want to trade with us, you'll have to buy from us. Let's barter!

We would announce to all the countries that have been accumulating dollar reserves in order to run a trade deficit with the United States, that effective the following year their deficit on goods and services would have to be reduced twenty percent. They may respond to this challenge by planning to increase their imports from us, reduce their exports to us, or some combination of both. Failure to meet this annual goal would result in our imposition of a requirement that all imports from the offending country would require an Import Certificate (IC) purchased from the US Treasury Department or other designated agency of the federal government. (The US Treasury Department has experience in auctioning off its own obligations; much the same process would be involved in auctioning off import certificates.)

Prospective importers from countries that fail to reduce their deficits in timely fashion would have to apply for an IC and follow the Treasury's instructions. Over a period of five years, the US Treasury Department would steadily reduce the amount of available import certificates so that the targeted country's trade exports to the United States would be no higher than 5% above their imports from the United States. The Treasury would publish the amount of ICs issued and available and the date of each auction. Each certificate would have to be utilized within a specified period.

We recommend that the proceeds from selling the Import Certificates be placed in an off-budget fund that the US Treasury would use to buy foreign currencies and foreign financial assets, putting money into the hands of foreign consumers, especially the consumers of the dollar mercantilist nations. These currency reserves could also be sold by the US Treasury whenever the dollar is declining too rapidly in foreign exchange markets.

Clearly the dollar mercantilist countries would be directly affected by our plan. In 2006 China had already accumulated $1,066 billion in currency reserves, preponderantly dollars, and was exporting 4.5 times more goods and services to the United States than it was importing. That year Japan had already accumulated $884 billion in currency reserves, preponderantly dollars, and was exporting 1.7 times more goods and services to the United States than it was importing.

Comparison Between the Plans

There are many differences between the two plans. Buffett's plan (as put into bill form by Senators Dorgan and Feingold) would involve our trade with all countries of the world, while our plan would only affect our trade with the dollar mercantilist countries. Buffett's plan would distribute the certificates to US exporters with no change in US government revenue, while our plan would have the US government gain revenue by auctioning the import certificates directly to importers. Buffett's plan would clearly and definitely balance trade over a period of 10 years. Our plan would balance our trade with the dollar mercantilist countries, but would not completely balance trade. The biggest difference, however, would be the effect of the plans on the international trading system.

Buffett's plan runs contrary to the spirit of World Trade Organization rules, since it subsidizes US exports. The current system of international regulations was designed to gradually reduce government interference with free trade. Even so, other countries have taken advantage of loopholes in the international regulations to directly subsidize their exports. The dollar mercantilist nations have been the most egregious, selling their currencies and buying dollars in order to make their exports cheaper and US exports more expensive in world markets. The European nations rebate value-added taxes to their exporters and charge them on American imports so that their goods actually sell for less in the United States than they do in Europe. Even though the rules are not fair, they have been improving and many would be hesitant to reverse them. Buffett's plan would enshrine the principle that countries have a right to subsidize their exports if that is necessary in order to balanced trade and so would weaken the system of regulations that has governed trade in recent years.

Our plan has the advantage that it is much more modest. It could more clearly be instituted without violating World Trade Organization rules since it would only impose import certificates upon countries having a large trade surplus with us. Article 12 of the Uruguay Round GATT agreement specifically lets countries running a threatening overall trade deficit restrict imports from any country with whom they are running a trade deficit.[9] Our plan would simply enforce the International Monetary Fund agreement that countries should not manipulate their currency values. The result would be a more balanced playing field under the current rules of international trade.

Our plan would directly force the dollar mercantilist governments to change their policies. Instead of discouraging their people's consumption of American goods and services, the dollar mercantilist governments would have to encourage their people to import more goods from the United States should they want to export goods and services to the United States. Our plan leaves the current system of international regulations intact. It would just end dollar mercantilism, the export-subsidy loophole unnecessarily permitted by the United States under the current system.

But is the current system of international regulations really worth preserving? It may be that decades from now people will look back with wonder at the foolishness of 20th century nations putting their faith in a system of rules. No system is ever perfect. Governments will always find loopholes to exploit.

The Buffett plan has within it the seeds of a different, but perhaps better international system, one based upon the fact that balanced trade, like barter, always benefits the parties involved. Under the new system, any country experiencing a trade deficit could decide to impose a system of import certificates in order to bring that trade back into balance. The new system would put an end to mercantilism. Any country that tried to subsidize one particular export-competing industry would be hurting its import-competing industries. There would no longer be a need for the World Trade Organization, nor for the GATT treaties, nor for any other of the forms and bureaucracies of the current regulatory-based trade system.

The new system could easily retain the dollar standard using the dollars that are already abroad. By the end of 2006, we estimate that foreign governments already had $3.2 trillion dollars in reserves. Unless the United States were to begin to run trade surpluses, these dollars would remain abroad where they could be used as the medium for international transactions.

Under the new system, countries that were running trade deficits would need to decide whether or not they wanted to impose import certificates in order to balance their trade. Not all countries would decide to do so. Developing or recovering countries might want to attract the financial capital that accompanies trade deficits.

No longer would it be possible for one country to deindustrialize and economically destroy its trading partners without its trading partners' consent. With balanced trade the rule, not the exception, no longer would the world economy be characterized by massive movements in the prices of currencies that would cause intense recessions and depressions. The mercantilist era of economic warfare would end. The era of economic instability caused by currency collapses would end. An era of international economic stability would begin.

Advantages of Import Certificates

Some people mistakenly think that export-linked ICs would be no different in their effects from across-the-board tariffs. But this is not true. ICs guarantee that the trade deficit is eliminated, while tariffs invite counter-tariffs.

Furthermore, ICs linked to exports change the psychology of the situation both among US manufacturers and also among foreign governments. Manufacturers, knowing that the trade deficits would move toward parity, would increase their investment in US production. Foreign governments, knowing that they would need to import more in order to export more, would increase their imports. ICs are the only way to solve the problem assuredly and consistently over a preset period of time.

Each year of ICs, our manufacturing industries would come roaring back, as would our level of manufacturing investment. The risk of a hard landing would diminish: our economy would gain the strength needed to withstand sudden pullouts of foreign financial funds. Gradual pullouts of foreign financial investment would probably be matched by increases in foreign fixed investment as foreign companies would rush to build and expand factories in the United States.

Objections to Import Certificates

When the Buffett plan was introduced as a bill in September 2006, Sherman Katz[10] of the Carnegie Endowment for International Peace and Sallie James[11] of the Cato Institute focused upon four overall criticisms:

1. *The plan would raise consumer prices paid by Americans.* This is true. At present the prices of imports into the United States are being subsidized by the dollar mercantilist countries in order to steal the market share of our industries. The result has been the deindustrialization of the United States. This plan would end those subsidized prices and that deindustrialization.

2. *The plan would raise US interest rates and thereby reduce investment in the United States.* Although interest rates would indeed go up, investment in those sectors of our

economy that export or compete with imports would surge. The loans being forced upon us by the mercantilist countries have indeed lowered interest rates, causing us to mortgage our future in order to buy consumer goods.

3. *The plan would anger our trading partners.* The Richman plan would only apply to those countries running large export surpluses with us, not our other trading partners. The Buffett plan could be adjusted to exempt some of our trading partners. If we wish to exclude the North American countries (Mexico and Canada), we could, perhaps, persuade them to adopt the same ICs themselves. Then North America would continue to be a free-trade zone, but all imports into North American countries would have to be accompanied by ICs.

4. *The plan would intrude government into business activity.* Not all business activity would be affected. The Buffett plan would affect exporters by giving them a bonus. The Richman plan would *not* involve exporters. Both plans would indeed place additional costs upon importers.

In general, the objections to Import Certificates come from those who do not recognize the unsustainable and dangerous nature of the current situation. They reason that lower prices paid by consumers are good, without realizing that the lower prices won't last but that the industries lost as a result of them may never return. They reason that lower interest rates mean higher investment, but don't realize that the dollar mercantilism that causes the lower interest rates also takes away investment opportunities for American manufacturing. Import Certificates, whether the Buffett plan or the Richman plan, may be the only way to solve the trade deficit problem without precipitating a crash in the value of the US dollar.

Governments should not be allowed to subsidize their exports and limit their imports by accumulating dollar reserves or reserves of any other currency. If they wish to protect themselves from a sudden fall in the value of their own currency, let them purchase SDRs (Special Drawing Rights) from the International Monetary Fund. The International Monetary Fund could, in turn, lend out those reserves to underdeveloped countries that want infrastructure investment.

STEP 3: TAX FOREIGN DOLLAR RESERVES

The U.S. income tax system provides a special tax break that exempts foreign governments from paying any U.S. taxes on dividends, interest, or any other income earned from their U.S. investments. Other governments have the same policy. It is a sort of gentleman's agreement among governments. *We won't tax you if you won't tax us.* This gentlemen's agreement is very one-sided inasmuch as the U.S. government has virtually no investments abroad while foreign governments, especially those practicing dollar mercantilism, have huge investments in the United States.

The United States should tax dollar mercantilism by placing the highest rate of tax possible on foreign government investments. If it were possible, we would tax foreign government investments at a 100% rate so that they would earn no interest or dividends whatsoever. We would also make it completely illegal for foreign governments to buy stock in US corporations, as they are currently doing through their Sovereign Wealth Funds. US capitalism should not be for sale!

It is not possible, however, to tax foreign government savings at a higher rate than private foreign savings are taxed. If we tried to do so, foreign governments could simply put their reserves into the eurodollar accounts of foreign banks and earn interest thereby when the foreign banks, in turn, put their dollars into US assets. Also, until the United States is well on its way to recovery from the trade deficits, it could be useful to encourage foreign governments to directly place funds into US assets where they could be frozen (see Figure 18).

Unfortunately, taxing foreign investments would not much discourage dollar mercantilism; the mercantilist governments put their money into dollar reserves in order to manipulate currencies, not in order to earn interest income. But doing so would earn plenty of revenue. In 2006, taxing foreign government income at a 30% tax rate would have earned about $45 billion in tax revenue from the interest paid to the $3.2 trillion of foreign government reserves. So long as dollar mercantilism continues, the amount of potential revenue from this measure will climb steadily. If other countries retaliate by taxing the income earned by the paltry $41 billion of US foreign currency reserves (at the end of 2006), the tax paid out by the US government would be negligible.

STEP 4: BUILD UP US FOREIGN CURRENCY RESERVES

Just as the dollar mercantilist countries buy our currency, our government should buy their currencies. This could be done by the Federal Reserve without requiring any new laws from Congress. Since 1962, the Federal Reserve has had the power to buy foreign currencies under its own account without being subject to any control by the US Treasury. The Federal Reserve could use that power to buy foreign currencies and bonds to match the buildups of dollar reserves by foreign central banks. (China does not permit foreign purchase of their government bonds, so the Federal Reserve would have to find other indirect ways to lend money to Chinese residents.[12])

Whenever the Federal Reserve responds in kind with reciprocal actions to the monetary mercantilist policies of foreign central banks, the effects would be exactly the same as if each central bank were minding its own business. (See the technical appendix at the end of this chapter for the mechanism behind this assertion.) By buying foreign treasury notes, the Federal Reserve would be gradually boosting available credit within the economies of our trading partners and increasingly the value of their currencies relative to the dollar so that they would increase their consumption of our exports.

This method would have to be practiced very gradually. The Federal Reserve would be borrowing by selling US Treasury Notes, using the dollars obtained to purchase foreign currencies, and then using those foreign currencies to purchase foreign financial assets. Such borrowing from Americans would likely boost American interest rates.

The Federal Reserve would want to be careful *not* to raise interest rates so high as to choke off investment, although somewhat higher interest rates could encourage personal savings. The Federal Reserve currently does an excellent job of balancing the growth in money supply so that it is neither inflationary nor deflationary. Intelligent leadership could eventually work out a balancing act that includes keeping mercantilists from artificially boosting the dollar as well.

Such Federal Reserve action would build up stores of foreign currencies that the Federal Reserve could use to slow the fall of the dollar should there be a sudden run on the dollar, and thus prevent a "hard landing."

Once our trade is in balance, the Federal Reserve should be given the job of keeping it in balance by immediately matching any foreign government buildup of dollar reserves with our own build up of reserves in their currency. In the future, Presidents should only appoint Federal Reserve chairmen who understand that the Federal Reserve's responsibility is not only to maintain a steadily increasing money supply, but also to prevent attacks upon the competitiveness of our economy by foreign central banks.

CHANGES NEED TO BE GRADUAL

The trade deficits were not built in a day and cannot be eliminated in a day. The gradual increase in foreign savings coming into the United States over the past three decades has not only produced huge trade deficits, but has also caused a decline in our manufacturing investment and in our domestic savings rates. The countries exporting to us have come to rely upon American markets to demand the goods that they produce and US consumers have come to rely on inexpensive imports combined with low interest rates.

It will take time to reverse those trends. In order to export and compete more effectively with imports, we will need more manufacturing investment. In order to finance domestic investment, we will need more domestic savings. Countries relying upon the US consumer will have to cut their taxes, expand their money supply, or otherwise make credit more readily available to their own citizens.

Any movement to reduce the trade deficits will necessarily reduce the other side of the coin, the foreign savings flowing into the United States. We will need additional domestic savings in order to counteract the loss of foreign savings. In the next chapters, we will discuss ways that the United States could improve its tax code in order to facilitate the needed bounce-back of domestic savings.

TECHNICAL APPENDIX: RECIPROCAL BUYING OF RESERVES

Whenever the Federal Reserve responds in kind with reciprocal actions to the monetary mercantilist policies of foreign central banks, the effects would be exactly the same as if each central bank were minding its own economy. We'll explain the economics involved with three examples. In these examples we'll assume that there are only two countries in the world with trade between them. We will call these countries US and Japan and we will call their currencies the dollar and the yen. We'll also assume that, in each country, the central bank is expanding the monetary base to meet the needs of its growing economy. For simplicity of discussion, we'll also assume that at the beginning the exchange rate is such that 1 dollar trades for 1 yen.

Example #1 – Japan and US each buy own bonds.

This is the normal situation. In this example the central bank of Japan buys 1 million yen of Japanese bonds and the central bank of the US (i.e. the Fed) buys 1 million dollars of US bonds. There would be no reason to suppose that these actions would affect either the exchange rate or the balance of trade. The effects would be expansion of aggregate demand in both countries just as described in any macroeconomics textbook:

1. *Monetary Base.* Both monetary bases would expand.
2. *Interest Rates.* There would be a reduction in both the Japanese and US interest rates because the Japanese central bank bid up the price of the Japanese bonds and the US central bank bid up the price of the US bonds.
3. *Credit Expansion.* Banks in both Japan and US would have new excess reserves that they would want to lend out.
4. *Aggregate Demand.* Consumers and investors in both countries would have more money that they could borrow and spend. They would spend some on products of their own country and some on products of the other country. The consumption and investment components of aggregate demand would rise in both countries with little expected change in net exports.

Example #2 – Japan and US both buy US bonds.

In this example, the Japanese central bank uses its 1 million yen to buy 1 million dollars and then uses the 1 million dollars to buy US bonds; the US central bank also uses its 1 million dollars to buy US bonds. These actions would give the US a lower interest rate, a higher dollar, and a negative trade balance:

1. *Monetary Base.* Both monetary bases would expand. The Japanese monetary base would expand by 1 million yen because the Japanese Central Bank created 1 million of new yen which it used to buy the 1 million dollars.

2. *Exchange Rate.* The US dollar would appreciate vis-à-vis the yen because the purchase of 1 million dollars by the Japanese central bank would increase demand for the dollar. This would increase the relative price of US products and decrease the relative price of Japanese products.

3. *Interest Rates.* There would be a double reduction in the US interest rate because both the US central bank and the Japanese Central bank were bidding up the price of the US bonds. There would be no expected change in the Japanese interest rate.

4. *Credit Expansion.* US banks would have new excess reserves that they would want to lend out.

5. *Aggregate Demand.* The consumption component of US aggregate demand would rise while the trade surplus component would fall. US consumers and investors would have more money that they could borrow and spend. Investment in the US could go either way. Falling interest rates would make fixed investment less expensive but the rising dollar would make investment opportunities less attractive. The trade surplus component of aggregate demand in Japan would increase.

6. *Balance of Trade.* US exports to Japan would decrease and Japanese exports to the US would increase. The only counterforce that could prevent this from happening would be a possible flow of private savings from the US to Japan. The reduced interest rate in the US would encourage a flow of private savings to Japan, but the appreciating dollar versus the yen would encourage a flow of

private savings from Japan to the US.

Example #3 – Japan and US each buy other country's bonds.
This is what the Fed could do whenever a foreign country buys dollars to increase its dollar reserves and trade surplus. In this example the Japanese central bank uses its 1 million yen to buy 1 million dollars and uses those dollars to buy US bonds; the Fed reciprocates and uses its 1 million dollars to buy 1 million yen and then uses those yen to buy Japanese bonds. The effects would be the same as in the normal situation of Example #1 where each country buys its own bonds:

1. *Monetary Base.* Both monetary bases would expand.
2. *Interest Rates.* There would be a reduction in both the US and Japanese interest rates because the Japanese central bank bid up the price of the US bonds that it bought and the US central bank bid up the price of the Japanese bonds that it bought.
3. *Everything Else.* Aggregate demand, exchange rate, and trade balance would be exactly the same as in Example #1.

It is clear from Example #3 that there are absolutely no negative economic effects if the Fed matches a foreign build-up of US dollar reserves with a reciprocal build-up of US reserves in the foreign currency. The effects would be exactly the same as when each bank buys its own country's bonds: No increased trade deficit. Mutual increases in consumption and investment in both countries. Mutual increases in the purchases of each other's exports. Whenever the Fed responds in kind with reciprocal actions to the trade-war attacks of foreign central banks, the effects would be exactly the same as if each central bank were minding its own economy.

Part II: The Tax System

*There are, broadly speaking, three different types of question about
a tax. What would increase welfare more – the use that taxpayers
would make of the money or the use the government will make of the
money? Is the burden of the tax distributed fairly? And what effect
will it have on work and saving?*

Attributed to Ursula K. Hicks

In Part I, we focused upon foreign savings coming into the United
States and how to reduce them. In this part we will focus upon domestic savings and how to increase them. Both are essential to a long-
term solution of the problems caused by the trade deficits.

In the first part of this book we showed that economists adopted
free trade and free movement of savings between countries as an
ideology that blinded them to the mercantilist practices of a number of
our trading partners. In this part, we show that economists have a
similar blindness to the consequences of the incentives of our dysfunctional tax system that discourage savings and investment in favor
of consumption.

Domestic savings are important because you cannot have real
investment that produces real economic growth without savings. In
recent years the United States economy has been imbalanced, with
excessive consumption and little saving.

Webster's New World Dictionary defines consumption as (1) destruction, waste, using up of something and (2) a disease that causes
the body or part of the body to waste away. Our leaders, both Democrat and Republican, seem bent on destroying the US economy through
tax policies encouraging the destruction, waste, and consumption of
capital, a process whose result, if continued, will make the United
States as a great power only a memory.

In Chapter 5, we propose a very simple but innovative change in
the current income tax code that would eliminate the perverse tax
incentive to consume capital gains. Not only would our innovative
proposal increase savings, but it would also eliminate many existing
tax loopholes.

In Chapter 6, we propose some very simple changes in the real-estate tax code that would encourage savings and investment in real-estate. Our proposals are based upon an important insight first explained by the lead author in a journal article, that the property tax is borne by the land owner. We are among the first economists to recognize that California's Proposition 13 solves almost all of the problems with the real estate tax. When combined with a homestead exemption, it would make the real-estate tax much more friendly to home ownership, savings, and fixed investment in real-estate.

In Chapter 7, we propose enhancing America's corporate sector so that American workers will have the tools they need to compete in the world economy. The corporate sector is the one sector of the American economy that did not stop saving when the inrush of foreign savings caused long-term interest rates to go down to near zero. We propose what many other economists before us have proposed, eliminating the corporate income tax and replacing it with a consumption tax, such as a Value-Added Tax, in order to help provide the needed capital for fixed investment in the United States and help level the international trade playing field. Other economists, however, have ignored the fact that eliminating the corporate income tax would create tax loopholes unless accompanied by changes in the capital gains tax, like the ones we propose in Chapter 5.

In Chapter 8, we will recommend the most sweeping change of all, replacing our present corporate and personal income taxes with a true consumption tax that would encourage savings and investment. We will compare several tax proposals that have been put forth in recent years.

As the trade deficits unwind, interest rates will necessarily shoot up to extremely high levels unless domestic savings come back at the same time. The changes that we propose in this section would encourage that needed comeback.

5. Taxation of Capital Gains

Nikita Khrushchev describes the disastrous consequences of Stalin's agricultural policies – the famines they produced, the deaths of millions, the decades long stagnation of Soviet agriculture. He writes, "On top of the outrageously low prices he set for the peasant's produce, Stalin also proposed that the collective farmers pay a special tax on any fruit trees they planted in private orchards. I remember a conversation I once had with Stalin about this tax. I told him that I'd been to see a cousin of mine who lived in Dubovitsa. She told me she was going to have to chop down her apple trees in the fall....(W)ith this new tax, it will be too expensive for me to keep them."[1]

As we have already observed in the case of flows of foreign savings to the United States, financial investment in the United States does not necessarily contribute to economic growth. The huge inflow of funds from abroad, while some of it found its way into productive investment, was disproportionately invested in financial assets. The effect was to bid up the prices of financial assets like shares of corporate stock. The US financial sector thrived. Meanwhile, Americans sold off their assets to foreigners and consumed the proceeds, encouraged by our dysfunctional tax system which gave a special tax discount to American sellers who consumed their capital, thus penalizing those who reinvested it.

In this chapter we propose a very simple but innovative change in the current income tax code that would eliminate the perverse tax incentive to cash in capital gains. Our proposal follows from an improved definition of income that we also propose in this chapter. The simple improvement that we propose in the way our income tax code treats capital gains would enhance America's future wealth and prosperity.

CONSUMPTION OF CAPITAL

There may be a tax that has worse economic effects than a tax on capital, but a tax on capital surely is one of the worst. A tax on capital, discourages the savings and investment upon which economic growth depends. Taxes on capital are like Stalin's taxes on productive resources (capital!) like fruit trees. They provide an incentive to cut down the trees. You get fewer apples; you get less output.

The current US income tax policy is not consistent with most economists' analyses of capital gains, and this is a blessing because most economists are wrong. Nearly all economists consider all increases in the value of capital to be income. For example, they consider an increase in the value of your home or the value of your share of a corporation to be income. Current tax policy, however, only taxes capital gains when property is sold. (*Accrued gains* are gains "on paper" when an asset goes up in value; *realized gains* occur when assets are sold and converted into money.)

Capital gains taxation policies in the United States represent a bad compromise between treating capital gains as income and treating them as capital. Under the current income tax law in the United States, unrealized or accrued capital gains are not taxed. After the capital is sold, net realized capital gains are considered income but are taxed at a maximum rate of 15%. The deduction of net realized capital losses is limited to $3,000. The rates of tax on ordinary income range from 10% to 35% and that on capital gains vary from 5% to 15%. Thus, capital gains are treated differently than income that takes the form of wages and salaries, interest income, and profits from business and real estate, which are taxed at ordinary rates.

This treatment has led to the creation of a myriad of tax shelters that are designed to turn ordinary income into capital gains so that it will be taxed at a lower rate. In a March 1984 paper, Bob McIntyre of Citizens for Tax Justice discussed the typical format of these shelters. The investments are usually financed through loans. The shelters take advantage of accelerated depreciation, whenever possible, so that they will pay less tax on income now, but a higher capital gains tax later. Then when the investment is sold, the investors take advantage of the especially low tax rates for capital gains.[2]

In recent years, corporations have been increasingly turning to stock buybacks as a way to turn corporate income into capital gains. According to a 2005 article in McKinsey Quarterly, the $230 billion in stock buyback announcements in 2004 more than doubled the rate of 2003 and there was no indication that the rate of buybacks was slowing.[3] In a buyback, the corporation buys back its own stock, thus consuming its own profits instead of reinvesting them. With fewer shares outstanding, the future income stream is split between fewer shares of stock, so the stock price tends to go up, thus producing a capital gain for the shareholders at the expense of the future growth of the company and of the nation. These buybacks are fueled by the lower tax rate that applies to capital gains.

A better approach to capital gains taxation would be based on the recognition that individuals sometimes treat capital gains as income, while at other times they treat these gains as capital. It is easy to distinguish between these two types of behavior, and a tax system that recognizes this distinction would avoid the flawed compromise made in current policies. Among other benefits, a revised capital gains taxation policy would provide stronger incentives to invest, while diminishing current incentives to consume capital gains. By eliminating the time-inconsistent inefficiencies of the current system, it would encourage more efficient capital investment and higher savings rates.

In this chapter we develop a new definition of income which provides us with a consistent way to tax capital gains that does not encourage the taxpayer to consume them.

DEFINITIONS OF INCOME

Economics has oscillated on the question of whether capital gains are income. Early definitions of income did not treat any capital gains as income. Currently, most economists view all capital gains, even gains that have not yet been realized through a sale, as income. In contrast, we define present income as wages, interest, profits, rent, and consumed future income. If capital gains are consumed, then future income is being consumed and should be taxed. If capital gains are reinvested, then they will produce future income which can be taxed when it occurs.

What are Capital Gains?

What causes capital assets to increase in market value? A capital gain or loss is the change in the capital value of an asset due to an unexpected change in its future income stream. If the gain were expected, the price paid for it would reflect all of the future income expected to be received or to accrue from its ownership. The value of a capital asset is simply the capitalized value of the income it is expected to yield. (See the technical appendix at the end of this chapter for the mathematics behind this assertion.) We could rephrase the question to: "What causes unexpected changes in the value of a capital asset?" The answer includes all of the following *unexpected* changes in the future income stream:

1. *Earnings surprises.* Anyone who follows the behavior of share prices on the New York Stock Exchange and every other stock exchange in the world knows that the prices of shares go up or down when there is an "earnings surprise." An earnings surprise occurs when a company reports its earnings for the most recent quarter as higher or lower than was expected. If those higher earnings are expected to continue, they would increase the market value of shares. It is a common practice for companies to report how good or bad they expect earnings to be in subsequent periods. If reported earnings and expected future earnings are higher than expected, the price of the company's shares rise. This results in a capital gain. The reverse is true if the company reports lower than expected earnings. Notice that the reported gain (or loss) has to be unexpected. Future earnings that are expected are already reflected in the current price. What are called "growth stocks" are shares in companies expected to grow at higher rates than the average, Their expected growth is already reflected in the current price of shares. An investor pays more for shares of corporate stock that are expected to grow by 20% a year than for shares expected to yield the same income year after year. Because the growth is anticipated, it is reflected in the current price.

2. *Reinvestment of earnings by corporations.* Corporations pay tax on their earnings whether they are paid out as dividends or reinvested. When they reinvest their earnings, future earnings can be expected to increase. When they do, the prices of shares rise, producing a capital gain.

3. *Inflation.* Earnings tend to increase as a result of inflation. As a

result, gains on capital assets held for long periods are often illusory.

4. *Changes in the rate of interest.* Long-term interest rates indicate the rate of return that can be expected from an asset that has a fixed rate of return. When interest rates fall, asset values rise. On the other hand, when interest rates rise, asset values fall.

5. *Another cause of gains and losses is the business cycle.* Our experience during the past sixty years suggests that there is no longer a business cycle; rises and falls in the level of business activity are the result of the monetary and fiscal policies of governments. It is true that there are so-called long cycles attributable to great innovations like the steamship, electricity, automobiles, home appliances, and computers. Economic growth is not a smooth and continuous process. It has ups and downs that produce capital gains and losses. The bunching of capital gains in the last year of an upturn and the reduction in gains reported in the first year of a downturn provide some evidence that changes in general business activity may account for capital gains and losses.

6. *Buying a bargain!* Capital gains also occur when investors buy an asset they consider to be "undervalued" and they turn out to be right. Likewise, capital losses can occur when investors "overvalue" an asset and their expectations turn out to be wrong. The purchase of any asset requires the assumption of risk. Government bonds are the closest thing to a riskless asset, but even those are subject to changes in interest rates and inflation.

Accrued and Realized Gains

Taxing capital gains as they accrue, as well as the income these gains represent when realized, would result in a double tax on income: a tax on the capital gain which is paid in taxes and a tax on the future yields which are economically equivalent to the accrued capital gain. Indeed, if you taxed the accrued capital gain at a 100% tax rate, the taxpayer would never receive the future income that the capital gain represents. For example, assume a taxpayer pays $1,000 for 100 shares of GM at a price of $10 per share, based on expected GM earnings per share of $1 per year. Suppose GM's earnings are expected to rise to $2 per year. The shares would rise in value to $20 per share or $2,000, and the shareholder would have an accrued gain of $1,000. If the accrued gain were taxed at the 100% tax rate, then the taxpayer would have to sell 50 shares, just to pay the tax, and he or she would get no benefit whatsoever from the improved income prospects of GM shares. Capital gains are not income. Instead, they represent the capitalized value of expected future income.

Taxing unconsumed capital gains has negative economic effects upon the economy, principally arising from the reduced stock of capital resulting from it. In the above example of the owner of GM shares, the taxpayer had to sell half of his or her shares just to pay the tax.

Taxing accrued but unrealized capital gains is no more justified than taxing medical doctors upon completion of their training on the capital value of their future income stream. Suppose doctors can reasonably anticipate earning an income of $200,000 after graduation, an income stream that has a capital value of $2 million. Let us say that the cost of their education, including income foregone, was $500,000. Using a 10% discount rate, they have an accrued capital gain of $1.5 million and would be liable to a tax of $225,000 before earning a dime! Their earnings would be taxed twice, first as a capital gain and later as income. If you tax accrued capital gains which are the capitalized value of an expected increase in future yields and you tax the yields as they are received, you are taxing the same income twice.

There is no coherent theoretical justification for differential taxation of accrued gains and of those "realized" gains that are then reinvested in similar capital. If I sell shares of Southwest Airlines on December 31, realizing a substantial capital gain, I will be taxed on that gain, even if I repurchase those shares for the identical price on January 2. The consequence of this incoherence in the tax code is a process of "lock in" whereby individuals are discouraged from selling or exchanging capital in order to avoid paying taxes on the gains.

The Consistent Hicks-Richman Definition of Income

Current policy creates distortions by taxing gains from reinvested capital and not taxing accrued gains. That said, there is a definite place for taxing some capital gains: those gains from capital that their owner decides to realize as income now, instead of in the future. Capital gains are income whenever their owner decides to consume the capital instead of continuing to invest it.

The basis of the Hicks-Richman definition of capital (gains) is our claim that reinvested capital and accrued gains are equivalent: both produce future income, and their growth ought *not* to be taxed in the present. Instead, the future income should be taxed in the future. All income should be taxed at the same rate. There should be no reduced rate for any one kind of income over any other.

The difference between our definition and the Haig-Simons definition is that we hold that capital gains from consumed capital are future income that the taxpayer has chosen to realize as present income, and that capital gains from reinvested capital are future income to be taxed in the future. Here's how the Hicks-Richman definition works when a taxpayer buys $100,000 worth of stock (or any other asset) and sells it for $150,000. The tax rate depends upon whether he or she reinvests the capital:

1. *Capital Gains from reinvested capital are not taxed.* If the taxpayer reinvests the full $150,000 in an *income-producing* asset, then he or she pays no tax. Instead, the reinvested capital gain would be subtracted from the basis of the new asset.[4]

2. *Capital Gains from consumed capital are fully taxed.* If the taxpayer does not reinvest any of the capital in other assets, then he or she pays the full rate of tax on the $50,000 capital gain.

3. *Capital Gains from partly consumed capital are partly taxed.* If the taxpayer reinvests half ($75,000) in an income-producing asset, then he or she pays tax on half of the capital gain ($25,000). The other $25,000 is a reinvested capital gain that is subtracted from the basis of the new asset.

The roots of our definition go back to J. R. Hicks, who defined income as consumption plus capital accumulation (by which he meant savings). The only reference Hicks made to capital gains was in the following paragraph. He wrote:

The income *ex post* of any particular week cannot be calculated until the end of the week, and then it involves a comparison between present value and values which belong wholly to the past. On the general principle of "bygones are bygones," it can have no relevance to present decisions. The income which is relevant to conduct *must always exclude windfall gains* [italics added]; if they occur, they have to be thought of as raising income for future weeks (by the interest on them) rather than as entering into any effective sort of income for the current week. Theoretical confusion between income ex post and ex ante corresponds to practical confusion between income and capital.[5]

We agree with Hicks that accrued capital gains are not income at all. We differ only when the taxpayer, during the year, sells the asset and consumes the gain. Income should be defined as earnings from wages, rents, interest, profits, and consumed capital gains.

The revised system of capital gains taxation that we suggest would shift the burden of capital gains taxation to those who consume capital. We have not provided a full analysis of the shift in government revenue, but it could potentially be revenue neutral, or even beneficial for the Treasury. For instance, taxpayers in upper brackets would pay more than twice as much tax on consumed gains. These increased tax revenues would be offset by the elimination of capital gains taxes based upon gains that are reinvested.

The Inconsistent Haig-Simons Definition of Income

The Hicks-Richman definition of income contrasts with the Haig-Simons definition of income which is currently accepted by most economists. According to that definition, personal income is the amount a person can consume during a period of time without being worse off at the end of the period than he was at the beginning. Under this definition, any change, positive or negative, in the value of the investor's capital assets whether realized or accrued (i.e., unrealized or paper gains) is counted as income or loss.

The tensions underlying this definition become obvious when one contrasts this definition with that used in national income accounting, where changes in the value of capital assets are not considered income at all. The national income consists of wages, rents, interest, and profits. In presenting his definition of income, Henry Simons, one of the mentors of the lead author of this book, recognized that at an earlier point in time, many economists believed that no capital gains counted as income. Simons criticized definitions that defined personal income as the taxpayer's share of national income (i.e., including only wages, rent, interest and profits), reciting:

> The view that personal income is merely a share in the total income of society is to be found in almost every treatise on economics;... On this view, gifts, capital gains, and other items must be excluded from the base of a personal tax because such items cannot be counted in the income of society as a whole.[6]

Although realized capital gains and losses are not considered in calculating national income, most economists believe that capital gains should be counted as income for purposes of personal and corporate income taxation. They reason that to exclude capital gains would be unfair to taxpayers whose incomes come from wages, rents, interest, and profits. In this view, even unrealized capital gains (referred to in the economic literature as accrued capital gains) are income but need to be excluded for administrative reasons (i.e., one should not be forced to sell some of his capital to pay the tax liability).

R. M. Haig wrote in 1921, "Income is the money value of the net accretion to one's economic power between two points in time."[7] As Simons points out the words "economic power" in Haig's definition are ambiguous. The use of the word "power" suggests a focus on the political, and Simons took this further in his discussion of the income tax: "Income taxation is broadly an instrument of economic control, a means of mitigating economic inequality."[8] He substitutes a policy-oriented (i.e., a political definition of income) for an economic definition of income. Income is one indication of economic power; capital or wealth is another. But the latter is the source of the former and they should not be confused.

Because the Haig-Simons definition is not an appropriate economic definition of income, it has created a range of challenges for capital gains tax administration. These difficulties alert us to the fact that the Haig-Simons definition of income is wrong. There is no similar level of difficulty with taxing wages, rent, interest, and profits.

Even Simons recognized some of these difficulties. Although his definition of personal income included accrued gains, Simons nevertheless believed realization to be "indispensable to a feasible income-tax system."[9] Simons is being less than forthright about this possibility. For at least one large class of investments, capital gains can readily be taxed before they are realized. Most capital gains come from corporate shares. The market prices of listed securities are easily calculated. There is a more fundamental problem afoot. That problem is that accrued gains should not be considered income at all. Accrued gains are capital not income.

Consistent with Simons' practicality argument, the current treatment of capital gains in the United States is to tax only realized gains. This approach is inconsistent with Simons' definition and with ours as well. Unfortunately, the boundaries it draws between taxable and non-taxable gains creates a range of economic inefficiencies. Among these problems are the so-called locked-in effect, the incentive to realize and consume capital gains, the problem of illusory gains, tax avoidance by holding the asset to death, the problem of establishing the basis for measuring the gain, the problem of capping the deductibility of losses, etc..

The Haig-Simons definition misses the fact that only some capital gains are present income that should be taxed as income. Other capital gains are future income that should be taxed in the future. One consequence of a better definition would be clearer and stronger incentives to invest and save.

A sort of Gresham's Law – that bad money drives out good money – seems to apply to bad economic ideas that are slanted to achieve one or another political objective. They drive out unbiased analyses. The UK, after considering capital gains not to be income for two centuries, added a tax on capital gains in 1992. Currently, the first £8,500 of chargeable gains is exempt and so are gains from the sale of one's home. The rates of tax are 10, 12, and 40 percent depended on the amount of taxable income reported in the personal income tax return. The Italians went further in the Italian Tax Reform of 1998 with a tax that included accrued gains. The attempt can only be described as farcical. It was a short-lived attempt to tax accrued gains and realized gains comprehensively and retrospectively.[10] It can be done; but why would any educated economist want to do it?!

Bartlett, Hall, and Rabushka Got it Half Right

In an August 2001 policy report for the National Center for Policy Analysis, Bruce Bartlett got it half right. In an analysis that is quite similar to our own, he pointed out the flaws of the Haig-Simons definition of income while explaining, just as we do, that taxing reinvested capital gains taxes future income twice.[11] The same argument was made by Robert E. Hall and Alvin Rabushka in their book about the Flat Tax. They wrote:

> The market value of the stock is the capitalization of its future earnings. Because the owners of the stock will receive their earnings after the corporation has paid the business tax, the market capitalizes after-tax earnings. A capital gain occurs when the market perceives that prospects for after-tax earnings have risen. When the higher earnings materialize in the future, they will be correspondingly taxed. In a system like the current one, with both an income tax and a capital gains tax, there is double taxation.[12]

However, Bartlett, Hall, and Rabushka may not have understood that capital gains are indeed present income when they and the capital that produced them are consumed. Instead of recommending, as we do, that capital gains be taxed when the capital is consumed, they recommend that capital gains be untaxed in every situation, a recommendation that would encourage the consumption of capital.

NEUTRALITY REGARDING TIMING OF INCOME

The Haig-Simons treatment of capital gains, as currently incorporated into our income tax code, paradoxically provides incentives not to realize gains (the locked-in effect) and incentives to realize and consume gains (the differential effect). If one holds on to an asset that has appreciated in value, the income therefrom, dividends or earnings, is taxed at full rates of tax (e.g., 35% maximum). However, if the capital gain is realized, keeping in mind that it is the capitalized value of expected future income, the rate of tax is substantially lower (15%

maximum) than the rate that will be applied to the future income it represents (35% maximum). The current special tax treatment thus encourages disinvestment and the consumption of capital.

Bartlett's proposal provides even more incentive to consume. If the taxpayer waits for the future income stream to be produced by the capital gain, then that income stream would be taxed, whereas if the taxpayer consumes the gain now, it would be tax free.

The tax treatment of capital gains that we propose, based upon the Hicks-Richman definition, is completely neutral with respect to the timing of income. If the future income is consumed now, it is taxed now. If the future income is *not* consumed now, then the capital that will produce it is *not* taxed now.

CONCLUSION

The Hicks-Richman definition of income would eliminate the confusion of capital and income inherent in the Haig-Simons definition. Not only that, but it would help the United States find the domestic savings needed to facilitate the gradual reduction of the inflow of foreign savings, relative to domestic savings, that accompanies the reduction of the trade deficit. It would just require a small change in the current income tax code and might not much change the amount of income tax that would be collected, because consumed gains would be taxed at a substantially higher rate for most taxpayers.

The tax change that we propose in this chapter is neutral regarding timing of income because it is based upon an improved definition of *income*. But the Hicks-Richman definition does not, by itself, solve all of the problems with the capital gains tax. There is still the problem that a capital gain can be the illusory result of inflation. There is also double-taxation where corporation profits are taxed first as profits and then later as dividends or capital gains.[13] In Chapter 7, we will recommend dealing with the resulting double-taxation by eliminating the corporate income tax altogether. As we shall discuss in Chapter 7, our proposed treatment of capital gains is a necessary prerequisite for eliminating the corporate income tax, else eliminating that tax would create many new tax loopholes.

Our proposal in this chapter is a simple change in just one aspect of the current personal income tax code. It would end one of the federal tax system's worst biases against savings. In the next chapter, we will propose some simple changes in the real-estate tax code that would make that local tax much more friendly to savings and investment.

TECHNICAL APPENDIX: VALUE OF A CAPITAL ASSET

The relationship between the value of any capital asset and the income derived from its ownership is the present value of the stream of future income expected by the investor from his ownership of the asset, i.e.,

$$\text{Capital value} = Y_1/(1+r) + \ldots + Y_n/(1+r)^n \qquad (1)$$

where Y_1 is the expected profit the year following the purchase of the asset. Y_n is the expected return in future years, and r, the discount factor representing what the market considers an adequate reward for the time value of money and risk. The value of capital or property according to this equation is the capitalized or discounted value of its expected returns.

What then is a capital gain or loss? A capital gain or loss is the change in the capital value of an asset due to an *unexpected change* in its future income stream. Future earnings that are expected are discounted in Equation 1. The value of a capital gain therefore is:

$$\text{Capital gain} = dY_1/(1+r) + \ldots + dY_n/(1+r)^n \qquad (2)$$

where dY_1 is the *unexpected increase* in the expected return next year and dY_n, the unexpected increase in expected returns in future years. (A capital loss similarly is the capitalized or discounted value of an unexpected decrease in expected returns.)

We may illustrate these definitions by the case of an individual who buys an existing business for $100,000, the price based on an expected average return of $10,000 per year. As a result of superior management decisions or happenstance, he achieves a return of $15,000 during the first year, which is expected to continue. As a result, the value of his business increases, say, to $150,000 at the beginning of the second year. He has an accrued gain of $50,000, the present value of the $5,000 increase in annual return.

6. The Real Estate Tax

*After William the Conqueror conquered England, he ordered an
assessment roll to be prepared which came to be known as the
Domesday Survey of 1084. It listed all the real and personal property in the kingdom and all other sources of income including public offices such as sheriffs and judges and tax collectors. Most of
the property in the kingdom was real estate, and its basis was its
"annual value": what it could be expected to yield per year. Even
the tax on officeholders was assessed on the estimate of income
which could be expected from the office (its annual value). The rate
of tax was so burdensome, six shillings in the pound or 30%, payable in three installments, that many freemen were unable to pay it,
causing small landowners to seek refuge in a feudal arrangement. A
lord or wealthy landowner took over the burden in exchange for
feudal services and/or contributions. Freemen became serfs in the
process. The Magna Carta may have been the first successful tax
revolt. It forced King John and subsequent kings of England to get
parliamentary approval for any special tax levy.*

In this chapter we propose a fix to the current real estate tax code that
would encourage savings and fixed investment by home owners and
others who purchase and improve real-estate. The real-estate tax is
the best tax that local governments can levy, but it could be made
better.

The construction of a new home, a rental property, a commercial
property such as an office building or hotel, or an industrial building is
a fixed investment, which like any other new investment, promotes
economic growth. But as currently constituted, the real estate tax discourages investment. It imposes unjustified tax burdens when taxing
bodies – counties, municipalities, and school districts – leave the rate
of tax unchanged during periods of rising assessments in their eager-
ness to obtain larger revenues. (The tax is calculated by multiplying
the assessment by the tax rate.) As we shall note below, the greed of
taxing jurisdictions during a period of rising values caused the tax revolt that led to Proposition 13 in California.

The conventional wisdom is that the real estate tax, by its very
existence, discourages construction and improvements to real estate.

This criticism is not true. The burden of the real estate tax is shifted backward to the landowner, the seller, at the time of purchase. It is only the uncertainty regarding future tax burdens that discourages construction and improvements to real estate.

Our society justly encourages home ownership. Our income tax code, for example, gives income taxpayers a special deduction on mortgage interest. However, the special provisions of the income tax code to encourage home ownership are counteracted by the uncertainty of real estate taxes. Those who buy their own homes never know how much they will be paying in real estate taxes in the future.

There is a simple solution which would solve all of the problems with the real estate tax. It would turn the real-estate tax into one that encourages savings and investment and home ownership. Real estate should only be reassessed when the property is purchased. The assessment should normally be the purchase price. Rate increases should be limited to the rate of inflation. There should also be a homestead exemption on the first $25,000 (or so) of the assessed value, to both encourage home ownership and also make the tax more progressive. With these simple changes, the real-estate tax would encourage home ownership and fixed investment in real estate. Not only that, but these changes could preserve the real estate tax from tax revolts and continue this tax which is, in the final analysis, the best tax available to local governments.

The Good Tax for Local Governments

The real estate tax is the only tax local governments can levy that doesn't cause an outflow of people and jobs or inhibit their inflow. All the other taxes – sales, income, excises, and business taxes – encourage an outflow of people and jobs if neighboring communities have lower rates of tax. Under a federal system, the cities, counties and school districts must have their own revenue sources, lest they become mere appendages of the states and federal government.

Replacing the real estate tax with other taxes would cause a rise in property values and a windfall for landowners, putting home ownership out of the reach of many. Yet every year, some political demagogue or other will propose getting rid of the real estate tax and substituting an income, wage, or sales tax, all of which have serious negative economic consequences for local governments. It is one thing for state governments to levy such taxes, although they, too, have to be concerned about interstate competition. It is another when those taxes can be avoided by traveling a few miles to another jurisdiction. Even states have to worry about intergovernmental competition. New York's rates of income, sales, and excise taxes had better not be much higher than New Jersey's if it is to avoid an exodus of people and businesses.

Burden of the Real Estate Tax

David Ricardo in his 1821 book, *The Principles of Political Economy and Taxation,* theorized that the burden of a tax on the rent of land has to be borne by the landlord because it doesn't affect the supply of land and therefore cannot be passed on to the consumer. On the other hand, a tax on the product of land drives marginal producers out of business which does affect the supply of products. As a result, a tax on products is passed on, at least partially, to the consumer.[1]

The modern view is essentially the same. Taxes on land (i.e. the capital value of rent) are borne entirely by the landlord, but taxes on buildings and other improvements are passed on, in part because they affect building on marginal land. Therefore, at least part of the tax on buildings falls on the tenant or occupier of the improvement.

Unfortunately, in some contexts this view is wrong. In the urban environment, there is, for all practical purposes, no marginal land, so the supply of housing is unaffected, and therefore all of the tax on land and buildings falls on the landlord. The burden of the real estate tax is borne by the landowner. Economists call this "backward shifting," in contrast to a tax which is shifted forward to the consumer.

From an economic perspective, paying $100,000 and having no tax burden or paying $80,000 with a tax burden of $2,000 a year are equivalent, assuming a discount rate of 10 percent. As a consequence, prospective buyers discount existing real estate taxes. Indeed, the buyer needs less capital, $80,000 compared with $100,000, so that buyers can more easily qualify for loans and home buying is encouraged.

Neutrality Respecting Business Location Decisions

If one community has lower real estate taxes than another, the former is *not* more attractive. Prices of land in the higher taxed community will be lower than prices in the lower-taxed community. Hence is derived the conclusion that the tax is economically neutral so far as the decision to locate is concerned. It also follows that the tax cannot be avoided by moving from the higher taxed jurisdiction. The cost of houses and buildings will be higher in the lower taxed jurisdiction. This isn't true of other taxes. For example, if a city imposes a gross receipts tax, wholesale businesses will move to the suburbs.

Because prospective buyers pay a price that reflects the tax, existing taxes do not interfere with decisions of individuals and businesses concerning where to locate. Furthermore, the tax does not affect the supply of housing because it does not impede development. The construction and therefore the supply of offices, apartments, factories, and retail facilities are not affected by the level of current taxes.

Of course, if it is generally expected that taxes will increase, market prices of real estate will fall in anticipation of the increased taxes. Any tax increase will lower property values. Similarly, lowering or eliminating the real estate tax would raise the prices of new and existing homes by the capitalized value of the tax and provide a windfall for property owners. Because property values would rise, a cut in the real estate tax would have little or no effect on rents. It would, however put new houses out of reach of many first time home-buyers.

Progressivity

The real estate tax falls more heavily on the rich than on the poor for two reasons. First, a large proportion of real estate consists of commercial and industrial properties whose owners as a class are in the higher income brackets. And second, many jurisdictions offer a homestead exemption. In Florida, this exemption is currently the first $25,000 of market value. A householder who lives in a $25,000 home pays no tax; at $50,000 half the property is exempt; at $100,000, the exemption is only 25% of the value; at $500,000, the exemption is only five percent. The real estate tax is the only progressive tax that is administratively feasible at the local level.

Elected officials and political groups often allege that the real estate tax is regressive because more expensive homes are relatively underassessed. This is in fact true. The problem is principally one of lags; more valuable properties tend to increase in value over time and low valued properties to fall in value over time. However, many wealthy taxpayers own more than one parcel of real estate directly and indirectly and own commercial and industrial properties which pay a large proportion of the tax. To put it bluntly, commercial and industrial properties are not owned by poor people.

It is frequently alleged that the tax discriminates against renters and favors homeowners. But, since building is little affected by the tax, the supply of housing is largely unaffected. Unless demand changes, rents are unaffected. If the real estate tax were abandoned, rents would not fall at all because neither the demand nor the supply would be affected. It would just be a windfall for landlords. The supply and demand for housing is simply not affected by existing real estate taxes. Not only is this true in the short-run when the supply of housing is fixed, but it is true in the long-run because the tax does not affect the rate at which new construction takes place. Much more likely to affect the amount of housing and other construction are zoning restrictions which limit the uses to which land can be put.

TAXING LAND, NOT IMPROVEMENTS: THE GEORGIST MOVEMENT

It has been argued that taxes should be on land not on improvements. The fact that taxes on land values cannot be shifted forward to renters or buyers was the basis for Henry George's proposal over a century ago to obtain all government revenues by a single tax on land values.[2] There are numerous communities around the world in which his proposals have been taken seriously. For example, his ideas were the basis of Pittsburgh's late graded tax with land taxed at a higher rate than buildings. The Georgist movement is still alive and well.

However, it is unnecessary to make a distinction between land values and improvements; taxes on both are backward shifted and borne by the landowner.[3] The buyer knows what his tax will be when he buys a parcel and what it will be when he improves it. So he deducts the capitalized value of the expected future tax on the entire parcel when making an offer.

Furthermore, assessors have great difficulty in apportioning the total value of a parcel between land and improvements. Indeed, they tend to overvalue improvements and undervalue land values. This can be deduced from the fact that downtown properties are often bought, the buildings demolished, and a new building constructed, indicating that the land value was at least equal to the value that the assessors put on the land and buildings. Assessors can accurately appraise the total value of a parcel because market prices reflect the total value of the parcel. They do not have any market indicator of the value of land unless it is vacant.

Determining how much obsolescence has taken place since the improvements were put in place is also difficult. But assessors do have sales data which indicate what value the market places on the entire parcel. Finally, the real estate tax base has turned out to be insufficient to support local governments, let alone the state and federal governments. The states have very wisely abandoned the real estate tax as a source of state revenue, leaving it almost entirely as a revenue source of local governments.

The Problem of Equitable Assessment

Professional assessors estimate the market value of a particular parcel of real estate by comparing recent sales of comparable properties. With the exception of California and Florida and perhaps a few other states, the price that the owner paid is considered but as the legal phrase goes, it is not controlling. It is only one of the elements taken into consideration by the assessors. A taxpayer is entitled to an assessment lower that his purchase price if he can show that comparable properties have received lower assessments. Similarly, municipalities can request an upward revision of an assessment if the price paid is lower than the value of comparable properties.

A rule of thumb has been developed that assessors may be deemed to have done a good job if half the properties sold in a community have ratios of assessed value to their sales prices within fifteen percent of the targeted ratio. This criterion acknowledges that even when assessors are doing a good job, fifty percent of the assessment ratios can be expected to be more than 15 percent away from the targeted ratio. Buyers pay more than the assessor's valuation, or they pay less. What is considered to be good assessment is an average dispersion of 15 percent. Obviously, assessment is not an exact science! But the lack of uniformity should be limited.

Good assessment using this rule is fairly easy to satisfy in communities where properties are fairly homogeneous and is hardly ever satisfied in communities in which the properties are very heterogeneous even when, or perhaps especially when, mass appraisal techniques are being employed. Studies by the lead author demonstrate this to be true.[4]

One should not be surprised that assessed values are uneven in most tax jurisdictions. The real estate market is, from an economic point of view, very imperfect, with sales prices of older properties varying greatly from the estimates of market value by the assessors. The best alternative is a California Proposition 13 type solution that makes fewer demands on the assessment organization. Switching over would require changing the assessment law in most states because many state constitutions require taxes to be levied uniformly.

THE PROPOSITION 13 INITIATIVE

In recent years, taxpayers have rebelled against real estate tax increases, blaming the tax itself, instead of the government officials that abuse the tax by excessive levies. The most dramatic and publicized "revolt" was the 1978 enactment of a constitutional amendment by referendum in California by the famous (in the eyes of some, infamous) Proposition 13 initiative.

In 1973, Southern California housing prices were $1,100 below the national average, but, as a result of land use restrictions and other legislation, land for housing became scarce and development costs skyrocketed. By 1978, housing prices had risen to more than $26,000 above the national average and homeowners' taxes likewise skyrocketed because increased values were rarely offset by reductions in the rates of tax.[5] Soaring housing prices and the unwillingness of local governments to cut rates proportionately led to rapidly increased tax bills, sometimes by as much as 20% to 30% in a single year. The tax limitation proponents found fertile ground in the resulting homeowner dissatisfaction.

Proposition 13 limited the maximum rate of tax to 1% of market value, excluding preexisting indebtedness, and limited the increase of assessed valuations to no more than 2% per year. Properties newly sold were to be assessed at their sales prices.

Positive Aspects

Proposition 13 overcame a number of drawbacks that cause the real estate to be held in bad repute and deter investment in real estate. It limits the ability of local governments and school districts to arbitrarily increase real estate tax levies and assessments. It eliminates the uncertainty in what future taxes will be. In buying a parcel of real estate, the buyer knows exactly what his assessment will be and the limits placed on local governments and school districts on their levies. It eliminates opportunities for corruption by elected officials and bureaucrats. Investors in rental, commercial, and industrial properties are assured that they will not be discriminated against because they are nonresidents. Residency is a factor only in determining whether the taxpayer qualifies for a homestead exemption.

Other great advantages of a Proposition 13 system are a reduction, almost elimination, of tax appeals and a reduction in the costs of administering the real estate tax. Fewer assessors are required to administer the tax. There is no need to reassess properties annually. Only newly sold properties require assessment, and their assessment is their sales prices. Properties undergoing major reconstruction also need to be reassessed, but the cost of the remodeling is simply added to the existing assessment. There are problems of fairness when properties are damaged by earthquakes, fires, and the like, or transferred involuntarily as a result of eminent domain, for example. And assessors will still be needed to determine the fair market value when property is transferred with payments in kind in place of cash, etc. In California, the number of assessors declined from 2,100 in 1977-78 to 1,550 in 1986-87.[6]

Moreover, Proposition 13 appears to have had no negative economic effects and appears not to have impeded purchases of existing or new houses. The California real estate market has continued to be the strongest in the nation. Indeed, it could be argued that Proposition 13 has encouraged home ownership because it eliminated uncertainty about future tax increases.

Lack of Uniformity

The major criticism of Proposition 13 was that over time it would cause substantial differences in the taxes paid by owners of comparable properties. Assuming that asset values rise, the longer one owns a property, the lower will be the ratio of assessed value to market value compared to more recently sold properties.

While this is true, it does not necessarily mean *inequitable* differences in the tax burdens of old and new property owners. The reason for this is the fact that land owners bear the entire burden of real estate taxes by the process that economists call backward shifting. As a result of this process, buyers of properties pay less than they would if comparable properties were similarly assessed.

To illustrate how this works, take the case of two *identical* homes, one purchased years ago and now assessed at $200,000, paying a tax of $4,000 per year, and the other just purchased for $300,000 and liable to a tax of $6,000 per year. What this economic argument says is that the buyer of the new home would have been willing to pay $320,000 if his tax were just $4,000, with $20,000 being the capitalized value of $2,000, his higher tax liability. The seller will receive $300,000, whereas without the tax differential, he would have received $320,000.

Moreover, the lack of uniformity is an advantage to the community when recovering from the crash that follows a real estate bubble. Newly sold properties would not be burdened with high assessments. As a result, those selling real estate would receive more for their assets than they would otherwise. In general, Proposition 13 keeps the real estate market on a more even keel.

Negative Impact Upon Local Government Revenue

On the negative side, Proposition 13 can constrain essential public services and can lead to a diminished role for local governments.

But, a slower increase in local government spending may be an advantage, not a disadvantage, from the citizen taxpayer's point of view. There has been no serious movement in California for Proposition 13's repeal.

The reaction of California local governments was to try to offset the loss of real estate tax revenues by increasing revenues from other sources, such as imposing greater burdens on developers and imposing user charges on services that property owners formerly received for "free." Real estate taxes in California were 42% of state and local tax revenues in 1977 and fell to 25.5% in 1985, a decrease of 39%. Nationwide there was a 15.5% reduction.[7] A study of tax limitations in Illinois led to the finding that the restraining effect on revenues of the limit on the growth of property taxes is stronger with the passage of time.[8] If education costs per pupil rise faster than the cost of living index in states that restrain tax increases to the rate of inflation, a larger proportion of revenues will have to be borne by the state or by the imposition of other taxes.

The great mistake of the California model was its retroactive provision, which rolled back assessments two years and thereby created a fiscal crisis for school districts and municipalities, forcing the state to subsidize local governments using, as the source of revenues, the general fund that relies principally on sales and income taxes.[9] Indeed, this probably set back the cause of finding similar solutions in many states and gave Proposition 13 a bad name.

A similar tax limitation statute, the *Save Our Homes* initiative, was instituted in Florida and took effect in 1997. Because it was not retroactive as Proposition 13 was, there was little impact on school districts and no fiscal crisis at any level of government. The limitation on the increase in assessments was either 3% per year or the rate of inflation, whichever was smaller. The limitation applied only to domiciled owner-occupied residences in Florida. Unfortunately, because it applied to a single class of real estate, and not all of that class, there was nothing saved in the cost of administration of the tax, one of the great proven advantages of the California model.

Adoption of a Proposition 13 type of real estate tax is an example of the trade-offs between different criteria of taxation. The advantage of a Proposition 13 system is that future tax liabilities are known with relative certainty and fewer assessors are needed, making the administration of the real estate tax less costly. But there is a sacrifice of uniformity, requiring changing the assessment law in most states, because many state constitutions require taxes to be levied uniformly.

Recovery After Asset Values Fall

As the trade deficit is reduced, foreign savings inflows will necessarily slow, which will drive up long-term interest rates and drive down asset values, including real estate values. In locations where all real estate is still reassessed periodically, local governments will find their real estate tax base declining, and will raise the percentage tax on real estate values. This will compound the slump in the real estate market.

However, in locations where Proposition 13-like laws had been enacted, local government revenues would not have risen so fast when assessed valuations were rising and will not require higher percentage rates when assessed valuations fall. In fact, the lower and more certain assessed valuations of newly purchased homes will encourage new buyers to enter the market after an asset valuation fall. Proposition 13 would, in general, keep the real estate market on a more even keel.

Also, it would keep local governments from growing too fast when asset values grow and from then raising their rates too fast after real estate values fall, exacerbating the severity of the fall in real estate values. The real estate tax gives local governments an important resource of their own. It can be made more progressive with the addition of the homestead exemption. It is the only progressive tax that local governments can impose without driving jobs and wealthy residents away to other communities. The problem with the tax is that it can discourage investment if the levy is expected to rise *after* a property has been purchased. But with a changeover to the Proposition 13 system, the real-estate tax becomes one that is certain, that is inexpensive to administer, and that does not discourage savings and investment.

In this chapter and the last, we proposed some small but significant changes to the personal income tax code and the real-estate tax code that would make those tax codes more friendly to savings and fixed investment. In the next chapter we will suggest a much more sweeping change which would have a much greater impact upon savings and fixed-investment. We will advocate replacing the corporate income tax with a consumption tax.

7. The Corporate Income Tax

A poor peasant acquired a magical goose that laid golden eggs. In short order the peasant became fabulously wealthy. However, his wealth made him greedy, and in his greed he began to imagine that the goose was full of gold. Eager to acquire this gold more quickly, he killed the goose and cut her open, only to find... no gold. This attempt to consume more than his income left him impoverished.[1]

When irresponsible legislators govern in Washington, government savings are negative even during times of full employment. When credit becomes readily available due to an inflow of foreign savings, households go on a buying spree that consumes the nation's capital stock. The only segment of American society that can be relied upon, year after year, to provide the savings needed for investment and growth is the business sector, principally corporations.

Table 2 shows that business savings accounted for 85% of total

Table 2. Gross US Savings in 2006 [Billions of dollars] (Credits +; debits -)	
Households and Institutions	**158**
Personal savings	-103
Savings to replace depreciation	260
Businesses	**1550**
Undistributed corporate profits	499
Savings to replace depreciation	1051
Government	**115**
Savings	-151
Savings to replace depreciation	266
Other (wage accruals less disbursements)	**13**
Total Gross Savings	**1834**
(Source: Table 5.1, NIPA, Bureau of Economic Analysis)	

gross domestic savings in 2006 ($1,550 billion out of a total of $1,834 billion). If depreciation is subtracted from gross savings to produce net savings, then undistributed profits were the only positive contributor. Undistributed corporate profits contributed $499 billion to American net savings, while personal savings were negative, subtracting $103 billion, and government savings subtracted $151 billion.

There are two very quick ways that our government could increase domestic savings: (1) move its own budget from deficit to surplus or (2) lower the taxes that it takes from corporations since corporations retain and invest a high percentage of their profits.

There are many other good reasons to eliminate the corporate income tax which we will discuss in detail in this chapter:

1. *It penalizes American workers in international markets.* Because most of America's international competitors have lower corporate income taxes, the high US corporate income tax makes US products less competitive and drives corporate headquarters overseas.

2. *It results in double taxation.* The same corporate income that is taxed as profits is taxed again when distributed to shareholders as dividends.

3. *It violates the principle of equity.* There is a violation of the principle of equity in that the short-term burden of the tax is on shareholders and the same rates apply to poorer and richer shareholders. The long-run burden of the tax is shared with workers and consumers, since it reduces investment and economic growth.

4. *It encourages borrowing over equity.* The corporate income tax causes businesses to favor debt over equity, increasing the likelihood of business bankruptcy.

PENALIZING AMERICAN WORKERS IN INTERNATIONAL MARKETS

The United States has higher corporate income taxes than most of its trading partners. Among the countries in the OECD database, only Japan with a top corporate tax rate of 39.5% has a higher rate than the United States with a top tax rate (federal and state combined) of 39.3%. All of the other countries have lower corporate income taxes as shown in Figure 19. Thus the high rates of corporate taxation discriminate against the American corporation.

The high US federal corporate tax rate of 35% puts US manufactures at a competitive disadvantage internationally in two different ways. First, products produced in the United States are normally subject to higher taxation than foreign products. Second, many US corporations have been moving their headquarters abroad to tax havens such as the Bahamas to avoid paying the second highest corporate income tax in the world on the share of their income that is produced oversees.

Lack of Border-Adjustability

Our trading partners have been able to lower their corporate income taxes by using the border-adjustable Value-Added Tax (VAT) to make up the lost revenue. Border-adjustable taxes (the VAT and the sales tax) apply to all goods sold within a country whether they are produced abroad or within that country. They are not applied to goods that are exported.

In Chapter 8 we will present a chart (Figure 20) which shows that the United States has the second lowest level of border-adjustable taxes among the countries in the OECD database. As a result, foreign

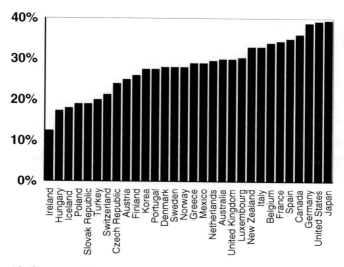

Figure 19. Corporate Income Tax Rates by Country.
In 2006, The United States has the second highest corporate income tax rate in the OECD database. (Source: OECD Tax Database, Table II.1)

goods sell for less in the United States than abroad, and American goods sell for more abroad than in the United States. (We'll discuss this further in Chapter 8.)

In the United States, the average sales tax is about 5% (if calculated on the same tax-inclusive basis as the VAT), while the average VAT of the other OECD database countries is about 18%.[2] This differential gives the American worker an uphill playing field in the international marketplace and the foreign worker a downhill playing field in the US marketplace.

In June 2007, Congressman Duncan Hunter introduced the *Border Tax Equity Act* designed to end the double taxation of US exports. Products produced in the United States but sold abroad pay all American taxes, except sales taxes, and then also pay consumption taxes abroad. Hunter's bill would direct the United States Trade Representative to negotiate a remedy within the World Trade Organization by January 1, 2009, in order to end the imposition of the VAT and import taxes on American goods sold abroad. If such a remedy were not achieved, then his bill would place tariffs on foreign goods equivalent to the additional taxes those countries charge on American goods.[3]

Given the fact that almost all countries have VATs, there is little chance that US negotiators will be able to change this particular WTO rule. But we can replace our corporate income tax with a VAT or a national sales tax. Doing so would not eliminate taxation of corporate income. Undistributed corporate profits would not be taxed, but corporate earnings would be taxed when distributed to shareholders as dividends or when consumed as capital gains by those selling shares and *not* reinvesting the proceeds.

Driving Corporate Headquarters Abroad

In the 2004 presidential campaign, Democratic Presidential candidate John Kerry made an issue of the many US corporations that have been moving their headquarters out of the United States to countries in the Caribbean in order to avoid paying US corporate income tax on corporate income produced outside of the United States. Even though US corporations get a tax credit for taxes paid to foreign governments, the US corporate income tax is so high that they still have to pay additional corporate income taxes to the US government.

Daniel J. Mitchell's solution to the problem was to eliminate US taxation on profits produced abroad. In a 2003 American Heritage Foundation research paper, he argued for a territorial tax regime in which the United States taxes corporate income produced in the United States but allows all income produced outside of the United States to be completely free from US taxes.[4]

Although Mitchell's solution would likely bring corporate headquarters to the United States, it would also encourage American corporations to build new factories abroad and then import the products into the United States for sale to American consumers tax free. Mitchell's solution would provide a very clear incentive for American companies to locate their investments in countries that had lower corporate income tax rates than the United States.

On the other hand, if the US corporate income tax were replaced by a border-adjustable consumption tax, such as a Value-Added Tax or a national sales tax, the entire problem would disappear. A border-adjustable tax applies to all products that are bought and sold in the United States, no matter where they are produced, but does not apply to products produced in the United States but sold abroad. Replacing the corporate income tax with a border-adjustable tax would likely bring multinational corporation headquarters to the United States and at the same time would make the American worker more competitive in the international market place.

Double Taxation of Corporate Income

Currently, corporate income is taxed twice. It is taxed when earned by the corporation and taxed again when it is received as dividends or as capital gains by the individual taxpayer.

All kinds of rationalizations have been used to justify this double taxation. The fact is that there is little difference between corporations and limited partnerships, yet the latter pays income tax only once. The income of limited partners is their share of the partnership's income and the partners include their share in the calculation of their personal incomes. Corporations are simply a form of business enterprise that allows a great number of people to invest in a common enterprise. It is a special kind of partnership with limited liability for the shareholders. It is, in fact if not in law, a limited partnership.

The double-taxation of corporate income discourages the corporate form of enterprise in favor of organizational forms that are not subject to the corporate income tax, like partnerships or private equity companies. Private equity buyouts of corporations are often motivated by the desire to avoid double taxation of earnings.

Some non-economists attempt to justify the corporate income tax on the ground that doing business as a corporation is a privilege made possible by the government: the privilege is to do business as a limited liability company. But, aside from passing a law authorizing the creation of a corporation, the government contributes nothing. Indeed, proprietorships, partnerships, limited partnerships, and corporations are all entities recognized in the law. This argument for the taxing of corporations is mere sophistry, an ostensible but not a real reason for imposing a special burden on shareholders. Doing business as a corporation is no more a privilege extended by government than is home ownership, proprietorship, partnership, or limited partnership.

The British once had an alternative system that taxes corporate income once only. Throughout most of its history, the United Kingdom treated corporate income as belonging to the shareholders, the corporation paying tax at the standard personal income tax rate, and the shareholders receiving a credit equal to the standard rate on dividends received. In effect, the corporate income and individual taxes were perfectly integrated so that corporate earnings would be taxed only once and the British taxpayer would pay the same percentage of tax on dividends as on any other income. Corporations paid tax at a standard rate as a sort of deduction at the source.

Deduction at the source can be traced back to before *The Aid to William and Mary of 1688* which required all "persons and bodies politic and corporate ... having any estate in goods, wares, merchandizes, or other chattels or personal estate" and all persons "having, using, or exercising any office, or imployment of profit" and all lands, tenements, and hereditaments, mines, manors, iron works, and forests were to be charged on the "true yearly value thereof." The tax was to be paid by the party in possession or, in the case of entities like corporations, by the entity. These provisions were incorporated in the Income and Property Taxes of 1803 to 1815 and in the income tax when it was restored in 1842, and they endured until the present system was adopted in 1965. There was none of the confusion of property and income so evident in the US income tax system. Capital gains were untaxed, and the corporation was not considered an entity separate and distinct from its owners, which it assuredly is not.

Since 1965, the British have embraced everything wrong with the American tax system, another application of Gresham's Law that the bad drives out the good when demagogues have their way.

In 2005, the President's Advisory Commission on Federal Tax Reform recommended two plans, one of which, "The Simplified Income Tax Plan," would eliminate double-taxation by having the taxpayer pay no income tax on dividend income received (if the corporation had produced the income in the United States).[5]

We do not recommend the British system or the "Simplified Income Tax Plan" system because we are trying to encourage corporations to retain and invest their earnings, not distribute them as dividends where they would likely be spent on consumption. The best way to eliminate the double-taxation is to eliminate the corporate income tax.

VIOLATION OF THE PRINCIPLE OF EQUITY

Economists differ greatly on the question of who bears the burden of the corporate income tax. The flippant answer is simply that corporations pay the tax. But corporations are not people, and ultimately the costs of the corporate income tax are borne by people. But which people? Are the costs borne by those who work for the corporation? By those who buy from it? By those who own it? Are corporations able to shift the tax forward to their customers in the form of higher prices? Do savers bear the burden as a result of lower interest rates? How about the economy as a whole? And complicating matters further, how does this vary between the short run and the long run? What about when foreign trade enters the mix? We quote the following passage from a paper by Alan Auerbach on corporate taxation, not because it is particularly clear, but to emphasize the complexity:

> For a variety of reasons, shareholders may bear a certain portion of the corporate tax burden. In the short run, they may be unable to shift taxes on corporate capital. Even in the long run, they may be unable to shift taxes attributable to a discount on "old" capital, taxes on rents, or taxes that simply reduce the advantages of corporate ownership. Thus, the distribution of share ownership remains empirically quite relevant to corporate tax incidence analysis, though attributing ownership is itself a challenging exercise.[6]

Because of its opacity, advocates and opponents of the corporate income tax sometimes assert that one or another group bears the burden. Some have argued that the tax is passed-on to consumers, others that the tax is shifted to workers. Our own belief is that the burden of the tax is borne by shareholders in the short run but is shared with savers, consumers, and workers in the long run.

Who Bears the Burden in the Short Run?

There is broad agreement that changes in the corporate tax rates burden only the shareholders in the short run. That is to say, changes in the rates of the corporate income tax will cause no immediate changes in prices or output when the corporate income tax is imposed, raised, lowered, or eliminated. The reason being that the firm's capital costs in the short run are what economists call "sunk costs." The stock of existing capital does not change in the short run; it takes a long time to increase or decrease the existing stock of capital significantly. Nor does the demand change. People's incomes do not change right away so their consumption (i.e., demand) is unchanged simply as a result of the change in the level of income tax. Therefore, in the short run the optimum levels of prices and production are unchanged and the tax is borne by shareholders. This leads to double taxation because shareholders are also taxed on distributed profits from the corporation, not to mention the "capital gains" generated when the corporation retains and reinvests profits.

Some economists object that even in the short run, the costs of the tax can be passed on to consumers. John Kenneth Galbraith, for example, has argued that corporations can set their prices arbitrarily.[7]

This assumes corporations have something like monopoly power. If they actually do, it is, in almost every case, the result of patents, copyrights, or other government protection. But the problem with this argument is that it assumes that, prior to the imposition of the tax, corporations were charging lower than profit-maximizing prices. If corporations were able to raise prices as a result of higher income tax, they must have had that power to do so in the absence of the tax because neither demand nor costs are changed immediately as a result of the change in corporate income tax rates. Moreover, what businesses can charge depends on the competition. If foreigners produce the same or slightly differentiated products, the power to raise prices is limited, since foreign competitors are not affected by the tax.

In the short run, the cost of plant and equipment are sunk costs, and marginal cost is based on the cost of variable factors that are employed, including labor, materials and other inputs. Supply does not change, demand does not change, and prices do not change. The burden of the tax in the short run is entirely on the shareholders. Conversely, a cut or elimination of the corporate income tax will benefit shareholders in the short run.

Most economists believe that the corporate income tax makes the overall tax system much more progressive because shareholders are preponderantly wealthy. But this is becoming less and less true as the ownership of shares has become and is becoming more widespread. Many forces are at work, including IRAs and other retirement accounts, the widespread ownership of pension funds, investment in mutual funds, and the growth of special purpose funds to pay for college education, health insurance, and so on. That shareholders as a group are more wealthy on the average conceals the fact that there are great ranges in the income of shareholders.

Within shareholders, the distribution of the corporate income tax burden is not progressive at all. Take for example two shareholders, one who is relatively wealthy and in the top 35% tax bracket for the personal income tax and the other who is much less wealthy and in the 15% tax bracket for the personal income tax. Given that the bracket rate of large corporations is 35% (federal tax rate on income over

$18 million) and that the tax rate for dividends is a fixed 15%, both the wealthy and less wealthy shareholder pay an effective tax rate of 45% on corporate dividend income. Thus, while the differential between their personal rates of taxation on normal income is more than 2 to 1 (35% to 15%), both pay the same 45% federal tax rate on distributed corporate income.

Who Bears the Burden in the Long Run?

The long-run effects of the corporate income tax are more important because higher tax rates tend to reduce investment, which is the key to economic growth. Investment not only includes the purchase of tools and structures, it also includes the development and implementation of the technological changes that drive economic growth. Investment is the golden goose that produces economic growth. When we tax corporations, we tax our future.

Indeed, if the tax rate on corporate income were 50 percent and the going rate of interest were 6 percent, corporations would require a 12 percent return on their capital just to earn what economists call the opportunity cost of capital. To earn 12 percent, the prices corporations charge for their goods and services would have to be higher than would be the case in the absence of the corporate tax, enough higher to enable them to earn 6 percent after tax. Corporations would have to expect to earn more than 12% in order to justify an investment. As a result, one effect of the corporate income tax is to reduce investment.

This reduction in investment, in turn, produces a number of additional effects principally on interest rates, wages, and productivity. In the literature on tax shifting, it is shown that the reduced demand for capital by corporations lowers the rate of return on investment in general, which lowers the return to savers. The demand for labor is less than it would be, so wages are lower than they would be with no tax. Less investment means that consumers pay higher prices and labor loses the higher wages associated with increased productivity.

The debate among economists about just who pays just how much of the long-term burden of the corporate income tax is ongoing. Put more broadly, the problem with this tax is that no one knows quite how the burdens are distributed in the long run, and it would be both clearer and fairer to distribute such burdens in a more transparent way.

Encouraging Borrowing Over Equity

Because interest is deductible as a business expense when calculating taxable corporate income, corporations can reduce their tax liability by increasing their proportion of borrowed capital to equity capital. This aspect favors corporations that are highly leveraged (i.e., that have a high debt to equity ratio), despite the fact that a heavy reliance on borrowed capital increases the vulnerability of such companies to cyclical downturns. Some economists have proposed ad hoc solutions to this problem.

Christian Keuschnigg and Martin Dietz proposed giving corporations a special deduction on their taxes equivalent to the money that they would normally earn in interest on their business equity. Specifically they proposed a "dual income tax" combining an allowance for corporate equity with a broadly defined flat tax on personal capital income.[8]

Proponents of the Flat Tax have come up with the opposite solution. Instead of lowering the cost of equity capital through a tax break, they propose raising the cost of borrowed capital by charging businesses the Flat Tax on all interest paid for borrowed capital.[9] Unfortunately, the Flat Tax solution would discourage investment by raising the cost of borrowing for investment. (We will discuss the Flat Tax further in Chapter 8.)

Each of these solutions has its problems. The Dual Income Tax would make the income tax code more complex; the Flat Tax would discourage borrowing for investment.

Why Not Eliminate the Corporate Income Tax?

Some economists argue that the corporate income tax should not be eliminated because doing so would produce tax loopholes and tax shelters. In the past when corporate tax rates were substantially lower than high marginal rates of the personal income tax (45 percent in the former and 70 percent in the latter), wealthy shareholders opposed paying dividends and favored retaining earnings and having them reinvested by the corporation. Currently, the rates are the same 35 percent. The corporation today cannot be used as a tax shelter.

As Clemens Fuest and Alfons Weichenrieder pointed out in a 2002 paper, when corporate tax rates fall below personal tax rates, individuals tend to avoid personal income tax by shifting their income from the personal to the corporate sphere.[10] Eliminating the corporate income tax without dealing with this problem would cause a return to the use of the corporation as a tax shelter. Reducing the corporate tax rate to zero would magnify this effect.

One way to deal with this problem is to continue taxing the corporation at the maximum personal income tax rate and to give shareholders a credit for the corporate income tax paid on their behalf. Double taxation is avoided. This would, by the way, benefit the less rich shareholders the most since the credit can be applied to taxes on other than dividend income as well. While this is similar to the historical United Kingdom tax treatment which gives a credit at the basic rate of tax to all shareholders on dividends received, it would differ by being a tax credit applicable to income from other sources, wages for example. But there is a better solution.

In our view, the optimum solution is to treat corporate earnings and partnership earnings the same. Neither should be taxed if reinvested. Once sheltered within a business, capital could then grow tax free until it is consumed. The corporation would assume a role similar to that of an Individual Retirement Account (IRA), a type of tax shelter that encourages savings and discourages consumption.

We want corporation income to go untaxed if it is reinvested, just as we want capital gains to go untaxed when the capital producing the gains is reinvested (see Chapter 5). Reinvested capital is future income that should be taxed in the future when it is realized and consumed.

When individuals wish to consume the income that has been sheltered in a corporation, they either take it as dividends or they sell shares to take capital gains. If both dividends and capital gains from consumed capital are taxed at precisely the same rate as normal personal income, then there is no real tax loophole, just a tax shelter that is good for society because it allows savings to grow tax free producing increased future income that will be taxed when consumed. The change in the capital gains tax treatment that we proposed in Chapter 5 would allow capital gains from consumed capital to be taxed at the same rate as normal income, thus permitting the elimination of the corporate income tax without creating new tax loopholes.

We recommend replacing the corporate income tax with either a Value-Added Tax (VAT) or a national sales tax since those taxes are border-adjustable in that they apply to imports, but not exports. It would make sense to target the tax to the products that are involved in international trade so that the maximum possible revenue could be obtained when the tax is applied to imports. US exports would be excluded from taxation by any border-adjustable tax.

In the next chapter we will discuss replacing both the corporate and personal income taxes with a single consumption tax. Two of the consumption taxes that we will discuss, the FairTax and USA Tax, are so progressive that there would actually be *improved* progressivity after eliminating the corporate income tax.

8. Solving the Low Savings Problem

As described in Genesis, Joseph came up with a plan for the Egyptian pharaoh to save grain during seven years of plenty so that Egypt would have grain during the following seven years of famine. As Prime Minister of Egypt, Joseph implemented the plan beautifully. During the famine, all of the nations of the world came to buy grain from Egypt.

In the last chapter, we argued that the corporate income tax amounts to a double tax on savings invested in the corporate sector and should be replaced by a consumption tax, either a Value-Added Tax or a national sales tax. This alone would go far to stimulate saving and investment. But in this chapter we consider a more sweeping reform, replacing both the corporate and personal income taxes with a single consumption tax in order to stimulate savings even more.

During the last few decades, there has been a minor revolution underway in the economics literature on income taxation. The trend has been steadily away from the income tax and towards some form of consumption tax. The chief problem with income taxes, as currently structured, is that they give incentives to consume income, and they penalize income that is saved and invested. Most economists, though not all, agree that a shift towards a consumption tax would increase long-run economic output and welfare by encouraging savings and investment.

Different formulations of the consumption tax have somewhat different economic effects, but all would increase long-term economic performance. This is because consumption taxes encourage savings which in-turn encourage fixed investments. The extent to which economic growth would be stimulated depends upon the extent to which fixed investment increases. The existence of investment opportunities is a *sine qua non*. But if trade is brought toward balance there will indeed be investment opportunities due to increased exports and diminished imports.

The idea of excluding savings from taxation goes as far back as Thomas Hobbes' *Leviathan,* published in 1651. John Stuart Mill in his *Principles of Political Economy* in 1848 argued that savings should be exempt from income tax, but he believed it impractical to measure an individual's consumption and instead recommended taxing savings at a lower rate.

Many economists today would agree with Mill. They recognize that savings are borrowed by investors and that new technology is developed as a by-product of investment. Investment and the new technology it creates have been the drivers of economic growth ever since the industrial revolution. The more investment, the more growth.

But not all tax experts would agree that the long-term growth effects make consumption taxes superior. In a 1984 paper, Bob McIntyre of Citizens for Tax Justice critiqued proposals for consumption taxes to replace the income tax. He argued that income taxes are more clearly based upon ability to pay. Specifically:

> Under income tax theory ... you the spender, and your neighbor, the saver, should be treated equally on your equal incomes because you each have the same ability to pay taxes and enjoy similar control over economic resources. A year later, when your neighbor's income is higher than yours due to the interest he earns on his savings, an income tax would ask him to pay more in taxes than you, since his control over economic resources has increased and his ability to pay taxes has become higher than yours. Whether your neighbor is paying a "single tax" or a "double tax," this result seems to square best with what assistant secretary Chapoton concedes to be "most people's conception of equity."[1]

He also correctly noted that at some times in our economic history, we have needed more consumption, not more savings. For example, in the midst of a recession or depression the economy needs more spending (either by government or consumers) to get it moving. President George W. Bush's tax cuts, for example, clearly helped get the US economy out of the 2001-2002 recession. But, temporary tax cuts work to get an economy out of a recession whether the tax involved is an income or a consumption tax.

Moreover, in the near future, we will clearly need more domestic savings if the trade deficit is to be brought under control. Economists recognize that savings lead to fixed investments and that fixed invest-

Table 3. Consumption Taxes Report Card

Tax	Encourages Savings	Border Adjustable	Progressive	Eliminates Paperwork
VAT	A	A	D	A
Flat Tax	D	F	C	C
GIT	F	C	B	D
FairTax	A	A+	A	A
USA Tax	A	F	A+	D

Grade: A=Excellent, B=Good, C=Fair, D=Poor, F=Fail

ments lead to economic growth. Thus, consumption taxes tend to produce higher rates of economic growth in the long run than income taxes.

At least five different taxes have been proposed in recent years as ways to move our tax system in the direction of a consumption tax: (1) the Value-Added Tax, (2) the Flat Tax, (3) the Growth and Investment Tax, (4) the FairTax, and (5) the USA Tax. These five taxes differ in the attributes shown in Table 5. We will discuss each of these tax proposals, in turn, and explain the reasons for the grades we gave each tax in that table.

THE VALUE-ADDED TAX

The Value-Added Tax, commonly known as the VAT, is a very widely used tax throughout the world, outside of the United States. It is such a successful tax that, once tried, it has never been withdrawn. Under a VAT, each business pays a flat percentage tax on the difference between the value of the products that it sells and the cost of the products that it buys from other businesses. The sum of the value-added by every productive unit in the country adds up to a total equal to Gross Domestic Product (GDP). The VAT doesn't tax savings, so it is a tax on the consumption of what is produced. (For more detail about the basis of a border-adjustable consumption tax, see the appendix at the end of this chapter.)

The fact that it is hidden from consumers – it is included in the price of goods with the consumers unaware of how much they are being taxed – makes this tax a very easy tax for governments to increase without consumers becoming aware of the increased burden that they are bearing. Partly as a result of imposing VATs, European nations have been able to raise their tax revenues significantly in recent decades in order to build extensive social-safety nets without much taxpayer protest. Although being hidden is considered an advantage by those who wish to increase tax revenue, it is considered a disadvantage by those who wish to keep tax rates low. Many conservatives have opposed it because they believe it encourages big government.

In 2005, the President's Advisory Panel on Federal Tax Reform calculated that a 15% VAT, made progressive at low income levels through work and family credits, would collect 65% of the revenue now collected by the personal and corporate income taxes combined. This particular version of the VAT would also exempt "non-commercial government services, primary and secondary education, existing residential housing, and charitable and religious services. Special rules would apply to financial services and other goods that are difficult to tax."[2] But the VAT would still not be progressive at higher income rates, so they suggested that if the VAT were adopted, which they didn't recommend, it be combined with a simplified version of the current corporate and income taxes, except with vastly lower tax rates.

Since a 15% VAT would replace 65% of the revenue now collected by the personal and corporate income taxes, it is possible to extrapolate that a 23% VAT would fully replace both income taxes. Such a tax rate would not be particularly high for a VAT. Four of the countries in the OECD database (Iceland, Sweden, Norway, and Denmark), as shown in Figure 20, already have VATs above 23%.

Encourage Savings = "A"

The VAT would eliminate the corporate income tax. Thus it would encourage corporate savings by leaving corporate profits with the corporation where they would likely be invested (see Table 2 of Chapter 7). This would likely result in an increase in corporate savings just because the corporations would have more money to save.

Eliminating the corporate income tax would also greatly reduce the opportunity cost of capital, which would, in turn, increase corporate investment. If the tax rate on corporate income were 50% and the going rate of interest were 6%, corporations would require a 12% return just to earn the opportunity cost of capital, but under the VAT, the corporation would just require a 6% return in order to earn the opportunity cost. The result would likely be greatly increased corporate investment.

Unlike corporations, individuals would not have more money to save, but they would have greater incentive to save because only the money that they would spend on consumption would be subject to the tax. Any savings would be tax free to be taxed only when consumed in the future.

The VAT would also encourage savings by allowing them to grow more rapidly since they would no longer have their growth slowed by

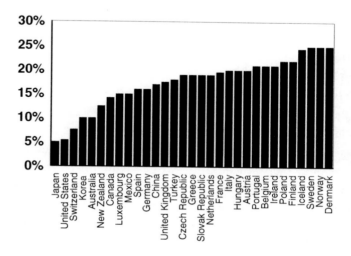

Figure 20. Border-Adjustable Consumption Taxes by Country.
In 2006, The United States had the second lowest border-adjustable tax rate (VAT+Sales Tax) with an average sales tax rate of 5.4% (tax inclusive). (Source: mostly OECD Tax Database, Table 12.[3])

taxation upon that growth. The current tax code slows the growth of savings by taxing corporate profits each year. Interest on savings are also taxed, unless those savings are in a retirement account.

Border-Adjustability = "A"

The international rules of trade of the World Trade Organization favor those countries that impose VATs. Their governments are permitted to rebate those taxes as an export subsidy to their exporters and to impose those taxes as an import duty upon imports.

The average sales tax is the United States is only 5.4% (calculated on a tax-inclusive basis). In contrast, almost all of our trading partners have much higher VATs which they use to subsidize their exports and tax their imports, as shown in Figure 20. Imposing a 23% VAT would turn the uphill playing field faced by the American producer in the international marketplace into a downhill playing field.

Take for example the situation where an American automobile company is competing with a Korean automobile company. Under the current income tax, the American company cannot pass on its taxes to the consumer or it would lose sales since the Korean company does not have to pay the US corporate income tax. On the other hand, with the VAT both the US company and the Korean company would have to pay the VAT when they sell a car in the United States. The American company would likely increase its profits and market share. It would also tend to invest some of its new profits in more efficient factories and to expand its research in order to improve its product line.

At the same time that the American company was investing, the American consumer would be saving tax-free and lending increased savings to the investor. These increased personal savings and the reinvested corporation profits could replace the savings that formerly came from abroad while producing the trade deficits.

The VAT should be made fully border adjustable by charging it to any nonresidents earning income from the United States. In other words, it should be withheld from dividend, interest and other income payments made by American businesses to nonresident foreigners. It should even be withheld from interest and dividends paid to foreign government dollar reserves, which are currently tax free. By the end of 2006, foreign governments already had $3,200 billion in dollar reserves earning interest directly or indirectly from the United States, and that amount was growing rapidly. All US tax treaties should be terminated or renegotiated to allow withholding of the VAT in these income payments.

Similarly, the VAT should be charged to returning tourists on products that they had purchased abroad and should be rebated to exiting foreign tourists on products purchased in the United States. It should also be rebated up to the VAT percentage to US residents who had paid tax to foreign governments on income, interest, or dividends received from abroad.

Progressivity = "D"

VATs are flat taxes in that the poor and rich pay the same flat percentage rate on consumption. The federal personal income tax with all its defects has the important virtue of being progressive in that richer people tend to pay higher percentage rates than poorer people. And those workers whose incomes fall below the poverty threshold receive a tax credit whether or not they pay any tax at all.

The VAT has been adopted by every country that is in the OECD database except for the United States. It has been made a bit progressive by applying lower rates to those products consumed most heavily by low income groups, such as foods, rents, and health expenditures. Henry Aaron of the Brookings Institution, while noting that the regressivity of the VAT can be reduced by multiple rates, wrote that most of the participants in a conference on the VAT in Europe agreed that it would be preferable to use other taxes and transfer payments to alleviate the VAT's undesirable distributional consequences.[4] Moreover, the 2005 President's Advisory Panel on Federal Tax Reform reported that when differential tax rates for different products are employed, European businesses tend to evade taxation by incorrectly claiming that their products belong in the lower-taxed category.[5]

Instead, the President's Advisory Panel on Federal Tax Reform put together a VAT proposal that was made progressive through supplemental family and work credits paid out directly to families. Some of the credits would be given to all families, others would be given only to those earning low wages. According to the President's Advisory Panel, these changes would make the VAT just about as progressive for the lowest 40% percentile of families in income as the taxes it replaces. However, above the 40% percentile level of income, the VAT would still be less progressive than the taxes that it would replace.[6]

A progressive tax is one in which the rich pay a higher percentage rate than the poor. The degree of progressivity is usually measured by calculating the burden of the tax as a proportion of the taxpayer's income. That taxes should be progressive relative to income is a value held almost universally. Both among the public[7] and in Congress, there is strong support for maintaining or increasing the progressivity of the income tax.

Because there is a trade-off in income taxes between progressivity and incentives to work and invest, there is disagreement over how progressive the tax system should be. A progressive tax on consumption would not necessarily have the same trade-off because an increased incentive to save at higher levels of taxation could stimulate growth even with a tax that is more progressive than the current US income tax.

Many economists make the case for progressivity on the ground that the utility of additional income decreases as income increases. Economic textbooks illustrate this concept by demonstrating that the first orange or apple is worth more to the consumer than a second, the second more than the third, and so on. Money like all other goods is subject to the law of diminishing utility. The first few thousand dollars are essential to keeping body and soul together while the last few thousand dollars of a multimillionaire are spent with little or no regard to cost. Some behavioral economists use the fact that happiness is little correlated with income to suggest that progressive taxes do little to diminish the welfare of anyone, and may increase overall happiness.[8] That said, interpersonal utility is difficult to measure – misers (if they still exist!) place a very high utility on money no matter how wealthy they are.

The real case for progressive taxation, as Henry Simons points out in his book *Personal Income Taxation,* is that it reduces inequality after taxes by imposing heavier rates of tax on those with high incomes. He enunciated the then-dominant economic view that society values greater equality or at least reduced inequality in the distribution of income, and therefore the tax system should be as progressive as possible, given awareness of the trade-off between progressivity and growth. At the margin, in his view, the marginal social value of the redistributive effects should equal the marginal social costs of retarded growth.[9] The problem is, how do we know when we have reached this optimum point? For a recent attempt to find it mathematically, see a recent paper by Juan Carlos Conesa and Dirk Krueger.[10]

While progressive taxation makes income after tax less unequal, raising incomes is also important. The growth of society's capital stock increases demand for workers, increases labor productivity, and raises wages. Indeed, the single best explanation given for different levels of income in different countries is the amount of capital per worker. Progressive taxes have the problem that their marginal rates of taxation are much higher, especially for the rich, than would be the marginal rates of proportional taxes. As a result, they can be expected to result in slower rates of growth.

Paperwork Reduction = "A"

The VAT is very inexpensive to administer; only businesses are taxed. Individual taxpayers do not pay it, and thus do not have to spend any time filling out tax returns. Businesses pay the tax on the value of the products they have sold after subtracting the value of the products that they have purchased from other business. Customs officials charge the tax to incoming products and give a rebate of the tax to exporters. The current tax code involves compliance costs of 12% to 15% of the tax collected, but the European experience with the VAT suggests that the compliance costs would just be 3% to 5% of the tax collected.[11]

THE FLAT TAX
The novel idea of the Flat Tax , which *Forbes Magazine* pub-

lisher Steve Forbes popularized in his unsuccessful run for President in 1996, was to tax businesses on their cashflows, not their profits. The cashflow is the amount that a business takes in after expensing investment and subtracting all of its expenses except interest costs. The tax was called "flat" because businesses would not pay tax on what they paid to labor, but individuals would file income tax forms and be taxed on their labor income at the same flat rate that businesses were taxed.

In 2007, Robert E. Hall and Alvin Rabushka published the second edition of *The Flat Tax*. The authors reported that a number of countries have adopted the Flat Tax beginning with Estonia in 1994 and followed by more than nine other countries since then, including Russia by the end of 2006.[12]

Hall and Rabushka and many other economists consider the Flat Tax to be a consumption tax, but they are wrong. The Flat Tax does not exclude savings from taxation. It taxes the value-added that is produced (which is income) while the VAT taxes the value-added that is consumed (which is consumption). As a result, the Flat Tax does not encourage savings as much as would a consumption tax.

The key aspect of the Flat Tax is the expensing of investment. The same effect could be obtained by having businesses take 100% depreciation the year that an investment is made. The other key aspect of the Flat Tax is charging businesses tax on the interest paid on any money that they borrow, a provision designed to encourage equity financing (see Chapter 7).

Encourage Savings = "D"

The Flat Tax would not encourage savings or investment in any of the four ways that a true consumption tax, like the VAT, would encourage them: (1) it would not eliminate the corporate profits tax which subtracts from corporate savings; (2) it would not greatly reduce the opportunity cost of capital, and thus would not much increase corporate investment; (3) it would not give individuals a direct incentive to save, and (4) it would not encourage savings by allowing savings to grow tax free. We'll discuss each of these in turn:

1. *No increased corporate savings.* The Flat Tax only gives cor-

porations more money to spend on savings during the first year of the tax, when they would be able to expense that year's depreciation. After that, they would still have to be paying tax on the profits produced by capital that had been expensed the first year, but would no longer be reducing their taxes by depreciation on their previously invested capital. They would thus have less and less profits to spend on investment during succeeding years of the tax. The Flat Tax frontloads corporate savings, but doesn't increase their savings in the long run.

2. *Little reduction in the opportunity cost of capital.* The opportunity cost of capital is the amount that a business would need to earn in order to break even from an investment. Under the Flat Tax, the opportunity cost of capital would not change very much. It would be reduced by the reduction in the corporate tax rate, but it would be increased because the Flat Tax would be applied to interest payments for borrowed money.

3. *No direct incentive to save.* Individuals, under the Flat Tax, would pay the same tax rate on income allocated to savings as on income allocated to consumption.

4. *Savings not allowed to grow tax free.* Profits and interest would be taxed each year as part of the cashflow tax paid by business. As a result, the growth of savings would be slowed by taxation.

The biggest mistake of the Flat Tax proponents, as far as savings is concerned, is their plan to completely eliminate any taxation on capital gains from the sale of shares of stock. As we demonstrated in Chapter 5, giving a reduced rate of taxation to capital gains actually encourages the consumption of capital stock, and thus discourages savings. A much better treatment would be the one we advocated in Chapter 5 in which capital gains are taxed at the same tax rate as other income when the capital producing the gain is consumed, but are not taxed at all if the capital producing the gain is reinvested.

Border-Adjustability = "F"

The Flat Tax is collected as an income tax and as such is charged only to US residents. Unlike the VAT, the international rules of trade would not allow it to be applied to imports but rebated to exports.

Unlike a sales tax it would not naturally be applied to imports but excluded from exports.

Progressivity = "C"

Critics of the Flat Tax argue that it is not as progressive as the taxes it would replace, even though the advocates of the Flat Tax have tried to make it more progressive through generous personal allowances. Figure 21 compares the 1996 personal and corporate income taxes with one of the most progressive Flat Tax options ever advocated (a $34,700 exemption in 1996 dollars for a family of four and retention of the Earned Income Tax Credit). The two curves were actually quite comparable except that the middle class would be taxed more heavily under the Flat Tax and the upper class would be taxed more heavily under the 1996 income tax system. The current version of the Flat Tax, as advocated by Hall and Rabushka, has a slightly less generous exemption ($27,500 in 2007 dollars for a family of four) and thus would be less progressive than the version shown.

Paperwork Reduction = "C"

One argument for the Flat Tax is its simplicity, but what complicates the income tax is not its progressive rate schedule. Once you have determined your taxable income, it takes little time to read your tax

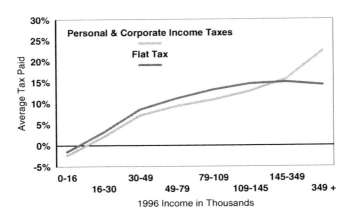

Figure 21. Tax Rates for 1996 Tax Code and the Flat Tax
In 1996, the personal and corporate income taxes combined taxed the rich at a higher rate than the middle class. Not so with the Flat Tax, given a 22.9% flat tax, a $34,700 exemption for a family of four, and retention of the EITC. (Source: U.S. Treasury, Office of TaxAnalyis, 1995a and 1996.)

from the tax tables. It is the countless rules for determining taxable income that make the income tax complicated.

The Flat Tax eliminates taxation of interest, dividend income, and capital gains from the sale of shares of stock from the personal tax form. However, for many taxpayers filling out tax returns would still be quite time consuming. Capital gains on rental property, plants, and equipment would still be subject to the tax. Those with royalties from copyrights and patents or with rental income would have to pay tax using the cashflow tax methods that apply to all businesses. And that is just the beginning. Congress, given time, would surely come up with many new complications. Although the Flat Tax would clearly reduce personal income tax paperwork, the only way to fully reduce it would be to eliminate personal income taxation altogether.

THE GROWTH AND INVESTMENT TAX

It is possible to modify the personal income part of the "Flat Tax" with graduated tax rates so that the rich would pay more. In fact just such a proposal was one of the two tax alternatives developed and recommended in 2005 by the President's Advisory Panel on Federal Tax Reform, The Growth and Investment Tax Plan (GIT). Essentially this graduated version of the Flat Tax combines a cashflow tax paid by businesses with a graduated income tax paid by personal taxpayers.[13]

Although the GIT, like the Flat Tax, is a cashflow tax for business, its rate of business taxation (30%) is much higher. As with the Flat Tax, labor, rather than business, pays the tax on labor income. Although capital gains are untaxed under the Flat Tax, they are taxed at a 15% rate under the GIT. Although dividends and interest are untaxed at the personal level under the Flat Tax, they are taxed twice under the GIT, first at a 30% rate by the business, second at a 15% rate by the individual. The GIT however would expand the availability of Roth IRAs so that taxpayers could shelter much of their income from the 15% personal tax.

Encourage Savings = "F"

Like the Flat Tax, the GIT does not encourage savings in any of the four ways that a VAT or other true consumption tax would encourage savings. Perhaps the worst effect of the GIT is that it introduces double-taxation of interest. This would particularly discourage savings that were kept in interest-bearing accounts. The GIT would increase the rate of taxation on interest income from the current rate which is set by the individual's marginal rate of taxation to a double-taxation rate of 40.5% (30% by the borrowing business, 15% by the lending individual). To ameliorate this problem, the GIT would expand the use of Roth-style retirement accounts.

Border-Adjustability = "C"

The truly innovative idea of the GIT is that the cashflow tax would be rebated to business on exports, but imports would not be deducted from cashflow. Any business or any subsidiary of a business operating in the United States would be subject to this taxation.

Although the tax panel argued in their report that border adjustability is not important since exchange rates adjust to balance trade (sigh!), they did try to make this tax proposal border adjustable. There must have been someone on the panel who had an inkling that US trade may actually be out of kilter.[14]

If the other nations of the world would agree to change the rules of international trade, then the GIT would be quite border-adjustable. Any business importing foreign goods or services would not be able to deduct the expense from taxation, but any business exporting goods or services would be rebated the entire 30% cashflow tax from their exports. If all exports and imports were to go through taxable companies, then the GIT would indeed provide substantial border-adjustability.

Unfortunately, the problem here is that the rules of International Trade are not made by the United States. As currently written, the GATT and WTO rules do not allow the proposed tax treatment, though they do allow a similar tax treatment for the VAT.

It is likely that our trading partners would object to treating the GIT as a VAT, especially with the high tax rate of the GIT (30%). The President's Advisory Tax Panel agreed that this aspect might not fly, but noted that if it did fly, it would result in an estimated $775 billion additional revenue over 10 years:

Multilateral trade rules originally developed as part of the General Agreement on Tariffs and Trade (GATT), and now incorporated into the rules of the World Trade Organization (WTO), affect the use of border adjustments. GATT/WTO rules treat border tax adjusting "direct taxes" as a prohibited export subsidy.... (G)iven the uncertainty over whether border adjustments would be allowable under current trade rules, and the possibility of challenge from our trading partners, the Panel chose not to include any revenue that would be raised through border adjustments in making the Growth and Investment Tax Plan revenue neutral. If border adjustments are allowed, then the plan would generate about $775 billion more revenue over the ten-year budget window than is currently estimated in the scoring of this plan.[15]

Unlike the GIT, a VAT or national sales tax would produce the huge boost of additional government revenue that accrues to a trade-deficit nation from a border-adjustable tax.

Progressivity = "B"

Unlike the Flat Tax, the tax rate for labor in the GIT is graduated with three tax brackets, 15% on incomes up to $80,000, 25% to $140,000, and 30% on incomes over $140,000. As a result, the GIT would be just as progressive as the corporate and personal income taxes that it would replace.

On the other hand, income from investments is not taxed progressively under the GIT. The capital gains tax is 15% for all taxpayers. As a result, those with incomes up to $80,000 would not get to take advantage of the huge (but foolish) tax-loophole available to rich taxpayers who consume their capital gains (see Chapter 5). The combined double-taxation rate for interest and dividends would be a flat 40.5%, with 15% paid by the personal taxpayer and the rest paid by the business that borrows the money or distributes the dividends. This increased tax burden would be somewhat alleviated through the promulgation of Roth-style retirement accounts in which interest and dividends would only be subject to the flat 30% rate of business taxation.

Paperwork Reduction = "D"

Although the intention of the President's Advisory Panel on Tax Reform was to make the GIT less complex than the current code, they did not succeed very well. For many taxpayers the burden of filling out tax returns under the GIT would be quite time consuming. Unlike the Flat Tax, the personal income tax part of the GIT taxes interest, dividend income, and capital gains from the shares of stock. With good intentions (to encourage charitable giving, to get people to buy their own homes, and to get people to buy their own health insurance) the President's Advisory Tax Panel also introduced several new deductions.[16] Given time, Congress would likely find ways to make the GIT just about as complicated as the current personal income tax code.

THE FAIRTAX

Congressman John Linder's FairTax proposal, as described in *The FairTax Book* by Neal Boortz and John Linder,[17] is the most comprehensive national sales tax proposal ever to be put forth. It would replace not only the personal income tax, but also the corporate income tax, the Social Security tax, the Medicare tax, the alternative minimum tax, and the estate and gift tax with a single 23% tax-inclusive sales tax. A 23% tax-inclusive rate is actually computed as a 30% sales tax since if you buy a $1 item and pay 30¢ in sales tax, you have paid 23% of the $1.30 in taxes. (Tax-inclusive terminology allows us to compare the FairTax with other taxes.) Proponents of the FairTax claim that a 23% tax-inclusive rate would raise about the same amount of government revenue as the taxes that it would replace.

Nothing sold new at retail would be exempt from the FairTax except educational tuition and items that were already in a business's inventory when the tax was instituted. Even governments buying automobiles, sick people paying medical expenses, and those buying a new home would pay the tax. Items sold used, though, would be exempt.

Encourage Savings = "A"

The FairTax would encourage savings in all of the ways that a VAT would encourage savings: (1) it would eliminate the corporate profits tax which subtracts from corporate savings; (2) it would greatly reduce the opportunity cost of capital, and thus would increase corporate investment; (3) it would give individuals a direct incentive to save because only the money that they would spend on consumption would be subject to the tax; and (4) it would encourage savings by allowing savings to grow tax free.

Border-Adjustability = "A+"

The FairTax is even more border-adjustable than the VAT since it replaces the non-border-adjustable Social Security and Medicare taxes as well as the non-border-adjustable income taxes. Like the VAT, it would not be charged on American products exported abroad, but it would be charged on foreign products imported into the United States. As we noted in our discussion of the VAT, the FairTax should be withheld from interest, dividend, and other income paid to nonresidents and should be rebated to US residents who had paid tax to foreign governments on income received from abroad.

Progressivity = "A"

Because the FairTax would replace the progressive personal income tax as well as the regressive Social Security and Medicare Taxes, it is actually more progressive for two-adult families than the taxes replaced as shown in Figure 22. The FairTax is especially progressive for the poor because all taxpayers, rich and poor alike, get a sizable "prebate" check or debit card payment at the beginning of each month equivalent to the amount that they would pay when buying necessities.

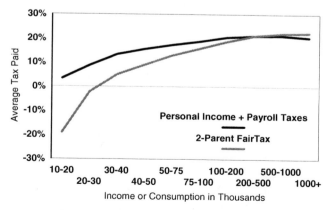

Figure 22. Tax Rates for Current Tax Code and the 2-Parent FairTax
Although the current personal income tax combined with payroll taxes as a share of cash income is progressive, it is less progressive for two-parent, 2-child families than the FairTax.

In 2007, that amount would have been based upon $10,210 spending per adult and $3,480 spending per child.

Figure 22 is not a perfect comparison. Ideally we would compare the two-adult two-child families of four shown for the FairTax with families of four under the current system, but we don't have statistics that isolate families of four under the current system, nor do we have statistics that break up all the taxes replaced by the FairTax by income level. In Figure 22, the black line shows the overall level of taxation under the current system for just the personal income tax and the payroll taxes according to 2006 tax year Brookings Institution statistics.[18]

As shown in Figure 22, two-parent families in the middle class would benefit greatly from a switchover to the FairTax. Families in the $30-40,000 category would only pay an average of 5%, not 13% (2.6% income tax; 10.8% payroll tax). Families in the $40-$50,000 category would pay an average of 9%, not 16% (4.8% income; 10.8% payroll). Families in the $50-75,000 category would pay an average of 13%, not 17% (6.6% income; 10.7% payroll).

If a family were to save money, buy anything used, or pay any educational tuition, they would reduce their tax rate further since saving, buying used items, or paying educational tuition would all be exempt under the FairTax. Conversely, if they were to spend more than their income, they would increase their tax burden.

Not all taxpayers would fare as well under the FairTax as the two-parent two-child family shown in Figure 22. A single parent with one child would receive half the prebate. Figure 23 compares how they would fare, as compared to the average taxpayer under the current tax system.

The one-adult, one-child family shown in Figure 23 could still reduce its taxation by saving money, paying tuition, or by buying used items. Some taxpayers might even find a partner to put their family into the two-parent bracket. But if they do not do any of these, they would pay approximately the same amount under the FairTax, as shown ias shown in Figure 23, as the average taxpayer pays under the current tax code.

It is commonly believed among economists that wealthy people save a much higher percentage of their income than the middle class. This was once true, but may not be true any longer. As the trade deficits have been growing, wealthy Americans have been selling off their stocks and bonds to foreigners. Although some wealthy people are accumulating wealth that would be exempt from the FairTax until consumed, others are living off of their wealth. Those who are accumulating wealth would pay lower taxes under the FairTax; those who are consuming their wealth would pay higher taxes.

The current tax system shown in Figures 22 and 23 might appear as more progressive if it were possible to determine who really pays the corporate income tax. In the long run (as we discussed in Chapter 7) that burden is distributed among all of those who suffer because of the investment that the corporate income tax stifles, but principally it is paid by the owners, the shareholders.

In 2005, the President's Advisory Panel on Federal Income Tax Reform criticized the FairTax's prebate as being a new entitlement. The report stated that the money distributed to all families would "make most American families dependent on monthly checks from the federal government for a substantial component of their incomes."[19] In-

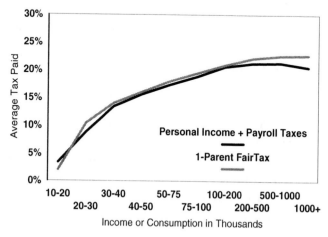

Figure 23. Tax Rates for Current Tax Code and the 1-Parent FairTax
A one-parent, one-child family would get half the prebate of a two-parent, 2-child family. They would pay a similar tax rate under the FairTax as under the current tax system.

deed, the poorest of the poor might rely upon the prebate for subsistence.

This particular entitlement, however, has a tremendous advantage over most of the other entitlements already in place in that it doesn't create a poverty trap consisting of disincentives against work. When poor people work, under the present system, their income rises and they lose eligibility for the various poverty programs. The effect is the same as a very high level of marginal taxation. Not only that, but the current system provides substantial incentives for mothers to remain single because an additional income would make the family ineligible for benefits. The resulting incentive system produces a poverty trap that prevents some of the poor from working their way out of poverty.

On the other hand, under a 23% FairTax, every taxpayer, rich or poor, gets to keep 77% of the additional dollar earned (even more if they save some of that additional dollar). This particular form of entitlement is similar to the negative-income tax recommended by libertarian-economists Milton & Rose Friedman in their book *Free to Choose* as a replacement for all of the current poverty programs.[20]

The Problem of Social Security

Although Boortz and Linder envision that social security payments would not be affected by a switchover to the FairTax, ending social security taxes would require developing a new formula for determining social security benefits. At first that formula would largely be based upon the payments by the recipient into the Social Security tax system before the institution of the FairTax, but as time went on, there would no longer be reliable income measures on which to base such a formula. Little by little, social security payments would move toward a flat rate that would be received by all retirees.

The poor would come to benefit from higher retirement incomes, but the middle class would end up receiving less than they would have received under the current system. Social Security would come to be seen as a welfare program instead of a system in which people are paying for their own retirement. Boortz and Linder point out that, to a certain extent, this new perception would be valid. They write:

Social Security is an income redistribution and welfare program. Low-income Americans receive a check that replaces 90 percent of their pre-retirement income. Workers paying taxes on a $50,000 income will receive a check for only 32 percent of their pre-retirement income, and those workers paying taxes on $90,000 will receive a check covering just 15 percent of their retirement income.[21]

Since all taxpayers plan to be elderly some day, the gradual movement toward flat payments for every recipient may not cause a reduction in the overall level of Social Security payments. Those who want more than the eventual flat payments to retirees would have plenty of years to save additional money for their own retirements, and the society would be richer as a result. Furthermore, given the fact that Social Security, as currently constituted, will eventually require either a cash infusion or a reduction of benefits, something will have to change regardless of whether the FairTax is enacted. Boortz and Linder point out that transferring Social Security to the broad based FairTax would actually preserve Social Security benefits.

The FairTax achieves greater progressivity than the current tax system largely by eliminating the regressive Social Security tax. While eliminating or modifying this regressive tax makes economic sense, the proposal is likely to make the FairTax a hard sell. The Social Security system is defended by powerful interest groups, and is justly characterized as the "third rail" of American politics.

But the current entitlement system is not sustainable. Perhaps the only way to reform it would be to do so as part of a sweeping overhaul, such as the institution of the FairTax. The prebate of the FairTax would provide a substantial new benefit for the poor and retired, while the elimination of the regressive Social Security tax and of income tax paperwork would provide a substantial increased benefit for those still working.

Eliminating the Social Security and Medicare payroll taxes would also reduce the unemployment rate for two reasons. First, the extensive paperwork of payroll taxes discourages small businesses from hiring employees. Second, according to the structuralist theory of unemployment developed by 2006 Nobel Prize winning economist Edmund S. Phelps, payroll taxes, unlike consumption taxes, increase structural employment, a particularly persistent form of unemployment. In a summary of his theory Phelps wrote:

> Another central theme is the thesis that assorted interventions in the
> labor market operate to raise the natural unemployment rate, not just
> to lower the wage. The taxation of employment is the leading example.
> (Barriers to firing a worker once hired are another.) More generally,
> the burden of taxation on wages relative to that on nonwage incomes
> (returns from existing bonds and equities, services of consumer
> durables, and entitlements) matters for employment. The theory says
> that a value-added tax is fairly benign for the natural rate, since it is a
> tax falling more or less proportionally on wage and nonwage income
> alike; the payroll tax (and the personal income tax too if nonwage
> incomes tend to escape or evade it) bears disproportionately on the
> reward to not quitting and not shirking, with the result that the natural
> unemployment rate is pushed up (as any fall of the wage curve is less
> than the fall of the demand curve).[22]

Is the 23% Tax Rate Reasonable?

Those looking at Figure 22 might wonder how it is possible for
tax rates to decline for almost all two-parent families, but yet for the
FairTax to generate enough money to replace not only the taxes shown
in the figure, but also to replace the corporate income, gift, and estate
taxes which in 2006 together generated $382 billion.[23] There are sev-
eral reasons why the 23% rate may be possible:

1 *Lower compliance costs.* The FairTax would eliminate unpro-
   ductive work. It would eliminate most of the approximately $140
   billion annually spent by individuals and businesses to comply with
   the current tax system.[24] It would also save the federal government some of the Internal Revenue Service's $11 billion budget.[25]
   At the same time the elimination of the corporate income tax could
   cause many multinational corporations to move their headquarters to the United States. Some of the white collar workers now
   working in tax code compliance and collection might find new
   jobs in these corporate offices.

2. *Less Tax cheating.* Tax cheating on the current income taxes is
   increasing. In 2001, the IRS estimated that between $281 and
   $322 billion went unreported on individual and business tax re-
   turns.[26] In general, the fewer the tax payers, the easier it is to
   catch tax cheating. With the FairTax only businesses, not indi-

vidual taxpayers, would pay the tax. Furthermore, there could easily be many safeguards against cheating by businesses. For example, the FairTax could be collected from all businesses exactly the same way as the VAT is collected, with the only difference being that it would show up on all sales receipts. When paying the FairTax to the government, each business would subtract the tax that it had paid to other businesses. As a result, retailers would keep their suppliers honest; if a supplier had not collected tax because of an under-the-table transaction, the retailer would have to pay it. The government could easily investigate whether retailers were being honest. They could send an undercover agent to a retailer, make a cash purchase, and then investigate the next month whether the transaction appeared correctly on the retailer's records.

3. *Higher Basis for Taxation.* Due to the low rate of US savings and the high US trade deficit, the FairTax has a higher basis for taxation than an income tax. Specifically, in 2006 the basis for the FairTax would have been $515 billion higher that the basis of the current corporate and personal income taxes, even though the FairTax would exclude undistributed corporate profits and other savings from taxation! (See the appendix to this chapter for the calculations behind this estimate.) The main reason is that the FairTax is border adjustable. In 2006, US imports exceeded exports by $760 billion. The foreigners who produced those imports were not taxed by the United States income taxes. The higher tax basis of a 23% FairTax would yield $118 billion of additional revenue.

4. *Economic growth.* As we pointed out in Chapter 7, a tax on corporate income is a tax on the nation's future growth. In contrast, the FairTax would leave more profits with corporations and would reduce the opportunity cost of capital. As a result, businesses would have more money to invest and more incentive to make investments. In February 2007, five economists from the Beacon Hill Institute at Suffolk University used their model of the economy to predict the effects of the FairTax. They concluded

that in just one year GDP would go up by 7.9% more than it otherwise would, largely due to the end of double-taxation upon the revenue produced by investment. In the first two years, consumers would consume less, but due to the growth of the American economy, by the third year they would already be consuming more than they would be consuming without the switchover.[27]

Dan R. Mastromarco, a principal in the Argus Group economics consulting firm, summarized the predictions of several of the studies that have been conducted:

> The FairTax increases the income of U.S. residents and the purchasing power of U.S. residents' income. Recent studies show that under the FairTax, a decade from now the economy would be about 20 percent larger, and real wages would increase far more than the current law.... A switch to the FairTax would cause real wages to rise by 13 percent for an 18 percent difference in remuneration; by 2030 real wages under the FairTax would be 9.3 percent higher than they otherwise would be. The shift to the FairTax would raise marginal labor productivity and real wages over the course of the century by 18.9 percent and long-run output by 10.6 percent. In the long run, low-income households would experience a 26.7 percent welfare gain, middle-income households a 10.9 percent welfare gain, and high-income households a 4.7 percent welfare gain.[28]

Several economists who have put together their analyses agree that the FairTax could indeed replace all of the taxes that it replaces with a tax-inclusive tax rate of about 23%.[29] But critics of the FairTax cite the 2005 President's Advisory Panel on Federal Tax Reform's claim that the FairTax rate would have to be between 25% and 41% (which they described in tax-exclusive terms as between 34% and 49%) just to replace the income taxes. In order to arrive at this exceptionally high estimate of the FairTax's replacement tax rate, they made two claims: (1) that FairTax advocates assume in their calculations that there will be absolutely no tax evasion, and (2) that governments would have to raise their taxes to pay the FairTax bills on their consumption and investment purchases.[30]

The first of these assumptions can be quickly dismissed. FairTax advocates begin their calculations using GDP statistics which already leave out the underground cash transactions that don't get reported on income taxes. The panel's second claim does have some validity, but not as much as the panel supposed. They were correct that governments would indeed pay the FairTax on their purchases, but they ignored the fact that governments would also have several of their own expenses reduced.

Take, for example, the statistics for government spending in 2004. That year, according to an analysis put together by Arthur, Laffer & Moore Econometrics, a 23% FairTax would have taken in $1,863 billion in revenue, which is $106 billion more than the $1,717 yielded that year by the combination of all the taxes that it would replace. Included in that amount was $335 billion collected from government spending on consumption and investment.[31] But governments, in 2004, would also have had cuts in their spending that could total about $203 billion:

1. *$65 billion*, their share of the Social Security and Medicare payroll taxes for their employees. Federal, state, and local governments are huge employers and would gain an immediate 7.65% windfall just from the payroll taxes that they would no longer have to pay.[32]

2. *$110 billion* or more because the businesses that they would be buying from would be facing lower costs and thus would be forced to charge at least 10% less due to competitive bidding.

3. *$28 billion* more by applying the FairTax to interest earned by foreign government dollar reserves in 2004 (assuming a 5% average interest rate). If foreign governments reciprocate by taxing US government currency reserves, the effect would be negligible, given the paucity of US reserves. Essentially, this would be tax collected upon dollar mercantilism. In 2004 the US foreign debt was $2,361 billion while foreign governments had about $2,424 billion in dollar reserves.[33]

Thus, the additional government spending due to the FairTax could just be $132 billion, an amount that could be accommodated given the Arthur, Laffer & Moore Econometrics calculation that the FairTax would have taken in $106 billion more revenue than that yielded by the taxes that it would replace.

Paperwork Reduction = "A"

The income tax and payroll taxes that the FairTax replaces are very difficult for individuals and businesses to comply with. Sales taxes like the FairTax, on the other hand, are very easy to comply with since individual taxpayers would not have to complete any paperwork whatsoever. All of the tax paying would be done by businesses.

The states with income taxes would likely change their own tax codes in order to make their taxes similar to the FairTax. Taxpayers would not stand for having to continue to file income tax returns with their states once they no longer have to file returns with the Federal government.

As we have already noted, the current tax code involves compliance costs of 12% to 15% of the tax collected. The FairTax could be collected exactly the same way as a VAT (except that the tax would be visible on all sales receipts). As we already noted when discussing the VAT, compliance costs in Europe are just 3% to 5% of the tax collected. Thus the FairTax could reduce compliance costs from the current 12% to 15% of tax collections to a much lower 3% to 5%.

The FairTax stands up well to the criticisms leveled against it. Just as its advocates state, it would eliminate the high cost of complying with the income tax code and it would lead to increased investment and long-term economic growth. At the same time, it would provide a substantial tax reduction to two-adult poor and middle class families.

THE USA TAX

For a long time the literature presented a false dichotomy between progressive taxation and taxing consumption. The old saw about why the United States does not use the VAT was that Republicans opposed it because it was too efficient and opaque when it came to collecting revenue, and Democrats opposed it because it was regressive. Although the FairTax is more progressive than the taxes it would replace, there is an even more progressive option, the USA Tax.

Progressivity = "A+"

Unlike the FairTax which must replace the regressive Social Security tax in order to be more progressive than the current system, the

USA Tax could achieve progressivity in the overall system without eliminating the Social Security tax. In fact, the USA Tax could be made more progressive than the current system with the highest bracket rate reaching 90% or more for the high-spenders, because the base of the tax is not income but consumption.

A progressive tax on consumption is not a new idea. One of its leading advocates was Irving Fisher who, with his brother Herbert, wrote a 1942 book about the progressive consumption tax.[34] In a recent journal article, John B. Shoven and John Whalley extol that book as a remarkable and pioneering contribution to the study of income taxation.[35]

In 1955, Cambridge economist Nicholas Kaldor published *An Expenditure Tax*.[36] Kaldor served as an advisor to the governments of India and Sri Lanka, which each briefly adopted the expenditures tax but had to abandon it as a failure. Unlike the tax we recommend here, it complemented but did not substitute for the income tax. It was intended to tax the rich who avoided income taxation, but neither of these countries had long experience with income taxation.

In 1977, the US Treasury issued its *Blueprints for Basic Tax Reform* which called for a cashflow tax (a kind of progressive consumption tax), to replace the income tax and also called for integration of the corporate and personal income taxes.[37] In 1995, Senators Sam Nunn and Pete Domenici proposed the Unlimited Savings Allowance Tax (USA Tax), a progressive consumption tax proposal that built upon the popularity of tax free Individual Retirement Accounts.

Progressive consumption taxes have their critics as well as their admirers. In 1978, most of the leading experts on income and consumption taxes attended a conference at the Brookings Institution. The proceedings were reported in a 1980 book entitled *What Should Be Taxed: Income or Expenditure?*[38] At that conference, the leading opponent of substituting a progressive consumption tax for the income tax was Richard Goode, a mentor of the chief author of this book. Goode's criticism of the progressive consumption tax, while cogent, has been overtaken by an event this book is concerned about, the decline in the rate of personal savings to less than 1% of personal income after taxes in both 2005 and 2006.

Goode argued that the income tax is superior, especially if its "existing remedial effects" are corrected. One of those defects, in our view, is its treatment of capital gains, as we discussed in Chapter 5. He also argued that failure to include savings and capital appreciation makes the progressive consumption tax more regressive. But progressivity depends on the rates of taxation. In theory, a progressive consumption tax could be graduated more severely than the current system without causing much, if any, reduction in savings or investment.

He noted that the US Treasury's *Blueprints* proposed to exclude gifts and bequests in the taxable consumption of the recipients. We agree that that is anomalous. There is no reason that gifts and inheritances that are consumed should be excluded from a progressive consumption tax.

Goode argued that both the income tax and the progressive consumption tax favor leisure and household production. But leisure is not free, especially the preferred ways of spending one's leisure time. Spending for leisure activities is taxed under both tax systems, even more under a consumption tax. In a section dealing with resource allocation, he noted that "The expenditure tax might be less biased in favor of leisure (or under demanding jobs), because some work is motivated by a desire to accumulate wealth rather than to consume." However, he argued, the higher rates of tax needed by the progressive consumption tax to obtain equal revenue would tend to counteract that incentive.

Goode was writing at a time when US savings were still high. Given the extremely low rate of personal savings in 2006, a consumption tax with comparable rates can raise just about as much, or even more revenue than an income tax with the same rates. (See the appendix to this chapter for the mathematics behind this assertion.)

In his 1984 paper, Bob McIntyre of Citizens for Tax Justice noted several specific shortcomings of progressive consumption tax proposals. Specifically, he wrote:

Particularly hard hit would be those who spend more than their incomes. Who might we expect to find in this last group? Some examples that come to mind include students borrowing to find their educational expenses; elderly people drawing down their savings to pay their living costs; unemployed individuals forced to deplete their bank accounts or borrow in order to put food on the table, and families taking out loans for major purchases.[39]

Here McIntyre made it sound like poor people would be especially hard hit by a consumption tax. He did not mention the fact that one of the hardest-hit groups would be rich people living off their inheritances! He also ignored the fact that a progressive consumption tax (the USA Tax or the FairTax) would likely leave poor people with more money, not less, and that those working to pay off their debts would be among the greatest beneficiaries.

We would modify the USA Tax to address one of McIntyre's concerns. We would count education as an investment in human capital. Those borrowing to pay their educational expenses would have those educational expenses deducted from their income. The extra income produced by their education can be taxed later.

Seidman, in his analysis of the USA Tax, provides a detailed explanation of how a progressive consumption tax would work.[40] We like his proposal, but also agree with the criticisms pointed out by Steven Pressman in his 1998 review of Seidman's book.[41] We would modify the USA Tax to meet these concerns:

1. *Revenue Shortfall.* Seidman's proposal results in a revenue shortfall in the early years because all capital transferred into IRAs could be deducted from the base income for taxation. We would modify the USA Tax by having all savings – stocks, bonds, business capital, savings accounts, real estate, cash, and so on – treated as capital assets as if they were all in an IRA. Under our proposal an IRA would simply be an accounting convenience. The owner of an IRA would not have to total any change in the value of the IRA but would just consider as income the difference between the amount removed from the IRA and the amount placed into the IRA.

2. *Role of Depreciation.* One of the weaknesses of Seidman's pro-

posal was its treatment of durable goods. We would modify his proposal so that when a person purchases a durable good, such as a car, with a standard life of a certain number of years (five, perhaps), he ends up paying taxes on only one-fifth of its purchase price each year. When the durable good is something that does not depreciate, a rule-of-thumb could be devised. For example, although the purchase of the home or art work could be counted against income, as a rule-of-thumb 1/30 of the purchase price could be considered to be its rental value and could be taxed as consumption each year.

3. *Income paid by a third party is taxed as income.* Another weakness of Seidman's proposal was that it might encourage corporate consumption. Whenever a business pays for something personal for the employee, it would report the benefit as employee income. Such expenses should include medical insurance and any consumption paid for by the business.

Encourage Savings = "A"

The USA Tax, like the VAT and FairTax would encourage savings in the same four ways: (1) it would eliminate the corporate profits tax which subtracts from corporate savings; (2) it would greatly reduce the opportunity cost of capital, and thus would increase corporate investment; (3) it would give individuals a direct incentive to save because only the money that they would spend on consumption would be subject to the tax; and (4) it would encourage savings by allowing them to grow tax free and by only subjecting them to single taxation, at a graduated rate, when they are consumed.

Border Adjustable = "F"

The USA Tax is not border-adjustable. Unlike the VAT, the international rules of trade would not allow it to be rebated to our exporters. Unlike the FairTax it would not naturally be excluded from exports but applied to imports.

Paperwork Reduction = "D"

Under the USA Tax with the modifications that we propose, all sources of income would receive equal treatment. The incentives of the current law to avoid taxes by converting income from one form to another would disappear. Taxpayers who roll over their assets into other assets would pay no tax. Income taxes would be postponed until the taxpayer consumed those wages, salaries, dividends, interest, rents, and capital gains. Thus, savings would not be taxed, but consumption would be taxed.

In order to calculate your taxable income, you would simply calculate your income and then subtract your educational expenses and the net additions to your assets. Specifically, your taxable income would consist of wages, rents, dividends, profits, plus the proceeds from the sale, depreciation or depletion of capital assets. Then you subtract all purchases of capital assets, including deposits in savings accounts and purchases of financial assets. Educational expenses would also be subtracted, as an investment in human capital. Society can postpone taxation until the education produces additional future income.

Adding to your wealth by saving part of your current income lowers your taxes. Any money that you saved during the year gets subtracted from your basis for taxation. Any money that you borrowed for consumption gets added to your basis for taxation. Any money that you used to pay back loans gets subtracted from your basis for taxation.

COMPARISON OF THE CONSUMPTION TAX PROPOSALS

While the tax system is not the only way to increase incentives for savings and investment, it is a feasible way to do so. Replacing the income taxes, both corporate and personal, with a true consumption tax would do so.

We examined five different proposals that were thought to be consumption taxes or to have strong consumption tax components. Two of them, the Flat Tax and the Growth and Investment Tax (GIT), are actually not consumption taxes and would not increase savings and investment much, if at all. Both of these proposals tax corporate cashflow instead of profits, and thus are more-or-less equivalent to a corporate income tax that expenses depreciation. The effect would be to increase business savings the first year after the switchover, but reduce business savings in succeeding years because there would no longer be a deduction for depreciation from earlier investments that were still producing income. Furthermore, both of these cashflow taxes charge businesses tax on interest paid when money is borrowed, which would tend to discourage borrowing for fixed investment.

At least the Flat Tax would significantly reduce the tax rate on business income and end double-taxation on dividends and interest. The GIT would not. Its only advantages over the Flat Tax are that it would be more progressive and could be border adjustable should the rules of international trade be interpreted in a way that would be favorable to it. The President's Advisory Panel on Federal Tax Reform, with much input from the President's Council of Economic Advisors, recommended the GIT as a way to increase growth and investment even though it would do neither!

The other three (the VAT, the FairTax and the USA Tax) are true consumption taxes that would greatly increase savings and investment and likely produce rapid economic growth. Any personal savings by individuals would be encouraged through exemption from taxation. Corporations would also be completely untaxed, which would not only increase their savings, but would also greatly reduce their opportunity cost of capital, encouraging them to increase their fixed investment.

Two of these (the FairTax and the USA Tax) are more progressive than the taxes that they replace and thus would fall more heavily on the rich and less heavily on the poor. The FairTax achieves its progressivity partly by replacing the regressive Social Security and Medicare taxes, not just the personal and corporate income taxes. The USA Tax does not need to replace the Social Security and Medicare taxes in order to be more progressive than the taxes it replaces.

Two of these (the FairTax and the VAT) would eliminate the personal income tax, thus greatly reducing taxpayer paperwork. Both of these are also border adjustable. These two taxes would provide a double-benefit as far as balancing trade is concerned. First, by making American producers more profitable and investment less expensive, they would result in greater business investment. Second, by removing the taxation upon savings, they would generate the increased personal and corporate savings needed to replace foreign savings.

However, it should be kept in mind that the expected reduction in the trade deficit would not occur unless dollar mercantilism is addressed at the same time. As we pointed out in Chapter 2, when President Clinton and the Republican congress moved the US budget into surplus in the late 1990s, they expected the increased American savings to cause the trade deficit to go down. But the inflow of foreign savings, mostly foreign government reserves, prevented those benefits from occurring and instead caused American interest rates to plummet and US markets to experience unsustainable bubbles.

As the United States brings trade toward balance, growing domestic savings will be needed to replace diminishing foreign savings. The point of this chapter, like the previous three, is that we should shift the US tax code toward policies that encourage savings. In this chapter we proposed the most sweeping reform of all, replacing both the personal and corporate income taxes with a single true consumption tax (the VAT, the FairTax, or the USA Tax). Doing so would encourage savings, fixed investment and long-term growth.

Technical Appendix: Tax Basis of Various Taxes

Each kind of tax has a different overall tax basis:

1. *Flat Tax and Current Income Taxes.* These are both non-border-adjustable income taxes. Their basis is National Income which equals GDP after subtracting Depreciation (Capital Consumption Allowances):

$$\text{Income Tax Basis} = \text{GDP} - \text{Depreciation} \qquad (1)$$

where GDP is equivalent to the total aggregate demand for the products produced domestically. In 2006, GDP was $13,194 billion and Depreciation was $1,589 billion. So their basis was $11,605 billion.

2. *USA Tax.* The USA Tax is a non-border adjustable consumption tax. It does not deduct depreciation but it does exclude savings, including business savings, from taxation. The tax basis for the USA tax is thus GDP after subtracting Gross Savings:

$$\text{USA Tax Basis} = \text{GDP} - \text{Gross Savings} \qquad (2)$$

In 2006, Gross Savings was $1,834 billion, so the basis of the USA tax was $11,360 billion.

3. *VAT and FairTax.* The VAT and FairTax are border-adjustable consumption taxes. Like the USA Tax, they do not deduct depreciation, but they do exclude savings, including corporate savings. Being border-adjustable, they tax Imports but exclude Exports from taxation. The tax basis for the VAT and FairTax is thus the same as the basis for the USA tax except that the trade deficit (Net Imports) is added:

$$\text{VAT or FairTax Basis} = \text{GDP} - \text{Gross Savings} + \text{Net Imports} \qquad (3)$$

In 2006, Net Imports were $760 billion, so the basis of these taxes was $12,120 billion. Thus the FairTax and the VAT, even without taxing corporate savings (undistributed corporate profits) had a tax basis that was $515 billion higher in 2006 than the combination of the personal and corporate income taxes. If the percentage rate of the VAT or FairTax were 23%, this additional basis would generate $118 billion in additional revenue.

Note: The statistics for depreciation and savings cited in this appendix were calculated from Table 2 of Chapter 7. The calculations on this page are for the overall basis. Targeted tax exemptions tend to reduce this basis.

Part III: A Strong America

It is popularly thought that the Chinese pinyin character for the word "crisis" is a combination of the characters for "danger" and "opportunity." However, according to the pinyin.info website, a better translation of the components would be "a time when things start to go awry."[1]

If you are an optimist, study the works of John Locke, Alexander Hamilton, and James Madison. If you are a pessimist, study the works of Karl Marx, Vladimir Lenin, and Mao Zedong.

The future could go either way. No two economic crises follow the same path. Nearly every prediction has some caveats like this one from the International Monetary Fund's *World Economic Outlook*:

> Notwithstanding recent financial market nervousness, the global economy remains on track for continued robust growth in 2007 and 2008, although at a somewhat more moderate pace than in 2006... Nevertheless, recent market events have underlined that risks to the outlook remain on the downside. Particular concerns include the potential for a sharper slowdown in the United States if the housing sector continues to deteriorate; the risk of a deeper and more sustained retrenchment from risky assets if financial markets continue to be volatile; the possibility that inflation pressures may revive as output gaps continue to close, particularly in the event of another spike in oil prices; and the low probability but high cost risk of a disorderly unwinding of large global imbalances....[2]

In a June 2007 annual report, the Bank for International Settlements, the bank used by central bankers, saw many events on the horizon that could trigger a global recession or depression, almost all of them linked to overly-accommodating credit policies producing overly-low interest rates. They hypothesized that the crisis could begin with inflation in the United States caused by rising wages combined with the falling rate of growth in productivity that results from low levels of business investment.[3]

The Bank for International Settlements saw American corporate fixed investment as "inexplicably weak" given the low interest rates and given the high profits currently being made by US corporations.[4]

We do not find this lack of investment as being at all inexplicable. American corporations have waning confidence in the future of American industry, given our government's continuing failure to deal with the trade deficits. American firms can reasonably expect foreign competition to invade their industries. If you cannot fight them, join them by investing abroad and importing from your own subsidiary as many have done. So long as the US government does nothing about the trade deficits, investment abroad remains more attractive than investment at home.

If neither crisis nor solution come soon, our manufacturing sector will continue to deteriorate, as we lose industry after industry, and our forced borrowing from the world will continue to mount until we have little but debt to show for our inaction in the face of the trade deficits. Besides that, we will have lost the skills needed to produce the goods we are importing.

Many readers will justifiably be skeptical about the political likelihood that the short-term and long-term corrective actions we consider necessary will be taken. In Chapter 9, we discuss what individuals can do to preserve their assets in the event of a soft or hard-landing or a continuation of the current situation. We are not financial advisers but we offer some suggestions for dealing with the likely eventualities. In Chapter 10, we summarize our program which we consider essential for a strong America.

9. How to Protect Your Assets

In the movie Sliding Doors, *Gwyneth Paltrow explores two possible futures, one that occurs if she makes it through the subway's sliding door in time to catch her train home and find her fickle boyfriend in bed with another woman, and the other if she doesn't catch the train. When she catches the train, she has to face the harsh reality much sooner. But the result is that she recovers more quickly.*

There are a number of scenarios as to how the problem of the trade deficits will be resolved. One scenario envisions a soft landing that would occur if US exports and savings increase gradually while US imports decrease gradually. Another envisions no landing as the situation in the United States continues to deteriorate along current lines. Another scenario envisions a hard landing that would occur if there is a run on the dollar and the dollar collapses on world currency markets. We will discuss each scenario in turn.

SOFT LANDING SCENARIO

Were the President and Congress to follow our recommendations with respect to the trade deficits, US productivity when competing with foreign goods and services in US and international markets would come roaring back and the United States would retain its status as the premier economy in the world.

If our plan were followed in the recommended order, then the adjustment could be quite mild. In response to our restoration of the tax on interest earned by private foreigners (our restoration of the foreign private savings withholding tax), China would move its dollar reserves out of foreign banks and into the United States where they could be frozen should China try to engage in economic warfare by rapidly pulling its reserves out of dollars in order to cause a US currency crash.

The Import Certificates that we propose would force the dollar mercantilist nations to divert some exports to domestic consumption and/or stimulate imports by making more credit more easily available to their own citizens and institutions. If they did not do so, they would experience economic recession or depression because Import Certificates demand that they import from us in order to enable their exporters to maintain a high level of exports to the United States.

Hopefully, the Bank of Japan would finally stop following a deflationary monetary policy and would make credit more easily available to consumers while causing mild inflation and allowing the yen to appreciate vis-à-vis the US dollar. Similarly, Chinese banks would make credit available to Chinese citizens at rates lower than the approximately 20% currently paid by consumers for borrowing outside the banking system. Chinese hospitals would be able to buy modern medical equipment without being forced to borrow the money from abroad.

Among the measures chosen by the Japanese and Chinese governments to promote these changes would be an appreciation of the yen and renminbi relative to the dollar. The citizens of these countries would be very pleased with this turn of events. The Chinese people, in particular, would benefit. Their standard of living would increase dramatically.

In the meantime, the tax system in the United States would change to encourage savings. The change could be small, such as a simple change in the capital gains tax that would discourage consumption of capital. Or it could be a much more major change such as the replacement of the corporate income tax with a VAT or the replacement of both the corporate and personal income taxes with a VAT or the FairTax. If one of these border-adjustable taxes were enacted, then American goods would be immediately made more competitive in international markets, the dollar would strengthen, and American savings would be greatly encouraged.

If this scenario occurs, then save your money and invest it in American manufacturing and in other American products and services that compete against foreign goods and services in US and world markets. Not only would the revised tax system reward your savings, but those who invest their savings in US products would see their investments pay off handsomely.

No Landing, Just Falling, Scenario

As we noted earlier, most economists still believe that free market forces will "automatically" fix the trade deficits. They are like ostriches living with their heads tucked in the sand. These economists are correct that, normally, a system of freely fluctuating exchange rates would indeed cause the currency of a trade-deficit country to lose value relative to the currencies of the trade surplus countries and thus stimulate exports and discourage imports and bring an end to trade deficits. They just don't understand that the trade deficits are being deliberately caused by governments. In their ignorance, they have been making failed prediction after failed prediction.

First, they thought that America's federal budget deficits were largely causing the trade deficits. They predicted that with fiscal austerity the trade deficits would decrease.[1] They were wrong. When President Clinton and the Republican congress brought the federal budget into surplus in the 1990s, the dollar mercantilist governments expanded their loans to the United States and the trade deficits grew.

When for a while America's trade surplus in services was growing while our industrial base was declining, they expected the trade surplus in services to continue to grow.[2] They were wrong. Due to the dollar mercantilists, the trade surpluses in services followed the trade deficits in goods on the downward trajectory.

When US assets were valued highly as a result of the low interest rates caused by the dollar mercantilists, they proclaimed that the trade deficits were really a good sign. Foreigners were sending their money to the United States because the United States was such a good place to invest.[3] They were wrong. It soon became evident that money invested abroad paid off much better than money invested in the United States, but still the inflows of savings from the dollar mercantilist governments increased.

The result has been a continuing decline in our industrial base and declining prospects for America's future. In August 2006 Dan R. Mastromarco, a principal in the Argus Group economics consulting firm, discussed the sad future that simulations of the US economic future were predicting:

> Recent simulations under the current system show capital per unit declining 5 percent over the course of the century for an 18 percent decline over the long-run in after-tax take-home pay.[4]

As foreigners continue to purchase US financial assets and the United States continues to lose industries, China will emerge as the dominant political and economic power in the world.

This scenario is the current situation. However, as wise economist and presidential advisor Herb Stein once said: "If something cannot go on forever, it won't." The huge trade deficits cannot and will not go on forever. As foreigners purchase more and more US assets, the income that they receive from those assets will grow and grow. Eventually the flow of this income out of the United States would cause a landing to occur, but one in which a debt-loaded United States is poor and weak.

If you see this scenario continuing for too long, consider emigration, preferably to a country that the Chinese do not want to deindustrialize! Invest your money abroad as much as possible. Especially buy shares in large-capitalization multinationals, foreign companies, international mutual funds and ETF (exchange-traded funds) that invest in shares of foreign companies. Also study Chinese so that, eventually, you will be able to communicate with your boss.

Hard Landing Scenario

This scenario is the likely outcome of our present policies. Eventually, not necessarily in the far distant future, the United States will be viewed as an undesirable place to invest private funds and government funds. The event could be triggered by a foreign government as part of a policy change. If China decided to torpedo the US economy, they could create a hard landing simply by dumping their enormous reserves on world foreign exchange markets.

Once the dollar starts to plunge, there would be such a rush to sell dollars on foreign exchange markets that the dollar would collapse in value. The United States would experience inflation. Interest rates would skyrocket. Trade would become balanced but at a severely reduced level of imports.

The skyrocketing oil prices and need to cut back on oil imports would force the United States to begin rationing gasoline, probably using an equitable electronic system like Martin Feldstein's 2006 "Tradable Gasoline Rights" proposal.[5]

If the Federal Reserve decides to inflate the money supply in order to pay off US debts with cheap dollars, we could experience runaway inflation. At the most extreme, the dollar might even be replaced with a new currency as has happened in Brazil multiple times. The Brazilian reis was replaced with the milreis, the milreis by the cruzeiro, the cruzeiro by the mil cruzeiro, the mil cruzeiro by the cruzado, the cruzado by the milcruzado, and finally the real.

The United States would not be alone. The US market is at the heart of the economic growth of developing and some developed countries. The world economy would go into recession or depression as a result of a sudden collapse in US demand for foreign products.

We need not speak of the political instability that would ensue from a worldwide depression. But the rise of totalitarian governments following World War I and during the Great Depression reminds us that the consequences would again be revolutionary and unpredictable. Scapegoats would be sought and the likely candidates would be free markets and the "usual suspects."

Although much more traumatic than the last scenario, in some ways the hard landing scenario is preferable to the seemingly unending decline: a decisive hard landing could end dollar mercantilism. American producers would likely come roaring back, especially if they produce goods in this country that can compete with foreign goods and services, both in the US market and in foreign markets.

Protecting Your Assets from the Crash

A few of us will profit from the dollar collapse by selling shares of stock short and dealing in derivatives. These new millionaires and billionaires will be the power brokers, the real survivors. Even if you are not a speculator, there is much you can do:

1. *Buy gold mining stocks.* Hedge your bets by buying gold, and other precious metals and shares of gold mining companies now. While this is not a sure thing, gold would tend to preserve more of its value than most other assets. In their 2004 book, *The Coming Collapse of the Dollar and How to Profit from It,* James Turk and John Rubino point out that investing in gold mining stocks is like investing in "gold in the

ground" and that such investments tend to appreciate even faster than gold itself.[6] Other mining stocks, oil company stocks, and farming stocks would also tend to retain their value even though a worldwide depression would tend to depress mineral and food prices.

2. *Buy Treasury Inflation-Protected Securities (TIPS).* The principal of a TIPS increases with inflation and decreases with deflation, as measured by the Consumer Price Index. When a TIPS matures, you are paid the adjusted principal or original principal, whichever is greater. TIPS are purchased directly from the US Treasury Department and some brokerages have mutual funds that specialize in them.

3. *Avoid buying fixed interest bonds and notes.* When interest rates rise, the market price of the bond or note declines.

4. *Stay away from US financial sector stocks.* Beware of investing in the US financial sector (banks, real estate companies, stock brokers, hedge funds, insurance companies). The big investment and commercial banks will probably come through without significant problem since they have been paying very close attention to risk management issues. But other banks and financial institutions will be caught holding assets that have lost much of their market values. Some hedge funds will make huge profits by betting against the dollar. But most hedge funds will be hit especially hard since they tend to hold risky assets.[3]

After the Crash

Those who have invested (or who work) in the retail and financial sectors of the US economy would be especially hard hit. Shareholders, bondholders, and homeowners would be hurt badly. But those who have managed to protect their assets would have tremendous opportunities to invest in the booming American agricultural, mining, and manufacturing industries. America should come roaring back, provided that our politicians do not get in the way of a recovery.

After the crash, two sorts of businesses will do especially well: businesses that either fix or buy and sell used goods and American businesses that can compete with foreign goods and services. Invest in such businesses with whatever assets that you have managed to preserve.

Used goods would often be selling for more than their pre-crash purchase price. It would be more profitable than ever before to fix up and sell things that were formerly just thrown away. Automobiles that would have once been junked would be repaired and made road-worthy. Junk metal lying around would be worth more than ever before. Some stores would change over from selling new goods to selling used goods on consignment.

American manufacturing companies would come roaring back, especially if they produce goods in the United States that can compete with foreign goods, both in the US market and in foreign markets. At the lower price of the dollar and, thus, of American labor, those companies would be able to make sizable profits competing with foreign goods. They would be expanding their factories and building new factories in the United States. Some of those factories would be built in vacant retail store buildings in former shopping malls.

Just because a hard landing occurs, all would not be lost. Many countries have come back strongly after currency crashes. Although the currency crash would be a bitter pill, it could eventually lead to an America that would be stronger than before. The recovery would be especially rapid if the currency crash were to occur sooner, rather than later. The longer it is delayed, the less industry we would have left to build upon.

10. Program for a Strong America

Otto von Bismarck once said, "God provides for fools, drunkards, and the United States of America."

The US chronic trade deficits have done great harm to American workers, causing wages to stagnate and worsening the distribution of income. To undo such harm is itself sufficient reason to take immediate action to reduce the trade imbalances. But that may be the least important reason. The United States is faced with great dangers arising from the resulting deindustrialization of the American economy and the industrialization and resulting increased military power of a potential enemy, China, a totalitarian state and an imperialistic power, which has declared aggressive designs on Taiwan, occupies Tibet, has murdered hundreds of thousands of its own citizens, and supports murderous regimes in Burma,[1] North Korea,[2] and Sudan.[3] There is also increasing danger, the longer the trade deficits last, of a currency collapse in the United States that could possibly destabilize the economies of the entire world.

We have identified the causes of the trade deficits and the fact that a great majority of economists have dealt with the problem in an ostrich-like way, turning a blind eye to the problem, unwilling to recognize the potentially deadly reality. They attribute the problem to the flow of savings from abroad, which indeed is true, and believe countries will find it in their interest to begin investing those savings at home, as though the huge continuing and growing deficits were transitory! They also believe that the cause of the flow of capital to the United States is the low rate of US savings.

We argue that the deficits have induced Americans to save less and reduced the incentives of businesses to invest in the United States. We agree with the need to increase domestic savings and investment, and we devote much attention to the tax reforms necessary to encourage domestic personal and business saving and investment. But we believe that steps toward solving the trade deficit problem must occur at the same time.

Leading economists appear unwilling to acknowledge that countries are investing in US financial assets deliberately to promote their exports and minimize their imports, which we have called dollar mercantilism. The fact that the world has been on a dollar standard gives them the excuse that they are merely accumulating dollar reserves. Reserves of a trillion dollars?! Reasonable reserves for countries experiencing huge chronic surpluses are in the hundreds of millions or less. It is we who need to start accumulating foreign exchange reserves.

ACTIONS THAT NEED TO BE TAKEN

The second author of this work had the pleasure of working closely with psychologist, computer scientist, and Nobel Prize winning economist Herb Simon with whom he coauthored several theoretical psychology papers. One of Simon's most important contributions to the artificial intelligence field was the method of means-ends analysis, a method that intelligent systems (including people) use to solve defined problems.[4] Essentially, the method involves a system of planning how to get from where you are to the place that you want to be. Solving each part of the problem often creates new smaller problems, so the method works best if a goal is set to address the largest part of the problem. If, on the other hand, the largest part of a problem is ignored, then a means-ends problem solver sometimes "tinkers around the edges" without making progress toward a solution.

In order to deal with the problems of the American economy right now, the goal must be set to reduce the trade deficit. If we simply try to increase domestic savings without taking direct actions against the trade deficit, as the federal government did when it reduced the budget deficit during the late 1990s, mercantilist governments may again increase their financial investments, driving our real interest rates down as far as necessary, in order to force the trade deficit to continue. The consequence of trying to boost domestic savings without reducing the inflow of foreign savings would be more asset bubbles rather than a reduction in the trade deficit.

We can solve the trade deficit by enacting the program that we suggested in Chapter 4. Specifically:

1. *Restore the withholding tax on foreign financial investments.* Delete §871(h,i,k) and §881(c,d,e) from the Internal

Revenue Service code and terminate or renegotiate the tax treaties so that private-foreigners would pay a 30% withholding tax on any interest earned in the United States on their financial investments. This action would increase United States annual income tax collections from foreigners, raise American interest rates (which would encourage Americans to save) and lower the exchange rate of the dollar (making American exports more competitive in world markets and when competing with foreign imports in American markets). It would also improve American national security by encouraging foreign governments to put their money into American banks where their reserves could be frozen should they come into conflict with the United States. (If income taxes were replaced with the VAT or FairTax, the same effect could be obtained by withholding the VAT or FairTax from interest paid to foreigners.)

2. *Impose Import Certificates to balance trade.* Either the Richman plan or Warren Buffett's plan would work. Our plan, would just involve the dollar mercantilist countries and would have the Treasury Department auction the Import Certificates directly to importers with the proceeds used to buy mercantilist-country currencies; Buffett's plan would involve all of US international trade (except that the NAFTA nations could be given the option of joining the certificate plan so that intra-North American trade would be exempted). Our plan gives the dollar mercantilist countries a direct incentive to increase their imports of US goods and services; Buffett's plan definitely equalizes US trade with the whole world over a period of five years. Our plan could be implemented without change in the current rules of international trade; Buffett's plan subsidizes US exports and replaces the current international regulations designed to produce free trade with a new system, not needing regulations, that would produce balanced trade.

3. *Other Measures.* There are other steps that should be taken as well. Specifically, we should tax foreign dollar reserves, and the Federal Reserve should match foreign buildups of

dollar reserves through reciprocal purchases of the offending currency.

Whichever steps we take will have to be gradual as it will take time for American consumers to change their saving habits in response to higher interest rates, for American producers to invest in new production, and for foreign governments to increase the consumption of their own people to make up for the diminution of their trade surplus with the United States.

It will not be easy to get these steps through Congress. The first step, ending the private-foreign-savings tax loophole, will likely be opposed by shortsighted bankers who would put their own short-term benefit ahead of their long-term benefit and the benefit to our country.

The Import Certificates will also be a tough sell. Domestic manufacturers and American workers understand the problem and would line up behind a solution that would work. Unfortunately, many American corporations have already built factories in the dollar mercantilist countries. They will not want to see the rules of the game change in a way that would reduce their profits from those foreign factories. The question will be whether the long-term interest of America will take precedence over the short-term harm to profits from foreign factories.

These steps would directly address the largest of our problems. But as with many complicated problems, the process of solving the major problem creates new problems that are smaller, but still important. The new problem is that bringing down the trade deficit will bring down the inflow of foreign savings and cause long-term interest rates to rise.

To a certain extent, domestic savings will come back as a consequence. Businesses, both domestic and foreign, will find new opportunities for fixed investment in the US manufacturing sector. That sector will boom regardless of how high interest rates go, but it would be much better for our economy if interest rates did not go up too high or too fast.

We can encourage the comeback of domestic savings if we fix

our dysfunctional tax system that encourages consumption of capital. A variety of steps are possible. Although our program could be enacted in a comprehensive way, it could also be put in place incrementally through gradual modifications of the existing tax code. The following steps could be taken:

1. *Tax capital gains based upon the Hicks-Richman definition of income.* The current personal income tax should be changed immediately because it is based upon an incorrect definition of income. Capital gains are only income if the capital upon which they are based is consumed. Capital gains from reinvested capital should not be taxed. Capital gains from consumed capital should be fully taxed. Capital gains from partly consumed capital should be partly taxed with the remainder of the capital gain subtracting from the basis of the reinvested capital. (If a true consumption tax is substituted for the personal income tax, as we suggest in item "4," then this provision would be irrelevant.)

2. *Move to a Proposition 13 Real-Estate Tax with a Homestead Exemption.* Real estate should only be reassessed when the property is purchased. The assessment should normally be the purchase price. Rate increases should be limited to the rate of inflation. There should also be a homestead exemption on the first $25,000 (or so) of the assessed value, to both encourage home ownership and also make the tax more progressive. These changes would make the real-estate tax more friendly to savings, home ownership, and fixed-investment.

3. *Eliminate the corporate income tax.* As personal savings have gone negative and the American federal government has run budget deficits, the one segment of the American economy that has continued to generate savings in recent years is the corporation. Eliminating the corporate income tax altogether would increase corporate savings leaving the corporation with more money for investment. It would also reduce the opportunity cost of capital faced by corporations and thus encourage them to invest in projects with lower expected payoffs. If

revenue were needed as a result of eliminating the corporate income tax, a VAT would be the best alternative because it would apply to imports as well as to domestically-produced goods. When the corporate income tax is eliminated, it will also be necessary to implement item "1", otherwise corporations would be used as tax loopholes in order to convert ordinary income into capital gains.

4. *Replace both income taxes with a true consumption tax.* Both the personal and the corporate income taxes should be replaced with a consumption tax. There are several alternative proposals available including the Value-Added Tax (VAT), the FairTax, and the USA Tax. The advantages of the VAT and FairTax are that they eliminate the personal income tax, greatly reducing the paperwork for US taxpayers and they are border-adjustable and so would level the international playing field for American producers. The FairTax and the USA Tax would be more progressive than the taxes replaced. The USA Tax is the most progressive of all, even without replacing the Social Security and Medicare taxes.

Essentially, we recommend that America tackle the trade deficit problem directly. This will create a smaller problem, the need for more domestic savings. We can increase domestic savings through a variety of changes in the tax code. Those changes could be minor, as proposed in Chapters 5 and 6, or more sweeping, as proposed in Chapters 7 and 8.

IMPROVEMENTS PROPOSED TO US TAX CODE

The solutions that we offer would eliminate tax loopholes, end double taxation, and simplify the tax codes. Specifically:

A. *These changes close tax loopholes:*
   1. The foreign-savings tax loophole lets private foreign savers earn tax-free interest on approximately $4 trillion of savings (as of 2006). This loophole is not only unfair to American savers but it also causes trade deficits.
   2. The foreign government savings loophole lets foreign governments earn tax free interest on approximately $3 trillion of

savings (as of 2006). This loophole directly subsidizes the deindustrialization of America by the dollar mercantilist countries.

3. American corporations have been buying back their shares, $230 billion in 2004 alone, partly to take advantage of the lower rate of taxation of consumed capital gains. The lower tax rate for consumed capital gains in the current personal income tax code counteracts the progressivity of the personal income tax and is causing the consumption of American wealth.

B. *These changes end double taxation:*

4. Individuals are double taxed on reinvested capital gains, first when they realize the gain and second when they earn income on the reinvested portion of the capital gain. The income received from the reinvested capital is taxed although its capital value had been taxed. This encourages taxpayers to consume the entire capital gain rather than have it taxed again on its income. Thus the current treatment encourages the consumption of capital rather than the holding of the asset for its future stream of income, especially when the income is taxed at a higher rate than capital gains are taxed.

5. Shareholders of corporations are double taxed, first when the income of the corporation is taxed and second when they pay tax on dividends or capital gains. Replacing the corporate income tax with a value-added or sales tax would eliminate this double taxation as well as enhance investment and level the international trade playing field. Eliminating the corporate income tax, however, would open up new tax loopholes if dividends remain taxed at lower rates as is now the case and if consumed capital gains remain taxed at lower rates than ordinary income is taxed.

C. *These changes simplify tax codes:*

6. Eliminating the lower rate of taxation of consumed capital gains would allow all income to be taxed at the same rate, eliminating much of the complexity of the current tax code.

7. Assessing properties at their sales price when purchased would

greatly simplify property tax codes and would make property tax rates less volatile when asset values rise and fall.
8. Replacing the income taxes with the VAT or the FairTax would greatly simplify the tax codes faced by US corporate and personal income tax payers.

INNOVATIONS TO ECONOMIC THEORY
In this book, we have made the following contributions to economic theory:

1. The economic theory that proves the advantages of free trade only applies when trade is relatively balanced. If trade is balanced, all parties benefit. But government-manipulated "free" trade can allow one country to steal industry from another. (See Chapter 1.)
2. The decline in US personal savings is not the cause of the inflow of foreign savings, but the result of that inflow. (See Chapter 2.)
3. Import certificates auctioned either by the US Treasury or distributed to exporters in proportion to exports, would jump start American manufacturing investment and balance trade. (See Chapter 3.)
4. The lack of differential between US taxation rates of private-foreign-savings and public-foreign-savings poses a security threat to the United States because it lets foreign governments put their reserves in foreign banks without interest penalty and without danger of their funds being frozen. (See Chapter 4.)
5. The proposed Hicks-Richman definition of income is an improvement over previous definitions because it correctly categorizes consumed capital gains as income and reinvested capital gains as future income which should not be taxed until the future. This improved definition leads to a proposed innovative method of taxing capital gains under an income tax that is neutral with respect to the timing of when capital is consumed. (See Chapter 5.)
6. Since real-estate taxes are borne by the land owner, changes

like California's Proposition 13 make the real-estate tax more certain, more fair, and less expensive to administer. (See Chapter 6.)

7. The changes we propose in the capital gains tax make it possible to eliminate the corporate income tax without creating tax loopholes. (See Chapter 7.)

8. The Flat Tax is not a consumption tax. It is a tax on the value-added of production (income) not the value-added of consumption. (See Chapter 8.)

9. The FairTax could be collected exactly the same way as the VAT, except that the tax would be visible on all sales receipts. This would greatly reduce the potential for tax cheating under the FairTax. The cost of tax compliance for the FairTax could then be predicted as being just 3% to 5% of tax collected, as compared to the 12% to 15% cost of compliance with the current income tax code. (See Chapter 8.)

A REASON FOR OPTIMISM

In the past, America has sometimes let problems fester until they became disasters. Slavery is a prime example. The growth of fascism in Germany is another. Dollar mercantilism may be a third. It very well may be that we won't have the political will to do anything about dollar mercantilism until after a hard landing leaves America with high inflation and a reduced standard of living.

But America has always come back. Whenever things have gotten bad enough, we always have found a Madison and Hamilton to pull our country together with a new constitution, or a Lincoln to fight the hotheads until union is restored, or an FDR to lead us through the depths of depression and war. None of these leaders acted alone. They all called upon the can-do spirit of a nation of problem-solvers. The solutions we suggest in this book could work to prevent the crash or could work after the crash to speed the recovery.

In 1929, economists were similarly caught with their heads firmly planted in the sand. The Federal Reserve did not yet see itself as responsible for maintaining a growing money supply. Finally, in 1932 Illinois Congressman A.J. Sabath and Treasury Secretary Ogden L.

Mills forced the Federal Reserve to take actions that would start making the depression better, not worse.[5]

The economics profession has again been caught with its collective head in the sand. But the American people know that something is wrong. There is growing awareness of Chinese government currency manipulations, one of the main drivers of the US trade deficits, and growing support for the FairTax, one of the best solutions to our faulty tax system. There is a solution within our reach today and it is not yet too late.

Notes

INTRODUCTION

1. *TheTrumpet.com*, "Greenspan: Euro Could Replace the Dollar," September 21, 2007, http://www.thetrumpet.com/index.php?q=4276.2514.0.0.
2. *CBS News*, "Greenspan Defends Low Interest Rates: Former Federal Reserve Chairman Talks To Lesley Stahl About Subprime Mortgage Meltdown," September 16, 2007, http://www.cbsnews.com/stories/2007/09/13/60minutes/main3257567_page2.shtml
3. United States-China Economic and Security Review Commission, *2007 Report to Congress Executive Summary* (November 2007), 4, http://www.uscc.gov/annual_report/2008/executive_summary.pdf
4. Joshua Aizenman and Jaewoo Lee, "Financial Versus Monetary Mercantilism - Long-run View of Large International Reserves Holding" (NBER Working Paper No. 12718, December 2006), http://www.nber.org/papers/w12718.
5. Alan Greenspan, *The Age of Turbulence* (NY: Penguin Press, 2007), 346.

CHAPTER 1

1. David Ricardo, *The Principles of Political Economy and Taxation* (London: J.M. Dent & Sons, 1911), 81.
2. Paul Krugman, "Is Free Trade Passé?" *Journal of Economic Perspectives* 1 (1987).
3. The initial statement of the strategic trade argument was by James A. Brander and Barbara J. Spencer, "Export Subsidies and International Market Share Rivalry," *Journal of International Economics* 18 (February 1985): 83-100. The article had about 900 citations in Google Scholar by June 2007.
4. For instance, by subsidizing Airbus, Europeans were able to increase competition in passenger airline production, driving prices down (which benefits European consumers among others). The subsidy also allowed Europe to capture a larger share of the aircraft market. For a more extended example, see Krugman "Is Free Trade Passé?".
5. Krugman, "Is Free Trade Passé?"
6. Krugman, "Is Free Trade Passé?"
7. Heng-Fu Zou, "Dynamic Analysis of the Viner Model of Mercantilism," *Journal of International Money and Finance* 16 (1997).
8. Zou, "Dynamic Anaylsis of the Viner Model of Mercantilism": 637-651.
9. For instance, Martin C. McGuire and Hiroshi Ohta, "Implicit Mercantilism, Oligopoliy and Trade," *Review of International Economics* 13 (2005): 165-184, find that:

>After the domestic cost structure is sufficiently close to the world
>price – or the world price is sufficiently high – the consumer in the
>mercantilist society actually benefits from sale of exports below
>domestic AC. For then foreign sales covers more and more fixed
>costs. Absorption of excess profit by new entrants increases
>domestic sales and, therefore, reduces domestic prices to the ben-
>efit of the domestic consumer. (p. 179-80)

In other words, by expanding the scale of the domestic market, the export-
favoritism of modern mercantilism can at times lead to better consumer as
well as producer outcomes in the mercantilist country.

10. David Collie, "Profit-Shifting Export Subsidies and the Sustainability of
Free Trade," *Scottish Journal of Political Economy* 40 (1993): 408-419.

11. See Giovanni Maggi, "Strategic Trade Policies with Endogenous Mode of
Competition," *The American Economic Review* 86 (1996): 237-258, and
Nolan H. Millera and Amit Pazgalb, "Strategic Trade and Delegated Com-
petition," *Journal of International Economics* 66 (2005): 215– 231.

12. See for example: Catherine L. Mann, *Is the U.S. Trade Deficit Sustainable?*
(Washington, DC: Institute for International Economics, 1999).

13. BIS 77th Annual Report (June 24, 2007), 141, http://www.bis.org/publ/
arpdf/ar2007e.htm.

14. We were not able to locate data for our trade balance with China in services
for the years from 1996 through 1998. As a result, the data for China por-
trayed in the table for the years from 1996 through 1998 does not include
the trade balance in services, just the trade balance in goods. The discrep-
ancy, however, is probably small. In 1999, our trade deficit in goods with
China was $68.8 billion while our trade deficit in both goods and services
was $67.4 billion.

15. Robert A. Blecker., "The Economic Consequences of Dollar Appreciation
for U.S. Manufacturing Investment: A Time Series Analysis," *International
Review of Applied Economics,* 21 (2007): 491-517. Blecker's Equation 1.5 of
Table 2 found that five factors predicted manufacturing investment rate in
the United States from 1973 through 2004 with a very close fit (adjusted
r2=.893). Those five factors were (1) real long term interest rate as defined
by Moody's Aaa corporate bond rate minus the GDP deflator, (2) the exchange rate for the dollar as measured by the Federal Reserve's comprehensive 'broad' index of the real value of the dollar, (3) the investment rate
of the previous year, (4) the GDP growth rate, and (5) cash flow as measured
by undistributed profits plus depreciation allowances. This was his closest fitting equation that included long-term interest rate as one of the vari-
ables. He was able to achieve a slightly closer fit when he substituted a
broader measure than interest rates for the cost of capital goods.

16. Robert A. Blecker, "Economy at Risk: The Growing U.S. Trade Deficit,"

(Statement presented at AFL-CIO/USBIC Conference Trade Summit 2006: Crisis and Opportunity, July 12, 2006), 2, http://www.american.edu/cas/econ/faculty/blecker/TD0706.pdf.

17. Dan R. Mastromarco, "U.S. International Tax Reform? Define 'Reform' for Me" *Tax Notes International* (August 7, 2006): 485, http://www.fairtax.org/PDF/USInternationalTaxReform-Mastromarco-8-7-06.pdf

18. US Department of Labor, Bureau of Labor Statistics, Office of Productivity and Technology, *Comparative Civilian Labor Force Statistics, Ten Countries, 1960-2006* (March 19, 2007), http://www.bls.gov/fls/lfcompendium.pdf.

19. Erica L. Groshen, Bart Hobijn, and Margaret M. McConnell, "U.S. Jobs Gained and Lost Through Trade: A Net Measure," *Current Issues in Economics and Finance* 11 (2005), http://www.newyorkfed.org/research/current_issues/ci11-8.pdf.

20. Paul Krugman, "Is Free Trade Passe," *Journal of Economic Perspectives* 1 (1987), reviews the early literature incorporating increasing returns into international trade theory. The introduction of increasing returns demolishes the simple comparative advantage argument for free trade, by creating special if difficult to identify circumstances in which export subsidies and other "strategic trade" (e.g. mercantilist) policies increase the welfare of the country implementing them. See also J.A. Brander and B.J. Spencer, "Export Subsidies and International Market Share Rivalry," *Journal of International Economics* 18 (1985).

21. Ben S. Bernanke, "The Level of Economic Well Being" (remarks by Chairman Ben S. Bernanke before the Greater Omaha Chamber of Commerce in Omaha, Nebraska, February 6, 2007), http://www.federalreserve.gov/BoardDocs/Speeches/2007/20070206/default.htm.

22. Helen Thompson, "Debt and Power: The United States' Debt in Historical Perspective," *International Relations* 21 (2007): 305–323.

23. Paul Krugman, "Will There Be a Dollar Crisis?" *Economic Policy* (July 2007): 435–467.

CHAPTER 2

1. Warren E. Buffett & Carol J. Loomis, "America's Growing Trade Deficit is Selling the Nation Out from Under Us. Here's a way to Fix the Problem -- And We Need to Do It Now," *Fortune,* November 10, 2003, http://money.cnn.com/magazines/fortune/fortune_archive/2003/11/10/352872/index.htm.

2. The data for 1975-1984 can be found in *Flow of Funds Accounts of the United States: Annual Flows and Outstandings 1975-1984,* http://www.federalreserve.gov/Releases/z1/current/annuals/a1975-1984.pdf. The

data for 1985-1994 can be found in *Flow of Funds Accounts of the United States: Annual Flows and Outstandings 1985-1994,* http://www.federalreserve.gov/Releases/z1/current/annuals/a1985-1994.pdf.

3. Private foreigners have to meet certain conditions in order to be exempt. Specifically the May 2004 version of IRS Publication 901 reads:

> Interest. If you are a nonresident alien who receives interest that is not effectively connected with the conduct of a U.S. trade or business, you do not include the interest in income if it is paid on deposits with banks, on accounts or deposits with certain financial institutions, or on certain amounts held by insurance companies. These amounts are exempt from U.S. tax even though they are considered to be income from a U.S. source. Also exempt from U.S. tax (although considered from U.S. sources) is certain portfolio interest on obligations issued after July 18, 1984. See Publication 519 for more information. (p. 32)

4. Mitchell B. Carroll, "The Historical Development of Income Tax Treaties," in *Income Tax Treaties,* ed. Jon E. Bischel (New York: Practising Law Institute, 1978), 53.

5. Giuseppe Ammendola, *From creditor to debtor: The US Pursuit of Foreign Capital - The Case of the Repeal of the Withholding Tax* (New York: Garland Publishing, 1994), 24. The passage that we quoted in turn includes a citation of U.S. House of Representatives, 98th Congress, 2nd Session, *Tax Treatment of Interest Paid to Foreign Persons,* Hearing before the Committee on Ways and Means (Washington, D.C.: U.S. Government Printing Office, May 1, 1984), 65.

6. The date of signature and the text of all US tax treaties can be found on the IRS website at http://www.irs.gov/businesses/international/article/0,,id=96739,00.html.

7. Robert McCauley, "Distinguishing Global Dollar Reserves from Official Holdings in the United States," *BIS Quarterly Review,* September 2006: 65, http://www.bis.org/publ/qtrpdf/r_qt0509e.pdf.

8. U.S. House of Representatives, 238.

9. U.S. House of Representatives, 244.

10. Howard Richman and Raymond Richman, "Dubai Ports Rejection Helped US Economic Growth," *Enter Stage Right,* (March 5, 2007), http://www.enterstageright.com/archive/articles/0307/0307dubaiportsrejec.htm.

11. Donald T. Regan, *For the Record: From Wall Street to Washington* (New York: Harcourt Brace Javanovich, 1988).

12. Robert L. Bartley, *The Seven Fat Years: And How to do it Again* (New York: The Free Press, 1992).

13. Daniel J. Mitchell, "Clinton-Era IRS Regulation Threatens Economy and Financial Markets" (Heritage Foundation Executive Memorandum #843,

2002).

14. Andrew F. Quinlan, "The IRS vs. Foreign Investment" (National Center for Policy Analysis Brief Analysis No. 43, 2003), http://www.ncpa.org/pub/ba/ba431.

15. Stephn J. Entin, "Proposed IRS Regulation a Threat to Foreign Investment, U,S. Banks, the Dollar, and the Economy" (IRET Congressional Advisory No. 142, 2002), www.iret.org, Downloaded on June 11, 2007.

16. Lawrence Goulder, "Implications of Introducing U.S. Withholding Taxes on Foreigners' Interest Income" in *Tax Policy and the Economy,* ed. Lawrence H. Summers (Cambridge, MA: MIT Press, 1990).

17. Eswar S. Prasad, Raghuram G. Rajan, and Arvind Subramanian, "Foreign Capital and Economic Growth" (NBER Working Paper No. 13619, November 2007): 31

18. Ben S. Bernanke, "The Global Saving Glut and the U.S. Current Account Deficit" (Sandbridge Lecture, Virginia Association of Economics, Richmond VA, April 14, 2005), http://www.federalreserve.gov/boarddocs/speeches/2005/200503102/default.htm.

19. George Wehrfritz, "China's Wealth Woes," *Newsweek International*, Sept. 4, 2006, http://peoplesgeography.com/2006/08/30/chinas-wealth-woes/.

20. Milton Friedman, "Rx for Japan: Back to the Future," *The Wall Street Journal*, Dec. 17, 1997, http://online.wsj.com/article/SB882308822323941500.html.

21. Richard Duncan, *The Dollar Crisis: Causes Consequences Cures* Revised and Updated (Singapore: John Wiley & Sons, 2005), 222.

22. These data come from the International Monetary Fund's World Economic Outlook Database which can be found online at http://www.imf.org/external/pubs/ft/weo/2007/02/weodata/index.aspx.

23. Hans Genburg et. al., *Official Reserves and Currency Management in Asia: Myth, Reality and the Future* (International Center for Monetary and Banking Studies, 2005), 8.

24. Peter Morici, "Dr. Morici: US Current Account Deficit widens in Third Quarter - Foreign Governments bankrolling US Consumers," *Finfacts Ireland*, December 18, 2006, http://www.finfacts.com/irelandbusinessnews/publish/printer_1000article_10008496.shtml

25. Robert McCauley, "Distinguishing Global Dollar Reserves from Official Holdings in the United States," *BIS Quarterly Review,* September 2006: 58, http://www.bis.org/publ/qtrpdf/r_qt0509e.pdf. According to a preliminary estimate from the BEA (see http://www.bea.gov/newsreleases/international/intinv/intinvnewsrelease.htm), foreign official reserves in the United States totaled $2.5 trillion at the end of 2006. According to our extrapolation from the IMF COFER database, foreign dollar reserves totaled about $3.2 trillion at the end of 2006 (see note 28 to this chapter). Thus, the BEA estimate was about 78% of the actual total at the end of 2006.

26. Ben S. Bernanke, "Global Imbalances: Recent Developments and Prospects" (Bundesbank Lecture, Berlin, Germany, September 11, 2007), http://www.federalreserve.gov/newsevents/speech/bernanke20070911a.htm.

27. Bernanke, "Global Imbalances", note 10.

28. According to the International Monetary Fund COFER database, those foreign governments who reported the allocation of their reserves in 2001 had $1,120 billion in dollars which was 71% of their total reserves. Those governments who did not allocate reserves had $483 billion in reserves. We extrapolate that about 71% of the $483 billion of unallocated reserves were dollars. In 2006 foreign governments reported $2,151 billion in dollars which was 65% of their total allocated reserves. There were $1,705 billions in unallocated reserves. Thus we extrapolate that about 65% of the unallocated reserves were dollars. Specifically, from the end of 2001 to the end of 2006, we estimate that foreign government dollar reserves increased from $1,436 billion to $3,211 billion, an increase of $1,775 billion.

29. The fact that China doesn't report the allocation of its reserves to the IMF is evident from the close parallels between the growth in China's reported reserves and the growth in the IMF's reported unallocated reserves. See Brad Setzer's blog etnry from June 9, 2007, for a chart illustrating this observation (http://rs.rgemonitor.com/blog/setser/202810). The report that China had $1.066 trillion in currency reserves at the end of 2006 comes from Forbes Magazine's online market feeds. See the following webpage: http://www.forbes.com/markets/feeds/afx/2007/03/06/afx3491447.html. One published estimate is that "roughly three-fourths" of Chinese foreign exchange reserves were in dollars in early 2006. See Peter S. Goodman, "China Set to Reduce Exposure to Dollar: Move Would Probably Push Currency Down," *Washington Post* (January 10, 2006), http://www.washingtonpost.com/wp-dyn/content/article/2006/01/09/AR2006010901042_pf.html.

30. Alan Ahearne, William R. Cline, Kyung Tae Lee, Yung Chul Park, Jean Pisani-Ferry, and John Williamson, "Global Imbalances: Time for Action" (Policy Brief PB07-4, Peterson Institute for International Economics, March 2007), http://www.petersoninstitute.org/publications/interstitial.cfm?ResearchID=720.

31. Bernanke, "Global Imbalances".

32. Ronald I. McKinnon, "The East Asian Dollar Standard" (Position paper for ANEPR conference, Tokyo, January 2004), 7, http://www.rieti.go.jp/cn/events/04011601/pdf/mckinnon.pdf.

33. David Backus, Espen Henriksen, Frederic Lambert, and Chris Telmer, "Current Account Fact and Fiction." (Paper presented at the annual meeting of the American Economic Association, Boston, January 6-8, 2006), http://www.aeaweb.org/annual_mtg_papers/2006/0108_1300_0101.pdf.

34. The source for foreign dollar reserves is the International Monetary Fund's COFER database with the assumption that the same percentage of

unallocated as allocated reserves are in dollars (see note 28 to this chapter). The source for US Treasury and Federal Reserve foreign currency reserves is *Treasury and Federal Reserve Foreign Exchange Operations October-December 2006.* See Table 1 on page 8, http://www.ny.frb.org/newsevents/news/markets/2007/fxq406.pdf.

35. Amy Menafee, "Where Do We Go from Dubai?" *Business & Media Institute,* March 15, 2006, http://www.businessandmedia.org/news/2006/news20060315.asp.

36. Ryan Stever, Goetz von Peter, and Christian Upper, "Highlights of International Banking and Financial Activity," *BIS Quarterly Review,* December 2006, http://www.bis.org/publ/qtrpdf/r_qt0612b.pdf.

37. Michael M. Phillips, "World Economy in Flux as America Downshifts: Huge Trade Gap Narrows as Dollar, Housing Slide; Exporting Lobster Traps," *Wall Street Journal,* September 20, 2007.

38 End of 2006 data for Japan and China are from http://www.forbes.com/markets/feeds/afx/2007/03/06/afx3491447.html. End of 2007 data for China are from "China's Foreign Exchange Holdings Top U.S. $1.53 Trillion" (Associated Press, January 11, 2008), http://www.iht.com/articles/ap/2008/01/11/business/AS-FIN-China-Foreign-Reserves.php. The end of 2007 data for Japan comes from "Japan's Forex Reserves Hit Fresh All-Time High: Government" (http://economictimes.indiatimes.com/Markets/Global_Markets/Japans_forex_reserves_hit_fresh_all-time_high_Government/rssarticleshow/2688857.cms).

39. Gabriele Parussini, "ECB, Politics, BusinessSpar over Euro Rate", *Dow Jones Newswires,* September 21, 2007, http://www.fxstreet.com/news/forex-news/article.aspx?StoryId=ab3e9dc1-0c21-492b-8b8b-0950f6fb58d1

40. Ambrose Evans-Pritchard, "China Threatens 'Nuclear Option' of dollar sales," *Telegraph.co.uk,* Aug. 10, 2007, http://www.telegraph.co.uk/money/main.jhtml;jsessionid=4OBX2LCBNMQ3BQFIQMFSFF4AVCBQ0IV0?xml=/money/2007/08/07/bcnchina107a.xml

41. "Currencies: How Big Could Sovereign Wealth Funds Be by 2015? (Morgan Stanley Research Global, May 3, 2007), http://www.morganstanley.com/views/perspectives/files/soverign_2.pdf

42. Mulloy, Patrick A., "Testimony Before the Senate Committee on Banking, Housing & Urban Affairs Hearing on 'Sovereign Wealth Acquisitions and other Foreign Government Investments in the U.S.: Assessing the Economic and National Security Implications. (November 14, 2007), http://banking.senate.gov/_files/111407_Mulloy.pdf

CHAPTER 3

1. Paul Krugman , "The East Is in the Red: A Balanced view of China's Trade,"

Slate Magazine , July 17, 1997.

2. Paul Krugman, *Pop Internationalism* (Cambridge, MA, MIT Press, 1996): vii.

3. Krugman, *Pop Internationalism,* 5.

4. United States-China Economic and Security Review Commission, "2007 Report to Congress Executive Summary" (November 2007), 3, http://www.uscc.gov/annual_report/2008/executive_summary.pdf. Hereafter referred to as USCESRC.

5. Quoted from China's State Council in USCESRC, 3.

6. Krugman, *Pop Internationalism,* 10.

7. See Paul Krugman, "Making Sense of the Competitiveness Debate," *Oxford Review of Economic Policy* 12 (1996): 17-25. It is Krugman who seems unaware that when trade is unbalanced, indeed one country, the one with a trade surplus benefits at the expense of the deficit country.

8. Paul Krugman and Maurice Obstfeld, *International Economics: Theory and Policy* 5th Edition (Glenview, IL: Little, Brown, 2000).

9. Paul Krugman, *The Age of Diminished Expectations:U.S. Economic Policy in the 1990s* (Cambridge MA: The MIT Press, 1990): 92.

10. Christopher J. Erceg, Luca Guerrieri, and Christopher Gust, "Expansionary Fiscal Shocks and the US Trade Deficit," *International Finance,* 8 (2005), http://www.blackwell-synergy.com/doi/abs/10.1111/j.1468-2362.2005.00164.x.

11. Lester Thurow, *Fortune Favors the Bold: What We Must Do to Build a New and Lasting Global Prosperity* (New York: Harper-Collins, 2003), 253.

12. Ben S. Bernanke, "The Global Saving Glut and the U.S. Current Account Deficit" (Sandbridge Lecture, Virginia Association of Economics, Richmond VA, April 14, 2005), http://www.federalreserve.gov/boarddocs/speeches/2005/200503102/default.htm.

13. Brian Bremer, "Will Beijing Honor a WTO Promise?" *Business Week*, December 11, 2006.

14. USCESRC, 4.

15. Jim Trippon, "Failure of United States Economic Mission to China Leaves America as Second Fiddle Says China Stock Digest Editor" (China Stock Digest press release, December 19, 2006), http://www.emediawire.com/releases/2006/12/emw492743.htm.

16. For a recent analysis of these patterns, and discussion of the position of the US current account deficit in relation to them, see Richard H. Clarida, Manuela Goretti and Mark P. Taylor "Are there Threshholds of Current Account Adjustment in the G7?" (NBER Working Paper 12193, April 2006), http://www.nber.org/papers/w12193. They find that "the present US current account deficit substantially exceeds — and has for some time — our estimated thresholds of current account deficit adjustment for the US."

(p.11) The paper concludes that a range of factors, including intervention by Asian central banks has cushioned deficit adjustment in recent years.

17. Nouriel Roubini and Brad Setser, *CESifo Forum*, 6 (2005): 8.

18. Jack Kemp, "Port Fiasco Could Lead to Port Security," *Townhall.com,* March 13, 2006, http://www.townhall.com/columnists/JackKemp/2006/03/13/port_fiasco_could_lead_to_port_security.

19. Ross Terrill, *The New Chinese Empire* (New York: Basic Books, 2003), 24.

20. William F. Jasper, "Has China really gone capitalist? American academic business, and government elites insist that China is changing, but the evidence shows that China's communist leadership remains in total control," *The New American* (December 11, 2006), http://www.thefreelibrary.com/Has+China+really+gone+capitalist%3F+America's+academic+business,+and...-a0156135302.

21. USCESRC, 6.

22. Richard Duncan, *The Dollar Crisis: Causes Consequences Cures* Revised and Updated (Singapore: John Wiley & Sons, 2005).

23. Irwin M. Stelzer, "The End of Free Trade: The Era of Increasingly-free trade comes to a close," *The Daily Standard*, May 22, 2007, http://www.weeklystandard.com/Content/Public/Articles/000/000/013/682bcbgz.asp.

24. Robert A. Blecker, *Beyond the Twin Deficits: A Trade Strategy for the 1990s* (Armonk NY: M.E. Sharpe, Economic Policy Institute Series, 1992), 119-120.

25. Robert A. Blecker, "Economy at Risk: The Growing U.S. Trade Deficit," (Statement presented at AFL-CIO/USBIC Conference Trade Summit 2006: Crisis and Opportunity, July 12, 2006), http://www.american.edu/cas/econ/faculty/blecker/TD0706.pdf.

26. Peter Morici, *Currency Manipulation and Free Trade*, (December 2004), http://www.steelnet.org/new/20041200.htm.

27. Peter Morici, "The Washington Dance on Trade," *Enter Stage Right* (February 6, 2007), http://www.enterstageright.com/archive/articles/0207/0207tradedance.htm.

28. Patrick J. Buchanan, *Where the Right Went Wrong* (New York: Thomas St. Martin's Press, 2004& 2005), 204

29. Buchanan, 201.

30. Chris Woodyard, "How Can you tell which car is more American?" *USA Today*, March 22, 2007, http://www.usatoday.com/money/autos/2007-03-22-american-usat_N.htm.

31. William R. Hawkins, "Economic Slowdown should prompt President to Reform Trade Policy," *American Economic Alert* (October 2, 2001), http://www.americaneconomicalert.org/view_art.asp?Prod_ID=71.

32. The Pew Global Attitudes Project. "World Publics Welcome Global Trade –

But not Immigration," (47-Nation Pew Global Attitudes Survey, October 4. 2007), http://pewglobal.org/reports/pdf/258.pdf

33. Automotive Trade Policy Council, "U.S. Automakers Endorse Japan Currency Manipulation Act; Applaud Stabenow Legislation to Force Action Against Japanese Currency Misalignment" (March 28, 2007), http://www.theautochannel.com/news/2007/03/28/041580.html

34. The text of the bill can be found online at http://www.govtrack.us/congress/billtext.xpd?bill=s110-1607

35. "Key Senators Predict a China/Japan Currency Bill in 2007" (*Washington Insider*, Motor & Equipment Manufacturers Association, March 30, 2007), http://www.mema.org/publications/articledetail.php?articleId=6703.

36. The International Monetary Fund Articles of Agreement can be found online at http://www.imf.org/external/pubs/ft/aa/aa.pdf.

CHAPTER 4

1. James C. Cooper, "The Trade Quagmire," *Business Week,* March 5, 2007.

2. Jon E. Bischel, "Basic Income Tax Treaty Structures" in *Income Tax Treaties,* ed. Jon E. Bishel (New York: Practicing Law Institute, 1978), 2.

3. The $4 trillion estimate of the amount of private foreign savings earning tax-free interest due to this loophole is obtained from two sources:

(a) According to the US Treasury, at the end of the year 2005, foreign official institutions were estimated to have approximately $1.8 trillion of the $6.7 trillion of US long-term securities held by foreign investors. Thus foreign private investors had approximately $4.9 trillion. According to the COFER database, foreign governments actually had $2.7 trillion in reserves at the end of 2005. Thus approximately .9 trillion of the 4.9 were actually foreign government reserves placed into accounts with foreign banks and then placed by those foreign banks into tax-free US accounts.

(b) The most recent IRS data release of interest earned by foreign individuals is from 2000 (http://www.irs.gov/pub/irs-soi/00frusi.pdf). That year, when the average interest rate on 10-year US Treasury T-Notes was 6.11%, private foreigners earned $128 billion tax exempt, indicating approximately $2.1 trillion of savings. Since 2000, increases in foreign government savings and increases in private foreign savings have each accounted for half of the current account deficit. Since foreign government savings went up by 2.4 times from 2000 to 2006, according to estimates based upon the International Monetary Fund COFER database, private foreigners savings in the United States have also gone up 2.4 times, up to $5.0 trillion. However, if an estimated $1 trillion of that amount is foreign government savings placed into private banks abroad

and then placed by those banks into US accounts under the bank's name, that would leave $4 trillion that would remain in private accounts, should those private accounts be taxed.
Our thanks to Jim Broten for help with making these estimates.

4. Robert McCauley, "Distinguishing Global Dollar Reserves from Official Holdings in the United States," *BIS Quarterly Review,* September 2006, http://www.bis.org/publ/qtrpdf/r_qt0509e.pdf.
5. Warren E. Buffett & Carol J. Loomis, "America's Growing Trade Deficit is Selling the Nation Out from Under Us. Here's a way to Fix the Problem -- And We Need to Do It Now," *Fortune,* November 10, 2003, http://money.cnn.com/magazines/fortune/fortune_archive/2003/11/10/352872/index.htm
6. Raymond L. Richman, "The Great Trade Debate," *Pittsburgh Tribune Review,* September 14, 2003, http://www.pittsburghlive.com/x/pittsburghtrib/s_154632.html.
7. Senator Byron L. Dorgan, *Take This Job and Ship It: How Corporate Greed and Brain-Dead Politics are Selling Out America* (New York: Thomas Dunne Books/St. Martin's Press, 2006), 247.
8. The text of the bill is available online at http://www.theorator.com/bills109/s3899.html.
9. Article XII of the Uruguay round of the GATT treaty can be found on the Internet at http://www.wto.org/English/docs_e/legal_e/articleXII.
10. Import Certificates Proposed to Shrink Trade Gap (New York Times, September 15, 2006). Summarized on the web at http://english.people.com.cn/200609/16/eng20060916_303321.html.
11. Sallie James, "A New Solution to the Trade Deficit 'Problem,'" (Posted on a Cato Institute Blog on September 15, 2006), http://www.cato-at-liberty.org/2006/09/15/a-new-solution-to-the-trade-deficit-problem/
12. Current information about Asian debt securities can be found at http://www.asianbondsonline.adb.org/how_to_buy_bonds/default.php. On 10/12/07 that site reported that foreign investors were not allowed to own Chinese government bonds.

CHAPTER 5

1. Nikita Khrushchev, *Krushchev Remembers,* trans. Strobe Talbott (Boston: Little, Brown and Company, 1970), 113.
2. Robert S. McIntyre, "Just Taxes & Other Options," *Less Taxing Alternatives* (March 1984): 28-29.
3. Richard Dobbs and Werner Rehm, "The Value of Share Buybacks," *McKinsey Quarterly* 3 (2005), http://www.cfo.com/printable/article.cfm/4392991/c_2984408?f=options.

4. If the tax system were changed so that owners of homes paid income tax on the rental value of the home (say 1/30 of the sales price) then we would allow shares of stock to be rolled-over into home purchases. In such a case, we would not count property taxes against the rental value of a home since buyers of real-estate buy free of the property tax, as we explain in Chapter 6.

5. J. R. Hicks, *Value and Capital* (Oxford: Clarendon Press, 1939), 179.

6. Henry Calvert Simons, *Personal Income Taxation* (Chicago: The University of Chicago Press, 1938), 47.

7. R. M. Haig, "The Concept of Income," in *The Federal Income Tax*, ed. R. M. Haig (New York, 1921) as quoted by Henry Calvert Simons, *Personal Income Taxation* (Chicago: The University of Chicago Press, 1938), 61.

8. Simons, 41.

9. Simons, 162.

10. Julian Alworth, Giampaolo Aruchi, and Roni Hamaui, "What's Come to Perfection Perishes: Adjusting Capital Gains Taxation in Italy," *National Tax Journal*, 56 (March, 2003).

11. Bruce Bartlett, "Why the capital gains tax rate should be zero" (National Center for Policy Analysis Policy Report No. 245, August 2001), http://www.ncpa.org/pub/st/st245/s245.pdf.

12. Robert E. Hall and Alvin Rabushka, *The Flat Tax* (2nd Ed.) (Stanford CA: Hoover Institution Press, 2007): 111-112.

13 The basis for calculating the gains from the sale of corporate shares is understated. The taxpayer is not credited with the investment by the corporation of retained earnings on which the corporation has paid tax. These earnings belong to the shareholders. If the corporation were treated as a limited partnership, the amount reinvested by the partnership would add to the shareholders' basis for calculating future gains. For example, in the case of mutual funds, any earnings that the taxpayers reinvest adds to their basis for the purpose of calculating capital gains.

CHAPTER 6

1. David Ricardo, *The Principles of Political Economy and Taxation*, 3rd Ed., (London: J. M. Dent, 1821, reprinted 1962): "A tax on rent would affect rent only; it would fall wholly on landlords, and could not be shifted to any class of consumers. The landlord could not raise his rent, because he would have unaltered the difference between the produce obtained from the least productive land in cultivation, and that obtained from land of every other quality" p. 110.

2. Henry George, *Progress and Poverty: An inquiry into the Cause of Industrial Depressions, and of Increase of wants with increase of wealth –the*

Remedy (London: Kegan Paul, Trench & Co., 1883).

3. Raymond L. Richman, "The Incidence of Urban Real Estate Taxes Under Conditions of Static and Dynamic Equilibrium," *Land Economics*, 43, May 1967.

4. For an overview of these studies see Raymond L. Richman, "The Reassessment," *Pittsburgh Tribune-Review* (April 7, 2002), http://www.pittsburghlive.com/x/pittsburghtrib/s_64790.html, and Raymond L. Richman, "Bring Back the Assessors," *Pittsburgh Tribune-Review* (March 6, 2005), http://www.pittsburghlive.com/x/pittsburghtrib/s_310083.html.

5. Frederick D. Stocker, ed. *Proposition 13 – A ten-year Retrospective* (Cambridge, MA: The Lincoln Institute of Land Policy, 1991), 2.

6. Stoker, 2.

7. George F. Break, "Ch. 5. Proposition 13's Tenth Birthday: Occasion for Celebration or Lament?" in *Proposition 13 – A ten-year Retrospective,* ed. Frederick D. Stocker (Cambridge, MA: The Lincoln Institute of Land Policy, 1991), Table 5.1, 180.

8. Robert F. Dye, Therese J. McGuire, and Daniel P. McMillen, "Are Property Tax Limitations More Binding over Time?" *National Tax Journal*, 63 (June 2005).

9. Ronald B. Welch, "Ch. 3. Property Tax Administrative Changes Resulting from Proposition 13," in *Proposition 13 – A ten-year Retrospective,* ed. Frederick D. Stocker (Cambridge, MA: The Lincoln Institute of Land Policy, 1991).

CHAPTER 7

1 *The Goose that Laid the Golden Eggs*, a fable attributed to Aesop.

2. The average sales tax rate in the United States was 5.7% in 2006 according to "Sales Tax and E-Commerce" (SmartEconomist.com: Report 175, August 2, 2006), http://www.smarteconomist.com/insight/175.

3. "Hunter Coauthors Legislation to Reduce Tax Burden on US Manufacturers" (Press Release from Congressman Hunter's Office issued June 7, 2007), http://www.house.gov/apps/list/speech/ca52_hunter/border_tax.shtml

4. Daniel J. Mitchell, "Making American Companies More Competitive (American Heritage Foundation Backgrounder #1691, 2003), http://www.heritage.org/Research/Taxes/BG1691.cfm

5. *President's Advisory Panel on Federal Tax Reform, Final Report* (November 1, 2005), http://www.taxreformpanel.gov/final-report.

6. Alan Auerbach, "Who Bears the Corporate Tax? A Review of What We Know" (NBER Working Paper No. 11686, May, 2005).

7. John Kenneth Galbraith, *The Affluent Society* (Boston: Houghton Mifflin, 1958).

8. Christian Keuschnigg and Martin D. Dietz, "A growth oriented dual income tax" *Int Tax Public Finan (2007) 14:191-221*

9. Robert E. Hall and Alvin Rabushka, *The Flat Tax* (2nd Ed.) (Stanford CA: Hoover Institution Press, 2007).

10. Clemens Fuest and Alfons Weichenrieder, "Tax Competition and Profit Shifting: On the Relationship between Personal and Corporate Tax Rates," (CESifo Working Paper No. 781, October 2002),

CHAPTER 8

1. Robert S. McIntyre, "Just Taxes & Other Options," *Less Taxing Alternatives* (1984): 24.

2. *President's Advisory Panel on Federal Tax Reform, Final Report* (November 1, 2005): 198, http://www.taxreformpanel.gov/final-report. Hereafter referred to as PAPOFTR.

3. The information in Table 12 of the OECD Database was supplemented with the following information from other websites. The average provincial sales tax for Canada was 7.8% (7.2% on a tax-inclusive basis) in 2005 according to www.comparativetaxation.treasury.gov.au/content/report/html/10_Chapter_8-02.asp. The average sales tax for the United States was 5.7% (5.4% on a tax-inclusive basis) according to www.smarteconomist.com/insight/175. The VAT for China was 15% according to www.uscib.org/index.asp?documentID=1676.

4. Henry J. Aaron, Ed., *The Value-Added Tax: Lessons from Europe* (The Brookings Institution, 1981).

5. PAPOFTR, 202.

6. PAPOFTR, 194.

7. Thomas Griffith, "Progressive Taxation and Happiness," *Boston College Law Review* 45 (2004): 1397–98.

8. Marjorie E. Kornhauser, "Educating Ourselves Towards a Progressive (And Happier) Tax: A Commentary on Griffith's Progressive Taxation and Happiness," *Boston College Law Review,* 45 (2004).

9. Henry Calvert Simons, *Personal Income Taxation* (Chicago: The University of Chicago Press, 1938).

10 Juan Carlos Conesa and Dirk Krueger, "On the optimal progressivity of the income tax code," *Journal of Monetary Economics,* 43 (2006): 1425-1450.

11. PAPOFTR, 201.

12. Robert E. Hall and Alvin Rabushka, *The Flat Tax* (2nd Ed.) (Stanford CA: Hoover Institution Press, 2007).

13. PAPOFTR, Chapter 7.

14. The argument that trade deficits balance themselves appears in PAPOFTR, 168-169 as well as PAPOFTR, 201. According to a personal communication

from Dan R. Mastromarco, Edward P. Lazear was the member of the panel who argued for border-adjustability.

15. PAPOFTR, 171-172.

16 PAPOFTR, 151-152.

17. Neal Boortz and John Linder, *The FairTax Book: Saying Goodbye to the Income Tax and the IRS* (New York: Regan Books, 2005), 126. The original FairTax legislation was written and the FairTax was initially introduced into public discourse by David R. Burton and Dan R. Mastromarco.

18. The data for the personal income plus payroll taxes are from a fact sheet published by the Tax Policy Center of the Urban Institute and Brookings Institution (http://www.urban.org/UploadedPDF/1001065_Tax_Units.pdf). These data are based upon the assumption that the employer's share of payroll taxes is passed on to the employee in the form of lower wages. In the long-run, the wage rate paid to the marginal worker is equal to the value that the marginal worker produces after subtracting the marginal cost of employing that worker.

19. PAPOFTR, 208.

20. Milton and Rose Friedman, *Free to Choose: A Personal Statement* (New York: Harcourt Brace Jovanovich, 1980), Chapter 4.

21. Boortz and Linder, 126

22. Edmund S. Phelps, "The Structuralist Theory of Employment," (AEA Papers and Proceedings, May 1995): 229-230, http://www.columbia.edu/~esp2/struct.pdf

23. Congressional Budget Office historical data, "Revenues by Major Source, 1962-2006": 4, http://www.cbo.gov/budget/data/historical.pdf

24. PAPOFTR, 1

25. GAO, *Internal Revenue Service: Assessment of Fiscal Year 2006 Budget Request and Interim Results of the 2005 Filing Season*, http://www.gao.gov/highlights/d05416thigh.pdf.

26. PAPOFTR, 4.

27. David G. Tuerck, Jonathan Haughton, Keshab Bhattarai, Phuong Viet Ngo, and Alfonso Sanchez-Penalver, *The Economic Effects of the FairTax: Results from the Beacon Hill Institute CGE Model* (Boston: The Beacon Hill Institute at Suffolk University, February 2007), http://www.beaconhill.org/FairTax2007/EconomicEffectsFTBHICGEModel4-30-07.pdf.

28. Dan R. Mastromarco, "U.S. International Tax Reform? Define 'Reform' for Me" *Tax Notes International* (August 7, 2006): 492, http://www.fairtax.org/PDF/USInternationalTaxReform-Mastromarco-8-7-06.pdf

29. See for example Arduin, Laffer & Moore Econometrics, *A Macroeconomics Analysis of the FairTax Proposal* (July 2006), http://www.fairtax.org/PDF/MacroeconomicAnalysisofFairTax.pdf and Paul Bachman, Jonthan Haughton, Laurence J. Kotlikoff, Alfonso Sanchez-Palalver, and David G.

Tuerck, *Taxing Sales Under the Fair Tax* (NBER Working Paper #12732, Dec. 2006).

30. PAPOFTR, 217. For a discussion of the mistakes made by POPOFTR when making their estimate, see Paul Bachman et al., *Taxing Sales Under the Fair Tax* (NBER Working Paper #12732, Dec. 2006).

31. Arduin, Laffer & Moore Econometrics, *A Macroeconomics Analysis of the FairTax Proposal* (July 2006): 6, http://www.fairtax.org/PDF/MacroeconomicAnalysisofFairTax.pdf

32. Bureau of Labor Statistics, *Employment and Wages, National Averages 2004,* Tables 7, 8, and 9, http://www.bls.gov/cew/cewbultn04.htm.

33. PAPOFTR, 221.

34. Irving Fisher and Herbert W. Fisher, *Constructive Income Taxation* (NY: Harper and Brothers, 1942).

35. John B. Shoven and John Whalley, "Irving Fisher's Spendings (Consumption) Tax in Retrospect," *The American Journal of Economics and Sociology*, 65, 2005.

36. Nicholas Kaldor, *An Expenditure Tax* (London: Allen & Unwin, 1955).

37. U.S. Department of the Treasury, *Blueprints for Basic Tax Reform* (Washington: U.S. Government Printing Office, 1977).

38. Joseph A. Pechman (Ed.), *What Should be Taxed, Income or Expenditure* (Washington: Brookings Institute,1980).

39. Robert S. McIntyre, "Just Taxes & Other Options," *Less Taxing Alternatives* (March 1984): 20.

40. Lawrence S. Seidman, *The USA Tax: A Progressive Consumption Tax* (Boston: MIT Press, 1997).

41. Steven Pressman, "Frontiers of Tax Reform," *American Economist*, 41, 1997.

PART III

1. See the following webpage: http://www.pinyin.info/chinese/crisis.html.

2. International Monetary Fund, *World Economic Outlook: Spillovers and Cycles in the Global Economy*, April 2007: p. 1, http://www.imf.org/external/pubs/cat/longres.cfm?sk=19780.0.

3. BIS 77th Annual Report (June 24, 2007), http://www.bis.org/publ/arpdf/ar2007e.htm. Chapter 8 discusses the dangers facing the world economy.

4. BIS, p. 141.

CHAPTER 9

1. See for example: Paul Krugman, *The Age of Diminished Expectations:U.S. Economic Policy in the 1990s* (Cambridge MA: The MIT Press, 1990): 92.

2. See for example: Catherine L. Mann, *Is the U.S. Trade Deficit Sustainable?*

(Washington, DC: Institute for International Economics, 1999).

3. See for example: David Backus, Espen Henriksen, Frederic Lambert, and Chris Telmer, "Current Account Fact and Fiction." (Paper presented at the annual meeting of the American Economic Association, Boston, January 6-8, 2006), http://www.aeaweb.org/annual_mtg_papers/2006/0108_1300_0101.pdf.

4. Dan R. Mastromarco, "U.S. International Tax Reform? Define 'Reform' for Me" *Tax Notes International* (August 7, 2006): 492, http://www.fairtax.org/PDF/USInternationalTaxReform-Mastromarco-8-7-06.pdf

5. Martin Feldstein, "Tradeable Gasoline Rights", *The Wall Street Journal*, June 5, 2006, http://www.nber.org/feldstein/wsj060506.html.

6. James Turk and John Rubino, *The Coming Collapse of the Dollar and How to Profit From it: Make a Fortune by Investing in Gold and Other Hard Assets.* (New York: Doubleday, 2004). Chapter 14 is an excellent guide

CHAPTER 10

1 Mary-Anne Toy, "China Under Pressure to Rein in Burma," *theage.com.au*, September 28, 2007, http://www.theage.com.au/news/world/china-under-pressure-to-rein-in-burma/2007/09/27/1190486480885.html.

2. Norbert Vollersten, "Prisoner Nation: Why North Koreans cheered Bush's 'axis of evil' designation." *Opinion Jounral from The Wall Street Journal Editorial Page*, February 5, 2003, http://www.opinionjournal.com/editorial/feature.html?id=110003030.

3. Frederick W. Stakelbeck, Jr., "Sudan's Chinese Guardian," *Front Page Magazine*, March 23, 2006, http://www.frontpagemag.com/Articles/Read.aspx?GUID={6478AC07-8985-413C-AC49-14F547D3C2ED}

4. Allen Newell and Herbert A. Simon, *Human Problem Solving* (Englewood NJ: Prentice Hall, 1972).

5. Milton and Rose Friedman, *Free to Choose: A Personal Statement* (New York: Harcourt Brace Jovanovich, 1980), 85-86.

Index

List of Figures

For purchasing info,

mp3 downloads,

and updates,

please visit

Ideal Taxes Association

at

www.idealtaxes.com